PISA

Programme for **I**nternational **S**tudent **A**ssessment

Sample Questions & Answers

Unicorn Books Pvt. Ltd.
F-2/16, Ansari Road, Daryaganj, New Delhi-110002
• E-mail: info@unicornbooks.in

Edition: 2020
ISBN 978-81-7806-4093

www.unicornbooks.in

Printed: Param Offsetters, Okhla, New Delhi-110020

FOREWORD

Parents, students, teachers, school leaders, governments and the general public need good information on how well their education systems prepare students for life. A growing commitment by governments to monitor the outcomes of education systems in terms of student achievement on a regular basis and within an internationally agreed framework led to the launch of the OECD's Programme for International Assessment (PISA) in 1997. There have so far been several PISA surveys starting from 2000 every three years. The results from PISA provide a new basis for policy dialogue and for collaboration in defining and implementing educational goals, in innovative ways that reflect judgements about the skills that are relevant to adult life.

What does PISA actually assess? This report/book brings together most of the publicly available questions in **reading**, **mathematics** and **science** and, together with the PISA assessment frameworks, gives a solid overview of the PISA test. Some of these questions were used in the PISA 2000, 2003 and 2006 surveys and others were used in developing and trying out the assessment.

Each chapter in this report has two distinct sections: the first presents the questions and the second presents the answers to these questions. This allows the reader to take the test!

This report was compiled by Susanne Salz and Diana Toledo Figueroa, with editorial assistance from Elisabeth Villoutreix and Juliet Evans.

TABLE OF CONTENTS

ANSWERS

CHAPTER 1

Introduction to the PISA

THE AIMS OF PISA

PISA aims to measure how far students approaching the end of compulsory education have acquired some of the knowledge and skills essential for full participation in the knowledge society. PISA surveys are carried out every three years in a large number of countries, that together make up close to 90% of the world economy. The first PISA survey was carried out in 2000 in 43 countries, the second in 2003 in 41 countries and the third in 2006 in 57 countries. The next assessment will take place in 2021. The primary objective is monitoring the outcomes of education systems in terms of student achievement to provide empirically grounded information which will inform policy decisions. PISA is steered by representatives from participating countries through the PISA Governing Board. The Directorate for Education at the Organisation for Economic Co-operation and Development (OECD) manages PISA and draws on the knowledge of a rich network of international experts.

THE PISA SURVEYS

PISA tests 15 year old students in reading, mathematics and science as well as measuring a wider range of factors including students' interest, attitudes and motivation. The assessment focuses on young people's ability to use their knowledge and skills to meet real-life challenges, rather than merely on the extent to which they have mastered a specific school curriculum. This approach is called 'literacy'. The definitions of literacy in reading, mathematics and science are explained in Chapters 2, 3 and 4 respectively. In order to test students' literacy in reading, mathematics and science, experts in different countries design assessment frameworks and questions that represent these frameworks. These questions are then carefully piloted in all countries before a final test is constructed that is appropriate and valid across the participating countries. Once the final booklets with test questions are created, they are given to students at a number of randomly selected schools in each country. Tests are typically administered to between 4,500 and 40,000 students in each country. The questions in the booklet are grouped into units. A unit consists of stimulus material such as texts, tables and/or graphs, followed by questions on various aspects of the text, table or graph. The questions use different formats: some are multiple choice, some require a short answer and some a longer constructed response. Students have two hours to answers these questions. In addition students are given a separate questionnaire containing questions about their families and different aspects of their learning, including their attitudes, aspirations and learning strategies.

THE PISA RESULTS

Scorers look at the PISA tests and use a detailed scoring guide to give no credit, partial credit or full credit for each answer. The results obtained in this way are analysed to provide many interesting insights. In addition to the performance of students in different countries, results are also analysed with regard to other factors such as gender, socio-economic background and differences between schools. In this way, PISA has produced an unprecedented comparative knowledge base of school systems and their outcomes, and allows these outcomes to be monitored over time. One of the key features of PISA is its policy orientation, with design and reporting methods determined by the need of governments to draw policy lessons. It is not possible to link the different information collected from students and school principals as the direct causes of PISA results, but it is possible to compare the degree of association of various factors in different countries with educational outcomes. These policy lessons are published by the OECD in numerous reports which can be found on www.pisa.oecd.org.

THE PISA QUESTIONS

This book presents all the publicly available questions used in the PISA surveys, as well as questions used in developing and trying out the surveys. Other questions have to remain confidential because they will be used in future PISA surveys to ensure comparability of the results over time. The next three chapters present the questions for the reading, mathematics and science tests respectively. Each chapter presents an overview of what exactly the questions assess. The second section of each chapter presents questions which were used in the PISA surveys, that is, the actual PISA tests for which results were published. The third section presents questions used in developing and trying out the surveys. These questions were not used in the actual surveys, but they are nevertheless illustrative of the kind of question PISA uses. The final section shows all the answers along with brief comments on each question. For the questions used in PISA surveys, the answer section includes a comment box showing the percentage of students who answered correctly across OECD countries, the difficulty of the question expressed in score points and which competency is being assessed. For other questions, the data on the percentage of students who answered correctly across OECD countries and the score points are not available or not considered reliable enough to be presented here. Therefore, the comment box states only which competency is being assessed.

CHAPTER 2

Reading Sample Tasks

The assessment of reading in PISA is not aimed at testing whether or not 15 year old students can read in a technical sense, since comparatively few young adults in modern societies have no skills in reading. The PISA definition of reading literacy goes beyond the notion of decoding information and literal comprehension towards more applied tasks. Reading literacy in PISA is defined as:

Understanding, using and reflecting on written texts, in order to achieve one's goals, to develop one's knowledge and potential, and to participate in society.

In the first PISA study in 2000, reading was the focus of the test and the majority of testing time was devoted to reading tasks. In the surveys in 2003 and 2006 reading was still assessed, but less comprehensively. Therefore the most detailed analysis was done in 2000. Reading will once again be the focus of the test in PISA 2009.

Students performance in reading is assessed in relation to different text formats, reading processes and situations. The primary distinction in text formats is between continuous texts and non-continuous texts. The former refers to prose organised in sentences and paragraphs and includes descriptions, narrations and argumentations amongst others. Non-continuous texts include lists, maps, graphs and diagrams. PISA assesses three types of reading processes. Students are expected to demonstrate their proficiency in (a) retrieving information, (b) interpreting texts and forming a broad general understanding of the text and (c) reflecting and evaluating its contents, form and features. The third element of assessment is the context or situation of the text. Four situations are distinguished: personal use, public use, occupational use and educational use. For example, a novel, personal letter or biography is written for people's personal use; official documents or announcements for public use; a manual or report for occupational use; and a textbook or worksheet for educational use. Each question used in a PISA survey falls into one category of each of the three aspects. Question 3.1 from the unit Graffiti, for example, assesses the process of interpreting texts, using a continuous text and a public situation. As the last two categorisations are generally fairly obvious, they will not be explicitly mentioned for the questions presented here.

To report the results, PISA uses a scale. In 2000 a reading scale with an average of 500 was used. On this scale, two-thirds of students scored between 400 and 600. The higher the score the better the students' reading skills are. In PISA 2000, when reading was the focus of the test allowing more time for assessment and more detailed results, separate scales were used for the three types of readings tasks and for the two types of text format. These scales showed the student's reading performance specifically in retrieving information, interpreting texts, reflection and evaluation as well as for continuous texts and non-continuous texts. More information on PISA proficiency scales can be found in Annex A.

This chapter presents 17 units. The first 11 units were used in PISA 2000, 2003 or 2006 surveys and internationally comparable results are published for these. Units 12 to 17 were used in developing and testing out the surveys. While it was decided not to include these units in the PISA surveys, they are nevertheless illustrative of the kinds of questions asked in PISA. The questions presented in this chapter are all publicly released PISA reading questions. Following the section with questions, answers for all questions are given. For units 1 to 11, a comment box includes score points, the percentage of students who answered correctly across OECD countries and the question category. For units 12 to 17, a comment box lists the question category. Because these units were not used in the PISA surveys the information regarding score points and percentage of students who answered correctly is not known or is not sufficiently reliable to be presented here.

READING UNIT 1: LAKE CHAD

Figure 1 shows changing levels of Lake Chad, in Saharan North Africa. Lake Chad disappeared completely in about 20,000 BC, during the last Ice Age. In about 11,000 BC it reappeared. Today, its level is about the same as it was in AD 1000.

Figure 2 shows Saharan rock art (ancient drawings or paintings found on the walls of caves) and changing patterns of wildlife

Source: Past Worlds: The Times Atlas of Archaeology, Times Books Limited 1988

Figure 1 Changing levels of Lake Chad, in Saharan North Africa

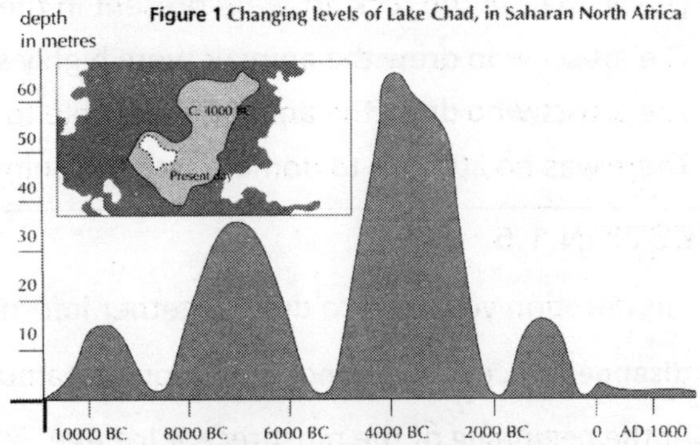

Figure 2 Saharan rock art and changing patterns of wildlife

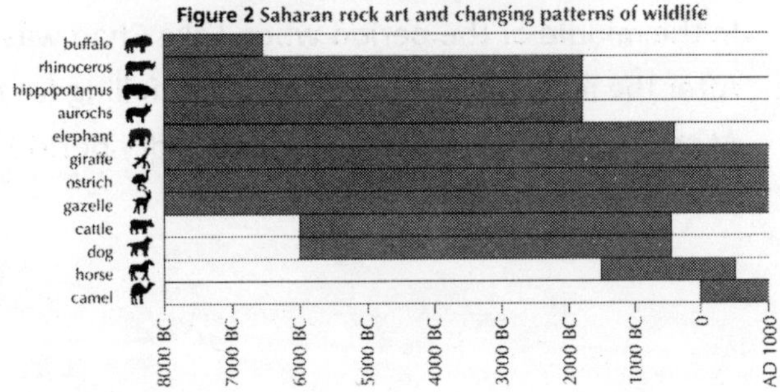

Use the above information about Lake Chad to answer the questions below.

QUESTION 1.1

What is the depth of Lake Chad today?

A. About two metres.

B. About fifteen metres.

C. About fifty metres.

D. It has disappeared completely.

E. The information is not provided.

QUESTION 1.2

In about which year does the graph in Figure 1 start?

....

QUESTION 1.3

Why has the author chosen to start the graph at this point?

....

....

QUESTION 1.4

Figure 2 is based on the assumption that

A. The animals in the rock art were present in the area at the time they were drawn.

B. The artists who drew the animals were highly skilled.

C. The artists who drew the animals were able to travel widely.

D. There was no attempt to domesticate the animals which were depicted in the rock art.

QUESTION 1.5

For this question you need to draw together information from Figure 1 and Figure 2.

The disappearance of the rhinoceros, hippopotamus and aurochs from Saharan rock art happened

A. At the beginning of the most recent Ice Age.

B. In the middle of the period when Lake Chad was at its highest level.

C. After the level of Lake Chad had been falling for over a thousand years.

D. At the beginning of an uninterrupted dry period.

READING UNIT 2 : FLU

ACOL VOLUNTARY FLU IMMUNISATION PROGRAM

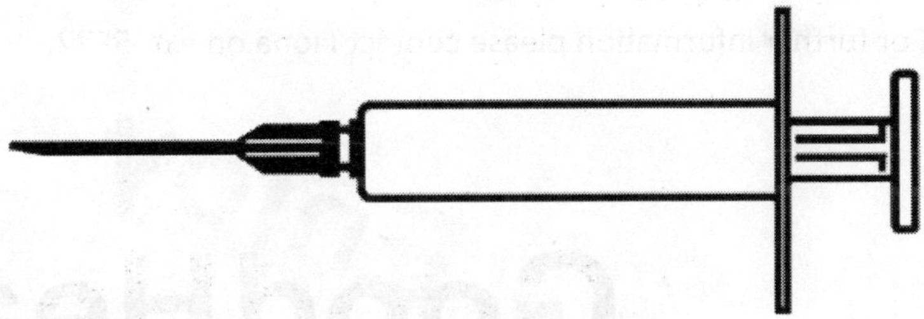

As you are no doubt aware the flu can strike rapidly and extensively during winter. It can leave its victims ill for weeks.

The best way to fight the virus is to have a fit and healthy body. Daily exercise and a diet including plenty of fruit and vegetables are highly recommended to assist the immune system to fight this invading virus.

ACOL has decided to offer staff the opportunity to be immunised against the flu as an additional way to prevent this insidious virus from spreading amongst us. ACOL has arranged for a nurse to administer the immunisations at ACOL, during a half-day session in work hours in the week of May 17. This program is free and available to all members of staff.

Participation is voluntary. Staff taking up the option will be asked to sign a consent form indicating that they do not have any allergies, and that they understand they may experience minor side effects. Medical advice indicates that the immunisation does not produce influenza. However, it may cause some side effects such as fatigue, mild fever and tenderness of the arm.

Who should be immunised?

Anyone interested in being protected against the virus.

This immunisation is especially recommended for people over the age of 65. But regardless of age, ANYONE who has a chronic debilitating disease, especially cardiac, pulmonary, bronchial or diabetic conditions.

In an office environment ALL staff are at risk of catching the flu.

Who should not be immunised?

Individuals hypersensitive to eggs, people suffering from an acute feverish illness and pregnant women.

Check with your doctor if you are taking any medication or have had a previous reaction to a flu injection.

If you would like to be immunised in the week of May 17 please advise the personnel officer, Fiona McSweeney, by Friday May 7. The date and time will be set according to the availability of the nurse, the number of participants and the time convenient for most staff. If you would like to be immunised for this winter but cannot attend at the arranged time please let Fiona know. An alternative session may be arranged if there are sufficient numbers.

For further information please contact Fiona on ext. 5577.

Enjoy

Good Health

Fiona McSweeney, the personnel officer at a company called ACOL, prepared the information sheet on the previous page for ACOL staff. Refer to the information sheet to answer the questions which follow.

QUESTION 2.1

Which one of the following describes a feature of the ACOL flu immunisation program?

A. Daily exercise classes will be run during the winter.

B. Immunisations will be given during working hours.

C. A small bonus will be offered to participants.

D. A doctor will give the injections.

QUESTION 2.2

We can talk about the content of a piece of writing (what it says).

We can talk about its style (the way it is presented).

Fiona wanted the style of this information sheet to be friendly and encouraging.

Do you think she succeeded?

Explain your answer by referring in detail to the layout, style of writing, pictures or other graphics.

....

....

....

QUESTION 2.3

This information sheet suggests that if you want to protect yourself against the flu virus, a flu injection is

A. More effective than exercise and a healthy diet, but more risky.
B. A good idea, but not a substitute for exercise and a healthy diet.
C. As effective as exercise and a healthy diet, and less troublesome.
D. Not worth considering if you have plenty of exercise and a healthy diet.

QUESTION 2.4

Part of the information sheet says:

Who should be immunised?

Anyone interested in being protected against the virus.

After Fiona had circulated the information sheet, a colleague told her that she should have left out the words "Anyone interested in being protected against the virus" because they were misleading.

Do you agree that these words are misleading and should have been left out?

Explain your answer.

....

....

....

QUESTION 2.5

According to the information sheet, which one of these staff members should contact Fiona?

A. Steve from the store, who does not want to be immunised because he would rather rely on his natural immunity.
B. Julie from sales, who wants to know if the immunisation program is compulsory.
C. Alice from the mailroom who would like to be immunised this winter but is having a baby in two months.
D. Michael from accounts who would like to be immunised but will be on leave in the week of May 17.

READING UNIT 3: GRAFFITI

I'm simmering with anger as the school wall is cleaned and repainted for the fourth time to get rid of graffiti. Creativity is admirable but people should find ways to express themselves that do not inflict extra costs upon society.

Why do you spoil the reputation of young people by painting graffiti where it's forbidden? Professional artists do not hang their paintings in the streets, do they? Instead they seek funding and gain fame through legal exhibitions.

In my opinion buildings, fences and park benches are works of art in themselves. It's really pathetic to spoil this architecture with graffiti and what's more, the method destroys the ozone layer. Really, I can't understand why these criminal artists bother as their "artistic works" are just removed from sight over and over again.

Helga

There is no accounting for taste. Society is full of communication and advertising. Company logos, shop names. Large intrusive posters on the streets. Are they acceptable? Yes, mostly. Is graffiti acceptable? Some people say yes, some no.

Who pays the price for graffiti? Who is ultimately paying the price for advertisements? Correct. The consumer. Have the people who put up billboards asked your permission? No. Should graffiti painters do so then? Isn't it all just a question of communication – your own name, the names of gangs and large works of art in the street?

Think about the striped and chequered clothes that appeared in the stores a few years ago. And ski wear. The patterns and colours were stolen directly from the flowery concrete walls. It's quite amusing that these patterns and colours are accepted and admired but that graffiti in the same style is considered dreadful. Times are hard for art.

Sophia

Source: Mari Hankala.

The two letters above come from the Internet and are about graffiti. Graffiti is illegal painting and writing on walls and elsewhere. Refer to the letters to answer the questions below.

QUESTION 3.1

The purpose of each of these letters is to

A. Explain what graffiti is.

B. Present an opinion about graffiti.

C. Demonstrate the popularity of graffiti.

D. Tell people how much is spent removing graffiti.

QUESTION 3.2

Why does Sophia refer to advertising?

....

....

....

QUESTION 3.3

Which of the two letter writers do you agree with? Explain your answer by using your own words to refer to what is said in one or both of the letters.

....

....

....

QUESTION 3.4

We can talk about what a letter says (its content).

We can talk about the way a letter is written (its style).

Regardless of which letter you agree with, in your opinion, which do you think is the better letter? Explain your answer by referring to the way one or both letters are written.

....

....

....

READING UNIT 4 : LABOUR

The tree diagram below shows the structure of a country's labour force or "working-age population". The total population of the country in 1995 was about 3.4 million.

The Labour Force Structure year ended 31 March 1995 (000s)[1]

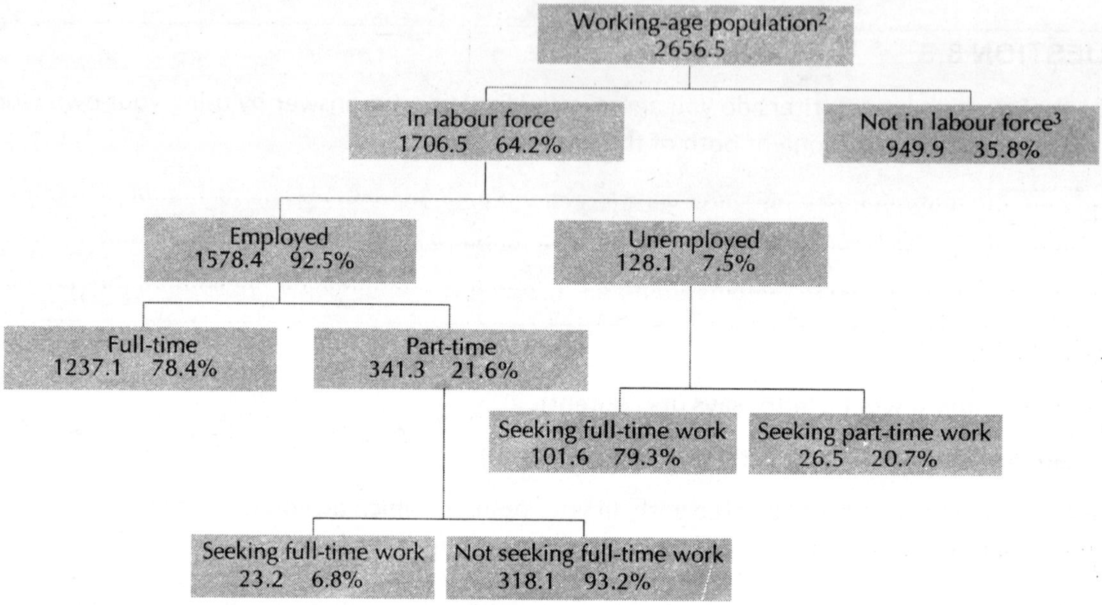

1. Numbers of people are given in thousands (000s).
2. The working-age population is defined as people between the ages of 15 and 65.
3. People "Not in labour force" are those not actively seeking work and/or not available for work.

Source: D. Miller, Form 6 Economics, ESA Publications, Box 9453, Newmarket, Auckland, New Zealand, p. 64.

Use the information about a country's labour force shown above to answer the questions below.

QUESTION 4.1

What are the two main groups into which the working-age population is divided?

A. Employed and unemployed.

B. Of working age and not of working age.

C. Full-time workers and part-time workers.

D. In the labour force and not in the labour force.

QUESTION 4.2

How many people of working age were not in the labour force? (Write the number of people, not the percentage.)

....

QUESTION 4.3

In which part of the tree diagram, if any, would each of the people listed in the table below be included?

Show your answer by placing a cross in the correct box in the table.

The first one has been done for you.

	"In labour force: employed"	"In labour force: unemployed"	"Not in labour force"	Not included in any category
A part-time waiter, aged 35	☐	☐	☐	☐
A business woman, aged 43, who works a sixty hour week	☐	☐	☐	☐
A full-time student, aged 21	☐	☐	☐	☐
A man, aged 28, who recently sold his shop and is looking for work	☐	☐	☐	☐
A woman, aged 55, who has never worked or wanted to work outside the home	☐	☐	☐	☐
A grandmother, aged 80, who still works a few hours a day at the family's market stall	☐	☐	☐	☐

QUESTION 4.4

Suppose that information about the labour force was presented in a tree diagram like this every year.

Listed below are four features of the tree diagram. Show whether or not you would expect these features to change from year to year, by circling either "Change" or "No change". The first one has been done for you.

Features of Tree Diagram	Answer
The labels in each box (e.g. "In labour force")	Change / (No change)
The percentages (e.g. "64.2%")	Change / No change
The numbers (e.g. "2656.5")	Change / No change
The footnotes under the tree diagram	Change / No change

QUESTION 4.5

The information about the labour force structure is presented as a tree diagram, but it could have been presented in a number of other ways, such as a written description, a pie chart, a graph or a table.

The tree diagram was probably chosen because it is especially useful for showing

A. Changes over time.

B. The size of the country's total population.

C. Categories within each group.

D. The size of each group.

READING UNIT 5 : PLAN INTERNATIONAL

PLAN International Program Results Financial Year 1996

Region of Eastern and Southern Africa RESA

Growing up Healthy	EGYPT	ETHIOPIA	KENYA	MALAWI	SUDAN	TANZANIA	UGANDA	ZAMBIA	ZIMBABWE	TOTALS
Health posts built with 4 rooms or less	1	0	6	0	7	1	2	0	9	**26**
Health workers trained for 1 day	1 053	0	719	0	425	1 003	20	80	1085	**4 385**
Children given nutrition supplements > 1 week	10 195	0	2 240	2 400	0	0	0	0	251 402	**266 237**
Children given financial help with health/dental treatment	984	0	396	0	305	0	581	0	17	**2 283**
Learning										
Teachers trained for 1 week	0	0	367	0	970	115	565	0	303	**2 320**
School exercise books bought/donated	667	0	0	41 200	0	69 106	0	150	0	**111 123**
School textbooks bought/donated	0	0	45 650	9 600	1 182	8 769	7 285	150	58 387	**131 023**
Uniforms bought/made/donated	8 897	0	5 761	0	2 000	6 040	0	0	434	**23 132**
Children helped with school fees/a scholarship	12 321	0	1 598	0	154	0	0	0	2 014	**16 087**
School desks built/bought/donated	3 200	0	3 689	250	1 564	1 725	1 794	0	4 109	**16 331**
Permanent classrooms built	44	0	50	8	93	31	45	0	82	**353**
Classrooms repaired	0	0	34	0	0	14	0	0	33	**81**
Adults receiving training in literacy this financial year	1 160	0	3 000	568	3 617	0	0	0	350	**8 695**
Habitat										
Latrines or toilets dug/built	50	0	2 403	0	57	162	23	96	4 311	**7 102**
Houses connected to a new sewage system	143	0	0	0	0	0	0	0	0	**143**
Wells dug/improved (or springs capped)	0	0	15	0	7	13	0	0	159	**194**
New positive boreholes drilled	0	0	8	93	14	0	27	0	220	**362**
Gravity feed drinking water systems built	0	0	28	0	1	0	0	0	0	**29**
Drinking water systems repaired/improved	0	0	392	0	2	0	0	0	31	**425**
Houses improved with PLAN project	265	0	520	0	0	0	1	0	2	**788**
New houses built for beneficiaries	225	0	596	0	0	2	6	0	313	**1 142**
Community halls built or improved	2	0	2	0	3	0	3	0	2	**12**
Community leaders trained for 1 day or more	2 214	95	3 522	232	200	3 575	814	20	2 693	**13 365**
Kilometres of roadway improved	1.2	0	26	0	0	0	0	0	53.4	**80.6**
Bridges built	0	0	4	2	11	0	0	0	1	**18**
Families benefited directly from erosion control	0	0	1 092	0	1 500	0	0	0	18 405	**20 997**
Houses newly served by electrification project	448	0	2	0	0	0	0	0	44	**494**

Source: Adapted from PLAN International Program Output Chart financial year 1996, appendix to Quarterly Report to the International Board first quarter 1997

The table on the previous page is part of a report published by PLAN International, an international aid organisation. It gives some information about PLAN's work in one of its regions of operation (Eastern and Southern Africa). Refer to the table to answer the questions below.

QUESTION 5.1

What does the table indicate about the level of PLAN International's activity in Ethiopia in 1996, compared with other countries in the region?

A. The level of activity was comparatively high in Ethiopia.

B. The level of activity was comparatively low in Ethiopia.

C. It was about the same as in other countries in the region.

D. It was comparatively high in the Habitat category, and low in the other categories.

QUESTION 5.2

In 1996 Ethiopia was one of the poorest countries in the world.

Taking this fact and the information in the table into account, what do you think might explain the level of PLAN International's activities in Ethiopia compared with its activities in other countries?

....

....

....

READING UNIT 6 : POLICE

A murder has been committed but the suspect denies everything. He claims not to know the victim. He says he never knew him, never went near him, never touched him... The police and the judge are convinced that he is not telling the truth. But how to prove it?

Scientific Police Weapons

At the crime scene, investigators have gathered every possible shred of evidence imaginable: fibres from fabrics, hairs, finger marks, cigarette ends...The few hairs found on the victim's jacket are red. And they look strangely like the suspect's. If it could be proved that these hairs are indeed his, this would be evidence that he had in fact met the victim.

Every individual is unique

Specialists set to work. They examine some cells at the root of these hairs and some of the suspect's blood cells. In the nucleus of each cell in our bodies there is DNA. What is it?

DNA is like a necklace made of two twisted strings of pearls.

Imagine that these pearls come in four different colours and that thousands of coloured pearls (which make up a gene) are strung in a very specific order. In each individual this order is exactly the same in all the cells in the body: those of the hair roots as well as those of the big toe, those of the liver and those of the stomach or blood. But the order of the pearls varies from one person to another. Given the number of pearls strung in this way, there is very little chance of two people having the same DNA, with the exception of identical twins. Unique to each individual, DNA is thus a sort of genetic identity card.

Geneticists are therefore able to compare the suspect's genetic identity card (determined from his blood) with that of the person with the red hair. If the genetic card is the same, they will know that the suspect did in fact go near the victim he said he'd never met.

Just one piece of evidence

More and more often in cases of sexual assault, murder, theft or other crimes, the police are having genetic analyses done. Why? To try to find evidence of contact between two people, two objects or a person and an object. Proving such contact is often very useful to the investigation. But it does not necessarily provide proof of a crime. It is just one piece of evidence amongst many others.

Anne Versailles

We are made up of billions of cells

Every living thing is made up of lots of cells. A cell is very small indeed. It can also be said to be microscopic because it can only be seen using a microscope which magnifies it many times. Each cell has an outer membrane and a nucleus in which the DNA is found.

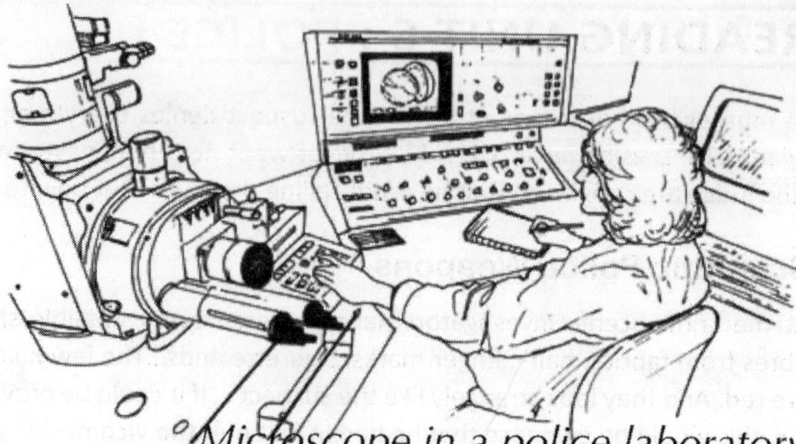

Microscope in a police laboratory

Genetic what?

DNA is made up of a number of genes, each consisting of thousands of "pearls". Together these genes form the genetic identity card of a person.

How is the genetic identity card revealed?

The geneticist takes the few cells from the base of the hairs found on the victim, or from the saliva left on a cigarette end. He puts them into a product which destroys everything around the DNA of the cells. He then does the same thing with some cells from the suspect's blood. The DNA is then specially prepared for analysis. After this, it is placed in a special gel and an electric current is passed through the gel. After a few hours, this produces stripes similar to a bar code (like the ones on things we buy) which are visible under a special lamp. The bar code of the suspect's DNA is then compared with that of the hairs found on the victim.

Refer to the magazine article on the opposite page to answer the questions below.

QUESTION 6.1

To explain the structure of DNA, the author talks about a pearl necklace. How do these pearl necklaces vary from one individual to another?

A. They vary in length.

B. The order of the pearls is different.

C. The number of necklaces is different.

D. The colour of the pearls is different.

QUESTION 6.2

What is the purpose of the box headed "How is the genetic identity card revealed"?

To explain

A. What DNA is.

B. What a bar code is.

C. How cells are analysed to find the pattern of DNA.

D. How it can be proved that a crime has been committed.

QUESTION 6.3

What is the author's main aim?

A. To warn.
B. To amuse.
C. To inform.
D. To convince.

QUESTION 6.4

The end of the introduction (the first shaded section) says: "But how to prove it?"

According to the passage, investigators try to find an answer to this question by

A. Interrogating witnesses.
B. Carrying out genetic analyses.
C. Interrogating the suspect thoroughly.
D. Going over all the results of the investigation again.

READING UNIT 7 : RUNNERS

Feel good in your runners

For 14 years the Sports Medicine Centre of Lyon (France) has been studying the injuries of young sports players and sports professionals. The study has established that the best course is prevention ... and good shoes.

Knocks, falls, wear and tear...

Eighteen per cent of sports players aged 8 to 12 already have heel injuries. The cartilage of a footballer's ankle does not respond well to shocks, and 25% of professionals have discovered for themselves that it is an especially weak point. The cartilage of the delicate knee joint can also be irreparably damaged and if care is not taken right from childhood (10–12 years of age), this can cause premature osteoarthritis. The hip does not escape damage either and, particularly when tired, players run the risk of fractures as a result of falls or collisions.

According to the study, footballers who have been playing for more than ten years have bony outgrowths either on the tibia or on the heel. This is what is known as "footballer's foot", a deformity caused by shoes with soles and ankle parts that are too flexible.

Protect, support, stabilise, absorb

If a shoe is too rigid, it restricts movement. If it is too flexible, it increases the risk of injuries and sprains. A good sports shoe should meet four criteria: Firstly, it must provide exterior protection: resisting knocks from the ball or another player, coping with unevenness in the ground, and keeping the foot warm and dry even when it is freezing cold and raining. It must support the foot, and in particular the ankle joint, to avoid sprains, swelling and other problems, which may even affect the knee. It must also provide players with good stability so that they do not slip on a wet ground or skid on a surface that is too dry.

Finally, it must absorb shocks, especially those suffered by volleyball and basketball players who are constantly jumping.

Dry feet

To avoid minor but painful conditions such as blisters or even splits or athlete's foot (fungal infections), the shoe must allow evaporation of perspiration and must prevent outside dampness from getting in. The ideal material for this is leather, which can be waterproofed to prevent the shoe from getting soaked the first time it rains.

Source: Revue ID (16) 1-15 June 1997.

Use the article on the previous page to answer the questions below.

QUESTION 7.1

What does the author intend to show in this text?

A. That the quality of many sports shoes has greatly improved.

B. That it is best not to play football if you are under 12 years of age.

C. That young people are suffering more and more injuries due to their poor physical condition.

D. That it is very important for young sports players to wear good sports shoes.

QUESTION 7.2

According to the article, why should sports shoes not be too rigid?

....

QUESTION 7.3

One part of the article says, "A good sports shoe should meet four criteria."

What are these criteria?

....

....

....

....

QUESTION 7.4

Look at this sentence from near the end of the article. It is presented here in two parts:

"To avoid minor but painful conditions such as blisters or even splits or athlete's foot (fungal infections),..."	*(first part)*
"...the shoe must allow evaporation of perspiration and must prevent outside dampness from getting in."	*(second part)*

What is the relationship between the first and second parts of the sentence?

The second part

A. Contradicts the first part.

B. Repeats the first part.

C. Illustrates the problem described in the first part.

D. Gives the solution to the problem described in the first part.

READING UNIT 8 : GIFT

THE GIFT

How many days, she wondered, had she sat like this, watching the cold brown water inch up the dissolving bluff. She could just faintly remember the beginning of the rain, driving in across the swamp from the south and beating against the shell of her house. Then the river itself started rising, slowly at first until at last it paused to turn back. From hour to hour it slithered up creeks and ditches and poured over low places. In the night, while she slept, it claimed the road and surrounded her so that she sat alone, her boat gone, the house like a piece of drift lodged on its bluff. Now even against the tarred planks of the supports the waters touched. And still they rose.

As far as she could see, to the treetops where the opposite banks had been, the swamp was an empty sea, awash with sheets of rain, the river lost somewhere in its vastness. Her house with its boat bottom had been built to ride just such a flood, if one ever came, but now it was old. Maybe the boards underneath were partly rotted away. Maybe the cable mooring the house to the great live oak would snap loose and let her go turning downstream, the way her boat had gone.

No one could come now. She could cry out but it would be no use, no one would hear. Down the length and breadth of the swamp others were fighting to save what little they could, maybe even their lives. She had seen a whole house go floating by, so quiet she was reminded of sitting at a funeral. She thought when she saw it she knew whose house it was. It had been bad seeing it drift by, but the owners must have escaped to higher ground. Later, with the rain and darkness pressing in, she had heard a panther scream upriver.

Now the house seemed to shudder around her like something alive. She reached out to catch a lamp as it tilted off the table by her bed and put it between her feet to hold it steady. Then creaking and groaning with effort the house struggled up from the clay, floated free, bobbing like a cork and swung out slowly with the pull of the river. She gripped the edge of the bed. Swaying from side to side, the house moved to the length of its mooring. There was a jolt and a complaining of old timbers and then a pause. Slowly the current released it and let it swing back, rasping across its resting place. She caught her breath and sat for a long time feeling the slow pendulous sweeps. The dark sifted down through the incessant rain, and, head on arm, she slept holding on to the bed.

Sometime in the night the cry awoke her, a sound so anguished she was on her feet before she was awake. In the dark she stumbled against the bed. It came from out there, from the river. She could hear something moving, something large that made a dredging, sweeping sound. It could be another house. Then it hit, not head on but glancing and sliding down the length of her house. It was a tree. She listened as the branches and leaves cleared themselves and went on downstream, leaving only the rain and the lappings of the flood, sounds so constant now that they seemed a part of the silence. Huddled on the bed, she was almost asleep again when another cry sounded, this time so close it could have been in the room. Staring into the dark, she eased back on the bed until her hand caught the cold shape of the rifle. Then crouched on the pillow, she cradled the gun across her knees. "Who's there?" she called.

The answer was a repeated cry, but less shrill, tired sounding, then the empty silence closing in. She drew back against the bed. Whatever was there she could hear it moving about on the porch. Planks creaked and she could distinguish the sounds of objects being knocked over. There was a scratching on the wall as if it would tear its way in. She knew now what it was, a big cat, deposited by the uprooted tree that had passed her. It had come with the flood, a gift.

Unconsciously she pressed her hand against her face and along her tightened throat. The rifle rocked across her knees. She had never seen a panther in her life. She had heard about them from others and heard their cries, like suffering, in the distance. The cat was scratching on the wall again, rattling the window by the door. As long as she guarded the window and kept the cat hemmed in by the wall and water, caged, she would be all right. Outside, the animal paused to rake his claws across the rusted outer screen. Now and then, it whined and growled.

When the light filtered down through the rain at last, coming like another kind of dark, she was still sitting on the bed, stiff and cold. Her arms, used to rowing on the river, ached from the stillness of holding the rifle. She had hardly allowed herself to move for fear any sound might give strength to the cat. Rigid, she swayed with the movement of the house. The rain still fell as if it would never stop. Through the grey light, finally, she could see the rain-pitted flood and far away the cloudy shape of drowned treetops. The cat was not moving now. Maybe he had gone away. Laying the gun aside she slipped off the bed and moved without a sound to the window. It was still there, crouched at the edge of the porch, staring up at the live oak, the mooring of her house, as if gauging its chances of leaping to an overhanging branch. It did not seem so frightening now that she could see it, its coarse fur napped into twigs, its sides pinched and ribs showing. It would be easy to shoot it where it sat, its long tail whipping back and forth. She was moving back to get the gun when it turned around. With no warning, no crouch or tensing of muscles, it sprang at the window, shattering a pane of glass. She fell back, stifling a scream, and taking up the rifle, she fired through the window. She could not see the panther now, but she had missed. It began to pace again. She could glimpse its head and the arch of its back as it passed the window.

Shivering, she pulled back on the bed and lay down. The lulling constant sound of the river and the rain, the penetrating chill, drained away her purpose. She watched the window and kept the gun ready. After waiting a long while she moved again to look. The panther had fallen asleep, its head on its paws, like a house-cat. For the first time since the rains began she wanted to cry, for herself, for all the people, for everything in the flood. Sliding down on the bed, she pulled the quilt around her shoulders. She should have got out when she could, while the roads were still open or before her boat was washed away. As she rocked back and forth with the sway of the house a deep ache in her stomach reminded her she hadn't eaten. She couldn't remember for how long. Like the cat, she was starving. Easing into the kitchen, she made a fire with the few remaining sticks of wood. If the flood lasted she would have to burn the chair, maybe even the table itself. Taking down the remains of a smoked ham from the ceiling, she cut thick slices of the brownish red meat and placed them in a skillet. The smell of the frying meat made her dizzy. There were stale biscuits from the last time she had cooked and she could make some coffee. There was plenty of water.

While she was cooking her food, she almost forgot about the cat until it whined. It was hungry too. "Let me eat," she called to it, "and then I'll see to you." And she laughed under her breath. As she hung the rest of the ham back on its nail the cat growled a deep throaty rumble that made her hand shake.

After she had eaten, she went to the bed again and took up the rifle. The house had risen so high now it no longer scraped across the bluff when it swung back from the river. The food had warmed her. She could get rid of the cat while light still hung in the rain. She crept slowly to the window. It was still there, mewling, beginning to move about the porch. She stared at it a long time, unafraid. Then without thinking what she was doing, she laid the gun aside and started around the edge of the bed to the kitchen. Behind her the cat was moving, fretting. She took down what was left of the ham and making her way back across the swaying floor to the window she shoved it through the broken pane. On the other side there was a hungry snarl and something like a shock passed from the animal to her. Stunned by what she had done, she drew back to the bed. She could hear the sounds of the panther tearing at the meat. The house rocked around her.

The next time she awoke she knew at once that everything had changed. The rain had stopped. She felt for the movement of the house but it no longer swayed on the flood. Drawing her door open, she saw through the torn screen a different world. The house was resting on the bluff where it always had. A few feet down, the river still raced on in a torrent, but it no longer covered the few feet between the house and the live oak. And the cat was gone. Leading from the porch to the live oak and doubtless on into the swamp were tracks, indistinct and already disappearing into the soft mud. And there on the porch, gnawed to whiteness, was what was left of the ham.

Source: Dollarhide, Louis, "The Gift", in Mississippi Writers: Reflections of Childhood and Youth, Volume 1, edited by Dorothy Abbott, University Press of Mississippi, 1985.

Use the story "The Gift" on the previous three pages to answer the questions which follow. (Note that line numbers are given in the margin of the story to help you find parts which are referred to in the questions.)

QUESTION 8.1

What is the woman's situation at the beginning of the story?

A. She is too weak to leave the house after days without food.

B. She is defending herself against a wild animal.

C. Her house has been surrounded by flood waters.

D. A flooded river has swept her house away.

QUESTION 8.2

When the woman says, "and then I'll see to you" (line 92) she means that she is

A. Sure that the cat won't hurt her.

B. Trying to frighten the cat.

C. Intending to shoot the cat.

D. Planning to feed the cat.

QUESTION 8.3

Do you think that the last sentence of "The Gift" is an appropriate ending?

Explain your answer, demonstrating your understanding of how the last sentence relates to the story's meaning.

....

....

QUESTION 8.4

"Then creaking and groaning with effort the house struggled up ..." (line 24)

What happened to the house in this part of the story?

A. It fell apart.

B. It began to float.

C. It crashed into the oak tree.

D. It sank to the bottom of the river.

QUESTION 8.5

Here are some of the early references to the panther in the story.

> "the cry awoke her, a sound so anguished..." (line 32)
>
> "The answer was a repeated cry, but less shrill, tired sounding..." (line 44)
>
> "She had...heard their cries, like suffering, in the distance." (lines 51–52)

Considering what happens in the rest of the story, why do you think the writer chooses to introduce the panther with these descriptions?

....

....

QUESTION 8.6

What does the story suggest was the woman's reason for feeding the panther?

....

....

....

....

QUESTION 8.7

Here is part of a conversation between two people who read "The Gift":

Give evidence from the story to show how each of these speakers could justify their point of view.

Speaker 1 ....

....

....

Speaker 2 ....

....

READING UNIT 9 : AMANDA AND THE DUCHESS

Text 1

AMANDA AND THE DUCHESS

Summary: Since Léocadia's death, the Prince, who was in love with her, has been inconsolable. At a shop called Réséda Soeurs, the Duchess, who is the Prince's aunt, has met a young shop assistant, Amanda, who looks amazingly like Léocadia. The Duchess wants Amanda to help her set the Prince free from the memories which haunt him.

A crossroads in the castle grounds, a circular bench around a small obelisk...evening is falling...

AMANDA

I still don't understand. What can I do for him, ma'am? I can't believe you could possibly have thought...And why me? I'm not particularly pretty. And even if someone were very pretty—who could suddenly come between him and his memories like that?

THE DUCHESS

No-one but you.

AMANDA, *sincerely surprised*

Me?

THE DUCHESS

The world is so foolish, my child. It sees only parades, gestures, badges of office...that must be why you have never been told. But my heart hasn't deceived me—I almost cried out at Réséda Soeurs the first time I saw you. To someone who knew more of her than just her public image, you are the living likeness of Léocadia.

A silence. The evening birds have now taken over from the afternoon birds. The grounds are filled with shadows and twittering.

AMANDA, very gently

I really don't think I can, ma'am. I have nothing, I am nothing, and those lovers...that was my fancy, don't you see?

She has got up. As if about to leave, she has picked up her small suitcase.

THE DUCHESS, gently also, and very wearily Of course, my dear. I apologise.

She in turn gets up, with difficulty, like an old woman. A bicycle bell is heard in the evening air; she gives a start.

Listen...it's him! Just show yourself to him, leaning against this little obelisk where he first met her. Let him see you, even if it's just this once, let him call out, take a sudden interest in this likeness, in this stratagem which I shall confess to him tomorrow and for which he will hate me—in anything but this dead girl who'll take him away from me one of these days, I'm sure...(She has taken her by the arm.) You will do that, won't you? I beg you most humbly, young lady. (She looks at her, beseechingly, and quickly adds:) And then, that way, you'll see him too. And...I can feel that I'm blushing again from saying this to you—life is just too mad! That's the third time I've blushed in sixty years, and the second time in ten minutes—you'll see him; and if he could ever (why not him, since he's handsome and charming and he wouldn't be the first?) if he could ever have the good fortune, for himself and for me, to take your fancy for one moment...The bell again in the shadows, but very close now.

THE PRINCE

Take the second turning on your left.

He bows, sadly and courteously, gets back on the bicycle and rides away. The bell is heard again in the distance. The Duchess comes out of the shadows, very much an old woman.

AMANDA, *gently, after a while* He didn't recognise me...

THE DUCHESS

It was dark...And then, who knows what face he gives her now, in his dreams? (She asks timidly:)

The last train has gone, young lady. In any case, wouldn't you like to stay at the castle tonight?

AMANDA, in a whisper

What should I say to him?

THE DUCHESS, gripping her arm

Simply say: "Excuse me, Sir, can you tell me the way to the sea?"

She has hurried into the deeper shadows of the trees. Just in time. There is a pale blur. It is the Prince on his bicycle. He passes very close to the pale blur of Amanda by the obelisk. She murmurs.

AMANDA

Excuse me, Sir...

He stops, dismounts from the bicycle, takes off his hat and looks at her.

THE PRINCE

Yes?

AMANDA

Can you tell me the way to the sea?

AMANDA, in a strange voice Yes, ma'am.

It is completely dark. The two of them can no longer be seen in the shadows, and only the wind can be heard in the huge trees of the grounds.

THE CURTAIN FALLS

Source: Jean Anouilh, Léocadia (end of Scene II). Published by La Table Ronde, 1984.

Text 2

Definitions of some theatrical occupations

Actor: plays a character on stage.

Director: controls and oversees all aspects of a play. He not only positions the actors, arranges their entrances and exits and directs their acting, but also suggests how the script is to be interpreted.

Wardrobe staff: produce the costumes from a model.

Set designer: designs models of the sets and costumes. These models are then transformed into their full size in the workshop.

Props manager: in charge of finding the required props. The word "props" is used to mean everything that can be moved: armchairs, letters, lamps, bunches of flowers, etc. The sets and costumes are not props.

Sound technician: in charge of all sound effects required for the production. He is at the controls during the show.

Lighting assistant or lighting technician: in charge of lighting. He is also at the controls during the show. Lighting is so sophisticated that a well-equipped theatre can employ up to ten lighting technicians.

On the previous two pages there are two texts. Text 1 is an extract from the play Léocadia by Jean Anouilh and Text 2 gives definitions of theatrical occupations. Refer to the texts to answer the questions which follow.

QUESTION 9.1

What is this extract from the play about? The Duchess thinks of a trick

A. To get the Prince to come and see her more often.

B. To get the Prince to make up his mind finally to get married.

C. To get Amanda to make the Prince forget his grief.

D. To get Amanda to come and live at the castle with her.

QUESTION 9.2

A. In the script of the play, in addition to the words to be spoken by the actors, there are directions for the actors and theatre technicians to follow.

B. How can these directions be recognised in the script?

....

QUESTION 9.3

The table below lists theatre technicians involved in staging this extract from Léocadia. Complete the table by indicating one stage direction from Text 1 which would require the involvement of each technician.

The first one has been done for you.

Theatre technicians	Stage direction
Set designer	A circular bench around a small obelisk
Props manager	
Sound technician	
Lighting technician	

QUESTION 9.4

The director positions the actors on the stage. On a diagram, the director represents Amanda with the letter A and the Duchess with the letter D.

Put an A and a D on the following diagram of the set to show approximately where Amanda and the Duchess are when the Prince arrives.

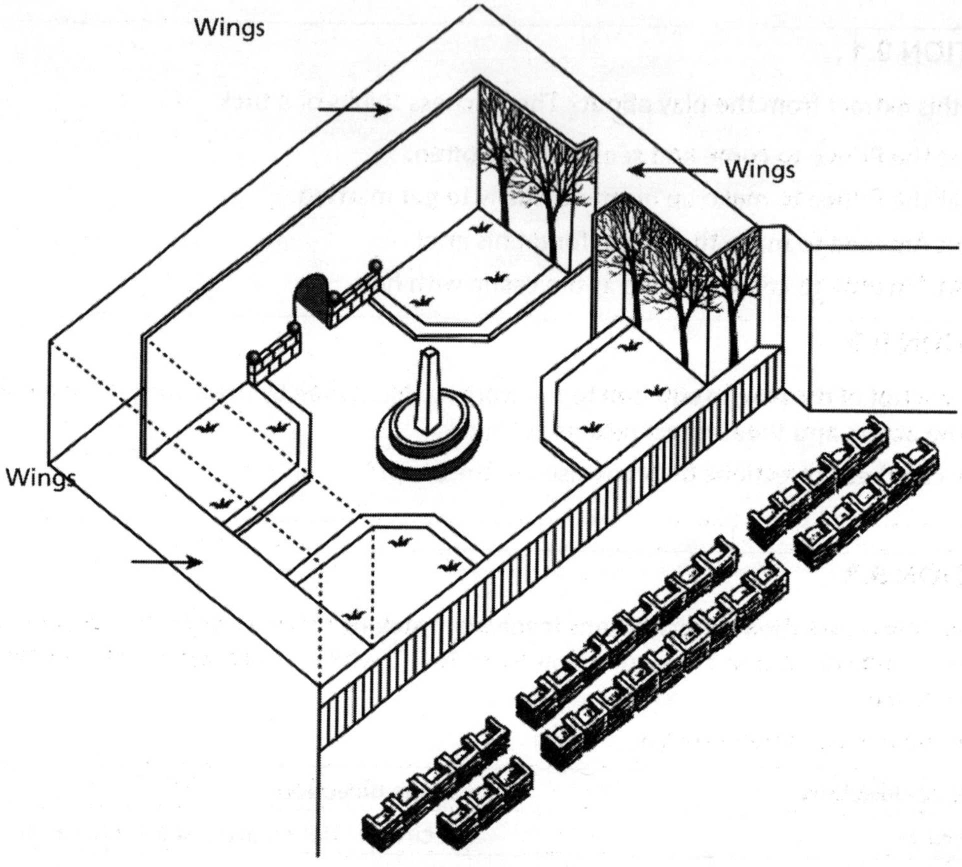

QUESTION 9.5

Towards the end of the extract from the play, Amanda says, "He didn't recognise me...". What does she mean by that?

A. That the Prince didn't A. t look at Amanda.

B. That the Prince didn't realise that Amanda was a shop assistant.

C. That the Prince didn't realise that he'd already met Amanda.

D. That the Prince didn't notice that Amanda looked like Léocadia.

READING UNIT 10 : PERSONNEL

CANCO

CANCO Manufacturing Company

Personnel Departmen

Centre on Internal and External Mobility

What is CIEM?

CIEM stands for Centre on Internal and External Mobility, an initiative of the personnel department. A number of workers of this department work in CIEM, together with members from other departments and outside career consultants.

CIEM is available to help employees in their search for another job inside or outside the Canco Manufacturing Company.

What does CIEM do?

CIEM supports employees who are seriously considering other work through the following activities:

- **Job Data Bank**

After an interview with the employee, information is entered into a data bank that tracks job seekers and job openings at Canco and at other manufacturing companies.

- **Guidance**

The employee's potential is explored through career counselling discussions.

- **Courses**

Courses are being organized (in collaboration with the department for information and training) that will deal with job search and career planning.

- **Career Change Project**

CIEM supports and coordinates projects to help employees prepare for new careers and new perspectives.

- **Mediation**

CIEM acts as a mediator for employees who are threatened with dismissal resulting from reorganisation, and assists with finding new positions when necessary.

- **How much does CIEM cost?**

Payment is determined in consultation with the department where you work. A number of services of CIEM are free. You may also be asked to pay, either in money or in time.

- **How does CIEM work?**

CIEM assists employees who are seriously considering another job within or outside the company.

That process begins by submitting an application. A discussion with a personnel counsellor can also be useful. It is obvious that you should talk with the counsellor first about your wishes and the internal possibilities regarding your career. The counsellor is familiar with your abilities and with developments within your unit.

Contact with CIEM in any case is made via the personnel counsellor. He or she handles the application for you, after which you are invited to a discussion with a CIEM representative.

- **For more information**

The personnel department can give you more information.

Use the announcement from a personnel department on the previous page to answer the questions below.

QUESTION 10.1

According to the announcement, where could you get more information about CIEM?

....

QUESTION 10.2

List two ways in which CIEM helps people who will lose their jobs because of a departmental reorganisation.

....

....

READING UNIT 11 : NEW RULES

EDITORIAL

Technology creates the need for new rules

SCIENCE has a way of getting ahead of law and ethics. That happened dramatically in 1945 on the destructive side of life with the atomic bomb, and is now happening on life's creative side with techniques to overcome human infertility.

Most of us rejoiced with the Brown family in England when Louise, the first test-tube baby, — most recently the births of healthy babies that had once been embryos frozen to await the proper moment of implantation in the mother-to-be.

It is about two such frozen embryos in Australia that a storm of legal and ethical questions has arisen. The embryos were destined to be implanted in Elsa Rios, wife of Mario Rios. A previous embryo implant had been unsuccessful, and the Rioses wanted to have another chance at becoming parents. But before they had a second chance to try, the Rioses perished in an airplane crash.

What was the Australian hospital to do with the frozen embryos? Could they be implanted in someone else? There were numerous volunteers. Were the embryos somehow entitled to the Rioses' substantial estate? Or should the embryos be destroyed? The Rioses, understandably, had made no provision for the embryos' future.

The Australians set up a commission to study the matter. Last week, the commission made its report. The embryos should be thawed, the panel said, because donation of embryos to someone else would require the consent of the "producers," and no such consent had been given. The panel also held that the embryos in their present state had no life or rights and thus could be destroyed.

The commission members were conscious of treading on slippery legal and ethical grounds. Therefore, they urged that three months be allowed for public opinion to respond to the commission recommendation. Should there be an overwhelming outcry against destroying the embryos, the commission would reconsider.

Couples now enrolling in Sydney's Queen Victoria hospital for in vitro fertilization programs must specify what should be done with the embryos if something happens to them.

This assures that a situation similar to the Rioses won't recur. But what of other complex questions? In France, a woman recently had to go to court to be allowed to bear a child from her deceased husband's frozen sperm. How should such a request be handled? What should be done if a surrogate mother breaks her child-bearing contract and refuses to give up the infant she had promised to bear for someone else?

Our society has failed so far to come up with enforceable rules for curbing the destructive potential of atomic power. We are reaping the nightmarish harvest for that failure. The possibilities of misuse of scientists' ability to advance or retard procreation are manifold. Ethical and legal boundaries need to be set before we stray too far.

Use the newspaper editorial "Technology creates the need for new rules" on the previous page to answer the questions below.

QUESTION 11.1

Underline the sentence that explains what the Australians did to help decide how to deal with the frozen embryos belonging to a couple killed in the plane crash.

QUESTION 11.2

List two examples from the editorial that illustrate how modern technology, such as that used for implanting frozen embryos, creates the need for new rules.

....

....

READING UNIT 12 : MORELAND

The Moreland Library System gives new library members a bookmark showing its Hours of Opening. Refer to the bookmark to answer the questions which follow.

Moreland Library System

HOURS OF OPENING *Effective from February 1 1998*

	Brunswick Library	Campbell Turnbull Library	Coburg Library	Fawkner Library	Glenroy Library
Sunday	1pm-5pm	Closed	2pm-5pm	Closed	2pm-5pm
Monday	11am-8pm	11am-5.30pm	1pm-8pm	11am-5.30pm	10am-5.30pm
Tuesday	11am-8pm	11am-8pm	11am-8pm	11am-8pm	10am-8pm
Wednesday	11am-8pm	11am-5pm	10am-8pm	11am-5pm	10am-8pm
Thursday	11am-8pm	11am-5.30pm	10am-8pm	11am-5.30pm	10am-8pm
Friday	11am-5pm	11am-5pm	10am-8pm	11am-5pm	10am-5.30pm
Saturday	10am-1pm	10am-1pm	9am-1pm	10am-1pm	9am-1pm

QUESTION 12.1

What time does the Fawkner Library close on Wednesday?

....

QUESTION 12.2

Which library is still open at 6 p.m. on Friday evening?

A. Brunswick Library

B. Campbell Turnbull Library

C. Coburg Library

D. Fawkner Library

E. Glenroy Library

READING UNIT 13: WARRANTY

Warranty Text 1

Camera Shots **Video House**
89 ELIZABETH STREET, MELBOURNE 3000
PHONE: 9670 9601 FAX: 9602 5527
http://www.camerashots.com.au
CUSTOMER
SARAH BROWN
151 GLENLYON STREET
BRUNSWICK VIC 3057

CAMERA SHOTS VIDEO HOUSE
89 ELIZABETH STREET
MELBOURNE VIC 3000
9670 9601

INVOICE 26802	**DATE** 18/10/99	**TIME** 12:10
ACCOUNT 195927	**SALES** 24 RAY	**REG.** 16

PRODUCT	DESCRIPTION	SERIAL No	LIST	QTY.	NET	TOTAL	EX.
150214	ROLLY FOTONEX 250 ZOOM	30910963		1	249.08	249.08	X
33844	TRIPOD			1	5.66	5.66	X
	Transaction . . . . . Amount	Change			Sub-Total	254.74	
	Visa/Bank Card $254.74				Total	254.74	

Thank you for your business

On the opposite page is the receipt that Sarah received when she bought her new camera. Below is the warranty card for the camera. Use these documents to answer the questions which follow.

Warranty Text 2

ONE YEAR WARRANTY : (Private Users)

VALID ONLY IN AUSTRALIA

VIDEO HOUSE & COMPANY PTY LTD – ACN 008 458 884 ('VIDEO HOUSE') warrants to the initial owner that the camera is free of any defects in material or workmanship. This warranty is not transferable.

Video House will service, repair or replace at its election, and free of charge, any part which is found upon inspection by Video House to be defective in material or workmanship during the warranty period(s).

PLEASE PRINT CLEARLY

NO. M 409668

Camera – Model

....

Serial No:

Name of Owner: SARAH BROWN

Address: 151 GLENLYON STREET

BRUNSWICK VIC 3057

Date Purchased:

Purchase Price:

Rubber Stamp of Dealer

PLEASE NOTE:

Post Immediately – Postage Stamp Necessary

This warranty card should be completed and returned to Video House within 10 days of purchase.

International Warranty Card issued on request.

QUESTION 13.1

Use the details on the receipt to complete the warranty card.

The name and address of the owner have already been filled in.

QUESTION 13.2

How long does Sarah have, to return the warranty card?

....

QUESTION 13.3

What else did Sarah buy while she was in the store?

....

QUESTION 13.4

The words "Thank you for your business" are printed on the bottom of the receipt. One possible reason for this is simply to be polite. What is another possible reason?

....

READING UNIT 14 : A JUST JUDGE

Just Judge Text

Refer to the story A Just Judge to answer the questions which follow it.

A Just Judge

An Algerian king named Bauakas wanted to find out whether or not it was true, as he had been told, that in one of his cities lived a just judge who could instantly discern the truth, and from whom no rogue was ever able to conceal himself. Bauakas exchanged clothes with a merchant and went on horseback to the city where the judge lived.

At the entrance to the city a cripple approached the king and begged alms of him. Bauakas gave him money and was about to continue on his way, but the cripple clung to his clothing.

"What do you wish?" asked the king. "Haven't I given you money?"

"You gave me alms," said the cripple, "now grant me one favour. Let me ride with you as far as the city square, otherwise the horses and camels may trample me."

Bauakas sat the cripple behind him on the horse and took him as far as the city square. There he halted his horse, but the cripple refused to dismount.

"We have arrived at the square, why don't you get off?" asked Bauakas.

"Why should I?" the beggar replied. "This horse belongs to me. If you are unwilling to return it, we shall have to go to court."

Hearing their quarrel, people gathered around them shouting:

"Go to the judge! He will decide between you!"

Bauakas and the cripple went to the judge. There were others in court, and the judge called upon each one in turn. Before he came to Bauakas and the cripple he heard a scholar and a peasant. They had come to court over a woman: the peasant said she was his wife, and the scholar said she was his. The judge heard them both, remained silent for a moment, and then said:

"Leave the woman here with me, and come back tomorrow."

When they had gone, a butcher and an oil merchant came before the judge. The butcher was covered with blood, and the oil merchant with oil. In his hand the butcher held some money, and the oil merchant held onto the butcher's hand.

"I was buying oil from this man," the butcher said, "and when I took out my purse to pay him, he seized me by the hand and tried to take all my money away from me. That is why we have come to you—I holding onto my purse, and he holding onto my hand. But the money is mine, and he is a thief."

Then the oil merchant spoke. "That is not true," he said. "The butcher came to me to buy oil, and after I had poured him a full jug, he asked me to change a gold piece for him. When I took out my money and placed it on a bench, he seized it and tried to run off. I caught him by the hand, as you see, and brought him here to you."

The judge remained silent for a moment, then said: "Leave the money here with me, and come back tomorrow."

When his turn came, Bauakas told what had happened. The judge listened to him, and then asked the beggar to speak.

"All that he said is untrue," said the beggar. "He was sitting on the ground, and as I rode through the city he asked me to let him ride with me. I sat him on my horse and took him where he wanted to go. But when we got there he refused to get off and said that the horse was his, which is not true."

The judge thought for a moment, then said, "Leave the horse here with me, and come back tomorrow."

The following day many people gathered in court to hear the judge's decisions.

First came the scholar and the peasant.

"Take your wife," the judge said to the scholar, "and the peasant shall be given fifty strokes of the lash."

The scholar took his wife, and the peasant was given his punishment.

Then the judge called the butcher.

"The money is yours," he said to him. And pointing to the oil merchant he said: "Give him fifty strokes of the lash."

He next called Bauakas and the cripple.

"Would you be able to recognise your horse among twenty others?" he asked Bauakas.

"I would," he replied.

"And you?" he asked the cripple.

"I would," said the cripple.

"Come with me," the judge said to Bauakas.

They went to the stable. Bauakas instantly pointed out his horse among the twenty others. Then the judge called the cripple to the stable and told him to point out the horse. The cripple recognised the horse and pointed to it. The judge then returned to his seat.

"Take the horse, it is yours," he said to Bauakas. "Give the beggar fifty strokes of the lash."

When the judge left the court and went home, Bauakas followed him.

"What do you want?" asked the judge. "Are you not satisfied with my decision?"

"I am satisfied," said Bauakas. "But I should like to learn how you knew that the woman was the wife of the scholar, that the money belonged to the butcher, and that the horse was mine and not the beggar's."

"This is how I knew about the woman: in the morning I sent for her and said: 'Please fill my inkwell.' She took the inkwell, washed it quickly and deftly, and filled it with ink; therefore it was work she was accustomed to. If she had been the wife of the peasant she would not have known how to do it. This showed me that the scholar was telling the truth.

"And this is how I knew about the money: I put it into a cup full of water, and in the morning I looked to see if any oil had risen to the surface. If the money had belonged to the oil merchant it would have been soiled by his oily hands. There was no oil on the water; therefore, the butcher was telling the truth.

"It was more difficult to find out about the horse. The cripple recognised it among twenty others, even as you did. However, I did not take you both to the stable to see which of you knew the horse, but to see which of you the horse knew. When you approached it, it turned its head and stretched its neck toward you; but when the cripple touched it, it laid back its ears and lifted one hoof. Therefore I knew that you were the horse's real master."

Then Bauakas said to the judge: "I am not a merchant, but King Bauakas, I came here in order to see if what is said of you is true. I see now that you are a wise judge. Ask whatever you wish of me, and you shall have it as reward."

"I need no reward," replied the judge. "I am content that my king has praised me."

Source: Leo Tolstoy, "A Just Judge" in Fable and Fairytales, translated by Ann Dunningham.

QUESTION 14.1

Near the beginning of the story we are told that Bauakas exchanged clothes with a merchant.

Why didn't Bauakas want to be recognised?

A. He wanted to see if he would still be obeyed when he was an "ordinary" person.

B. He planned to appear in a case before the judge, disguised as a merchant.

C. He enjoyed disguising himself so he could move about freely and play tricks on his subjects.

D. He wanted to see the judge at work in his usual way, uninfluenced by the presence of the king.

QUESTION 14.2

How did the judge know that the woman was the wife of the scholar?

A. By observing her appearance and seeing that she did not look like a peasant's wife.

B. By the way the scholar and the peasant told their stories in court.

C. By the way she reacted to the peasant and the scholar in court.

D. By testing her skill in work that she needed to perform for her husband.

QUESTION 14.3

Do you think it was fair of the judge to give the SAME punishment for all the crimes?

Explain your answer, referring to similarities or differences between the three cases in the story.

....

....

....

....

QUESTION 14.4

What is this story mainly about?

A. Major crimes.

B. Wise justice.

C. A good ruler.

D. A clever trick.

QUESTION 14.5

For this question you need to compare law and justice in your country with the law and justice shown in the story.

In the story crimes are punished under the law. What is another way in which law and justice in your country are SIMILAR to the kind of law and justice shown in this story?

....

....

In the story the judge gives fifty strokes of the lash for all the crimes. Apart from the kind of punishment, what is one way in which law and justice in your country are DIFFERENT to the kind of law and justice shown in this story?

....

....

QUESTION 14.6

Which one of the following best describes this story?

A. A folk tale.

B. A travel story.

C. An historical account.

D. A tragedy.

E. A comedy.

READING UNIT 15 : IN POOR TASTE

from Arnold Jago

Did you know that in 1996 we spent almost the same amount on chocolate as our Government spent on overseas aid to help the poor?

Could there be something wrong with our priorities?

What are you going to do about it?

Yes, you.

Arnold Jago, Mildura

Source: The Age newspaper, Melbourne, Australia, 1st April, 1997.

The letter above appeared in an Australian newspaper in 1997. Refer to the letter to answer the questions below.

QUESTION 15.1

Arnold Jago's aim in the letter is to provoke

A. Guilt.

B. Amusement.

C. Fear.

D. Satisfaction.

QUESTION 15.2

What kind of response or action do you think Arnold Jago would like his letter to prompt?

....

....

....

READING UNIT 16 : BULLYING

Bullying Text

Parents Lack Awareness of Bullying

Only one in three parents polled is aware of bullying involving their children, according to an Education Ministry survey released on Wednesday.

The survey, conducted between December 1994 and January 1995, involved some 19,000 parents, teachers and children at primary, junior and senior high schools where bullying has occurred.

The survey, the first of its kind conducted by the Ministry, covered students from the fourth grade up. According to the survey, 22 per cent of the primary school children polled said they face bullying, compared with 13 per cent of junior high school children and 4 per cent of senior high school students.

On the other hand, some 26 per cent of the primary school children said they have bullied, with the percentage decreasing to 20 per cent for junior high school children and 6 per cent for senior high school students.

Of those who replied that they have been bullies, between 39 and 65 per cent said they also have been bullied.

The survey indicated that 37 per cent of the parents of bullied primary school children were aware of bullying targeted at their children. The figure was 34 per cent for the parents of junior high school children and 18 per cent for those of the senior high school students.

Of the parents aware of the bullying, 14 per cent to 18 per cent said they had been told of bullying by teachers. Only 3 per cent to 4 per cent of the parents learned of the bullying from their children, according to the survey.

The survey also found that 42 per cent of primary school teachers are not aware of bullying aimed at their students. The portion of such teachers was 29 per cent at junior high schools and 69 per cent at senior high schools.

Asked for the reason behind bullying, about 85 per cent of the teachers cited a lack of education at home. Many parents singled out a lack of a sense of justice and compassion among children as the main reason.

An Education Ministry official said the findings suggest that parents and teachers should have closer contact with children to prevent bullying.

School bullying became a major issue in Japan after 13-year-old Kiyoteru Okouchi hanged himself in Nishio, Aichi Prefecture, in the fall of 1994, leaving a note saying that classmates had repeatedly dunked him in a nearby river and extorted money from him.

The bullying-suicide prompted the Education Ministry to issue a report on bullying in March 1995 urging teachers to order bullies not to come to school.

Source: Kyodo, The Japan Times Ltd., Tokyo, 23rd May, 1996.

The article above appeared in a Japanese newspaper in 1996. Refer to it to answer the questions below.

QUESTION 16.1

Why does the article mention the death of Kiyoteru Okouchi?

....

....

QUESTION 16.2

What percentage of teachers at each type of school was not aware that their students were being bullied?

Circle the alternative (A, B, C or D) which best represents this.

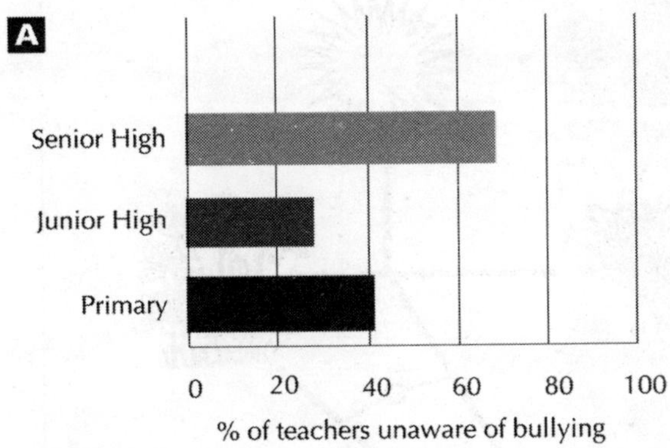

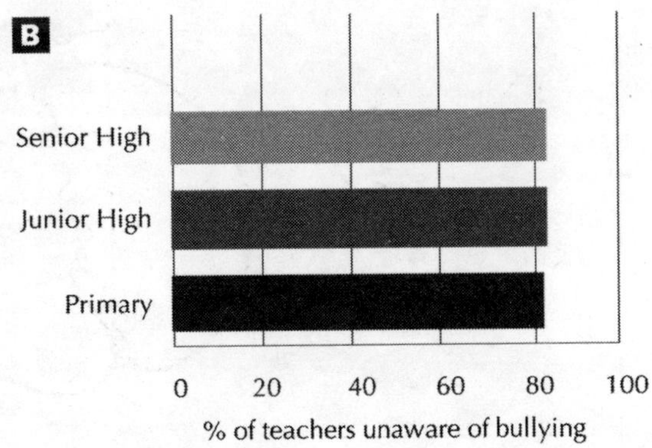

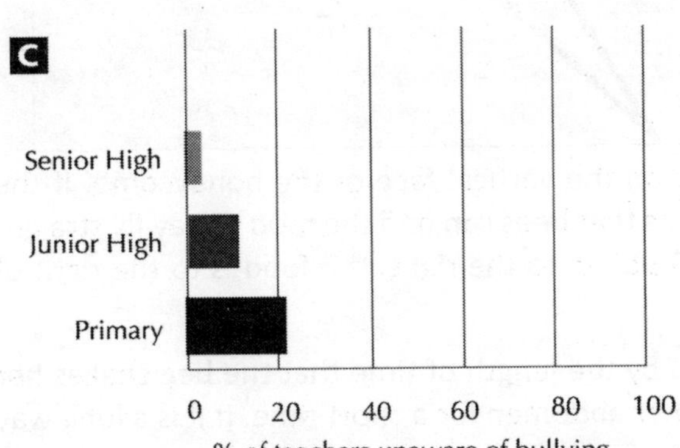

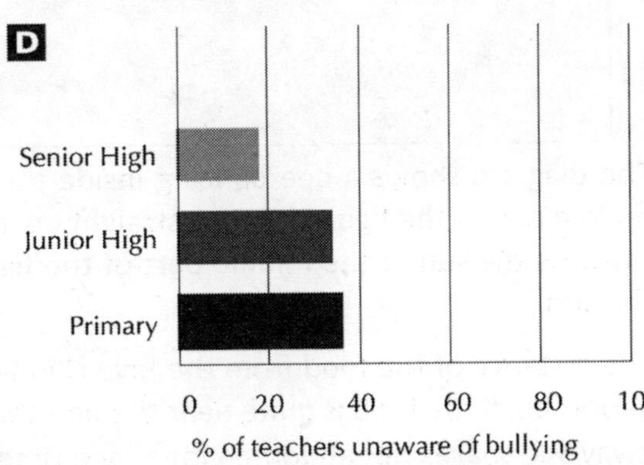

READING UNIT 17 : BEES

Bees Text

The information on this page and the next page is from a booklet about bees. Refer to the information to answer the questions which follow it.

Collecting Nectar

Bees make honey to survive. It is their only essential food. If there are 60,000 bees in a hive about one third of them will be involved in gathering nectar which is then made into honey by the house bees. A small number of bees work as foragers or searchers. They find a source of nectar, then return to the hive to tell the other bees where it is.

Foragers let the other bees know where the source of the nectar is by performing a dance which gives information about the direction and the distance the bees will need to fly. During this dance the bee shakes her abdomen from side to side while running in circles in the shape of a figure 8. The dance follows the pattern shown on the following diagram.

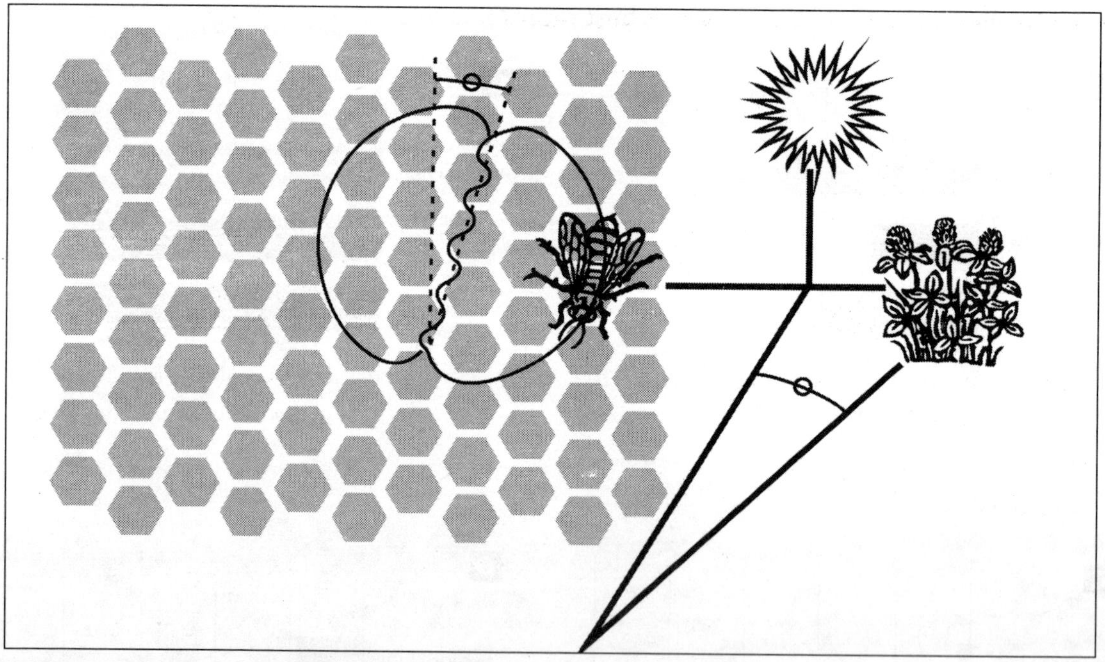

The diagram shows a bee dancing inside the hive on the vertical face of the honeycomb. If the middle part of the figure 8 points straight up it means that bees can find the food if they fly straight towards the sun. If the middle part of the figure 8 points to the right, the food is to the right of the sun.

The distance of the food from the hive is indicated by the length of time that the bee shakes her abdomen. If the food is quite near the bee shakes her abdomen for a short time. If it is a long way away she shakes her abdomen for a long time.

MAKING HONEY

When the bees arrive at the hive carrying nectar they give this to the house bees. The house bees move the nectar around with their mandibles, exposing it to the warm dry air of the hive. When it is first gathered the nectar contains sugar and minerals mixed with about 80% water. After ten to twenty minutes, when much of the excess water has evaporated, the house bees put the nectar in a cell in the honeycomb where evaporation continues. After three days, the honey in the cells contains about 20% water. At this stage, the bees cover the cells with lids which they make out of beeswax.

At any one time the bees in a hive usually gather nectar from the same type of blossom and from the same area. Some of the main sources of nectar are fruit trees, clover and flowering trees.

Source: "Hum Sweet Hum", National Foundation for Educational Research, 1993.

GLOSSARY

house bee	*a worker bee which works inside the hive.*
mandible	*mouth-part.*

QUESTION 17.1

What is the purpose of the bees' dance?

A. To celebrate the successful production of honey.
B. To indicate the type of plant the foragers have found.
C. To celebrate the birth of a new Queen Bee.
D. To indicate where the foragers have found food.

QUESTION 17.2

Write down three of the main sources of nectar.

1. ....
2. ....
3. ....

QUESTION 17.3

What is the main difference between nectar and honey?

A. The proportion of water in the substance.
B. The proportion of sugar to minerals in the substance.
C. The type of plant from which the substance is gathered.
D. The type of bee which processes the substance.

QUESTION 17.4

In the dance, what does the bee do to show how far the food is from the hive?

....

....

CHAPTER 3

Mathematics Sample Tasks

The mathematics questions in PISA aim at assessing the capacity of students to draw upon their mathematical competencies to meet the challenges of their current and future daily lives. Citizens have to use mathematics in many daily situations, such as when consulting media presenting information on a wide range of subjects in the form of tables, charts and graphs, when reading timetables, when carrying out money transactions and when determining the best buy at the market. To capture this broad conception, PISA uses a concept of mathematical literacy that is concerned with the capacity of students to analyse, reason and communicate effectively as they pose, solve and interpret mathematical problems in a variety of situations including quantitative, spacial, probabilistic or other mathematical concepts.

Mathematics was the focus of the PISA 2003 survey, meaning that more time was dedicated to mathematics testing which allowed a more detailed analysis of the results. The 2006 mathematics results are compared to the 2003 benchmarks, as will be the case for results from future surveys.

In 2000 and 2006, mathematics was also assessed, but less comprehensively than in 2003. Key assessment characteristics were established for the 2000 survey and underwent minor modifications for the following surveys.

Mathematics is defined in relation to three dimensions: the content, the mathematical *processes* and the *situations*. The first dimension, the content of mathematics, is defined primarily in terms of "overarching ideas" and only secondarily in relation to curricular strands. Strands such as numbers, algebra and geometry are commonly used in curricula. The overarching ideas used in PISA reflect the orientation towards real-life situations. For the first survey in 2000 two overarching ideas were assessed: *change and growth* and *space and shape*. These two were selected to allow a wide range of curriculum strands to be represented, without giving undue weight to number skills. In the assessments in 2003 and 2006 four overarching ideas were assessed: *quantity, space and shape, change and relationships and uncertainty*. This is in line with the contemporary view of mathematics as the science of patterns in a general sense. The PISA overarching ideas reflect this: patterns in *space and shape*, patterns in *change and relationships*, patterns in *quantity* form central and essential concepts for any description of mathematics, and they form the heart of any curriculum, at any level. But to be literate in mathematics means more. Dealing with uncertainty from a mathematical and scientific perspective is essential. For this reason, elements of probability theory and statistics give rise to the fourth overarching idea: *uncertainty*.

The second dimension is the *process* of mathematics as defined by general mathematical competencies. Questions are organised into three *"competency clusters"* (reproduction, connections and reflection) defining the type of thinking skill needed. The first cluster – *reproduction* – consists of simple computations or definitions of the type most familiar in conventional mathematics assessments. The second requires *connections* to be made to solve relatively straightforward problems. The third competency cluster – *reflection* – consists of mathematical thinking, generalisation and insight, and requires students to engage in analysis, to identify the mathematical elements in a situation and to pose their own problems. In general, these processes are in ascending order of difficulty, but it does not follow that one must be mastered in order to progress to the other: it is possible for example to engage in mathematical thinking without being good at computations. These competencies are applied as part of the fundamental process of mathematisation that students use to solve real-life problems. Mathematisation can be broken up into five steps:

- Starting with a problem in reality.
- Organising it according to mathematical concepts and identifying the relevant mathematics.
- Gradually trimming away the reality to transform the real-world problem into a mathematical problem that faithfully represents the situation.
- Solving the mathematical problem.
- Making sense of the mathematical solution in terms of the real situation.

The third dimension is the situation in which mathematics is used. PISA identifies four situations: personal, educational or occupational, public (related to the local community or society) and scientific. Each question used in a PISA survey falls into one category of each of the three dimensions. Question 10.1 from the unit Carpenter, for example, is part of the connections competency cluster, using content of the overarching idea quantity and set in an occupational situation. As the last two categorisations are generally fairly obvious, they will not be explicitly mentioned for the questions presented here.

To report the results of PISA 2000 a single mathematics scale was used. The average score on this scale is 500 with two-thirds of students scoring between 400 and 600. In 2003, when mathematics was the major domain, separate scales for each of the four content areas were created in addition to the overall mathematics scale. As in 2000, the average on each scale is 500 with two-thirds of students scoring between 400 and 600. In the 2006 survey, a single mathematics scale was used to gauge performance. The results are compared to the benchmark of 500 score points established by PISA 2003. More information on PISA proficiency scales can be found in Annex A.

It is the policy of PISA that students should be allowed to use calculators and other tools as they are normally used in school. However, the test questions are chosen so that the use of calculators is not likely to enhance a student's performance in the assessment. This chapter presents 50 units. The first 26 units were used in the PISA surveys. Units 27 to 50 were used in developing and testing out the surveys. While it was decided not to include these units in the PISA surveys, they are nevertheless illustrative of the kinds of questions asked in PISA. The questions presented in this chapter are all publicly released PISA mathematics questions. Following the section with questions, answers for all questions are given. For units 1 to 26, a comment box includes score points, the percentage of students who answered correctly across OECD countries and the question category. For country results, refer to Annex B. For units 27 to 50, a comment box lists the question category. Because these units were not used in the final PISA surveys the information regarding score points and percentage of students who answered correctly is not known or it not sufficiently reliable to be presented here.

MATHEMATICS UNIT 1: FARMS

Here you see a photograph of a farmhouse with a roof in the shape of a pyramid.

Below is a student's mathematical model of the farmhouse roof with measurements added.

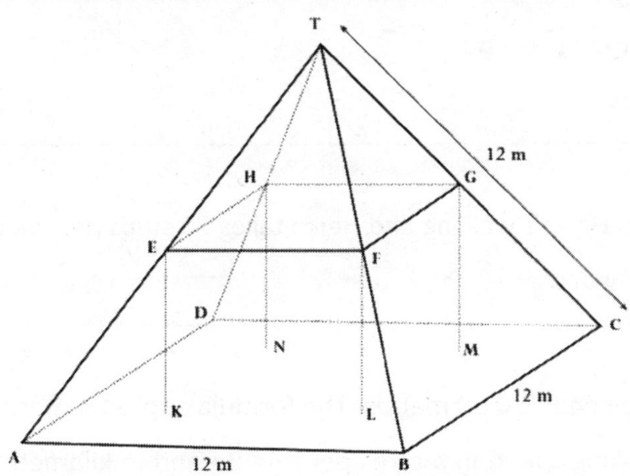

The attic floor, ABCD in the model, is a square. The beams that support the roof are the edges of a block (rectangular prism) EFGHKLMN. E is the middle of AT, F is the middle of BT, G is the middle of CT and H is the middle of DT. All the edges of the pyramid in the model have length 12 m.

QUESTION 1.1

Calculate the area of the attic floor ABCD.

The area of the attic floor ABCD = ____________ m^2

QUESTION 1.2

Calculate the length of EF, one of the horizontal edges of the block.

The length of EF = _____________ m

MATHEMATICS UNIT 2 : WALKING

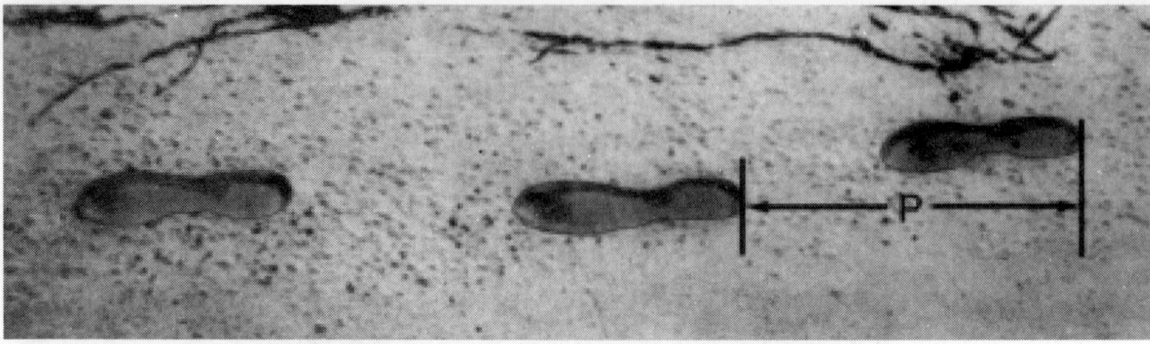

The picture shows the footprints of a man walking. The pacelength P is the distance between the rear of two consecutive footprints.

For men, the formula, $\frac{n}{P} = 140$, gives an approximate relationship between n and P where,

n = number of steps per minute, and

P = pacelength in metres.

QUESTION 2.1

If the formula applies to Heiko's walking and Heiko takes 70 steps per minute, what is Heiko's pacelength? Show your work.

QUESTION 2.2

Bernard knows his pacelength is 0.80 metres. The formula applies to Bernard's walking.

Calculate Bernard's walking speed in metres per minute and in kilometres per hour. Show your working out.

MATHEMATICS UNIT 3: APPLES

A farmer plants apple trees in a square pattern. In order to protect the apple trees against the wind he plants conifer trees all around the orchard.

Here you see a diagram of this situation where you can see the pattern of apple trees and conifer trees for any number (n) of rows of apple trees:

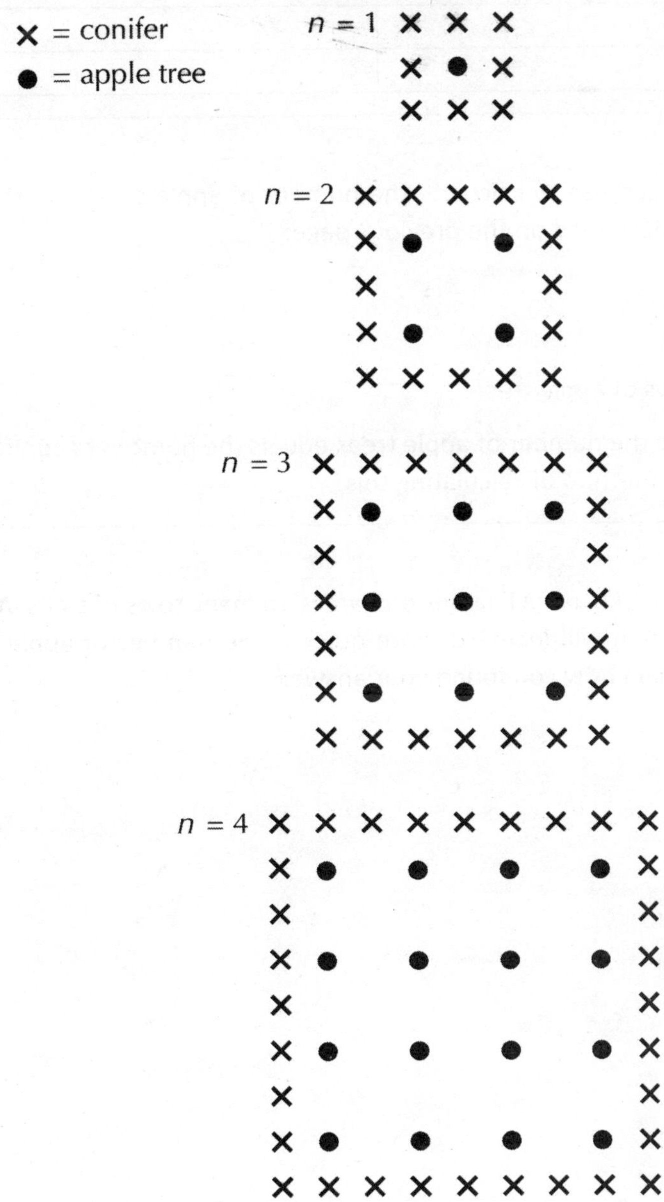

QUESTION 3.1

Complete the table:

n	Number of apple trees	Number of conifer trees
1.	1	8
2.	4	
3.		
4.		
5.		

QUESTION 3.2

There are two formulae you can use to calculate the number of apple trees and the number of conifer trees for the pattern described on the previous page:

Number of apple trees = n^2

Number of conifer trees = $8n$

where n is the number of rows of apple trees.

There is a value of n for which the number of apple trees equals the number of conifer trees. Find the value of n and show your method of calculating this.

QUESTION 3.3

Suppose the farmer wants to make a much larger orchard with many rows of trees. As the farmer makes the orchard bigger, which will increase more quickly: the number of apple trees or the number of conifer trees? Explain how you found your answer.

MATHEMATICS UNIT 4 : CUBES

QUESTION 4.1

In this photograph you see six dice, labelled (a) to (f). For all dice there is a rule:

The total number of dots on two opposite faces of each die is always seven.

Write in each box the number of dots on the bottom face of the dice corresponding to the photograph.

(a)	(b)	(c)
(d)	(e)	(f)

MATHEMATICS UNIT 5 : CONTINENT AREA

Below is a map of Antarctica.

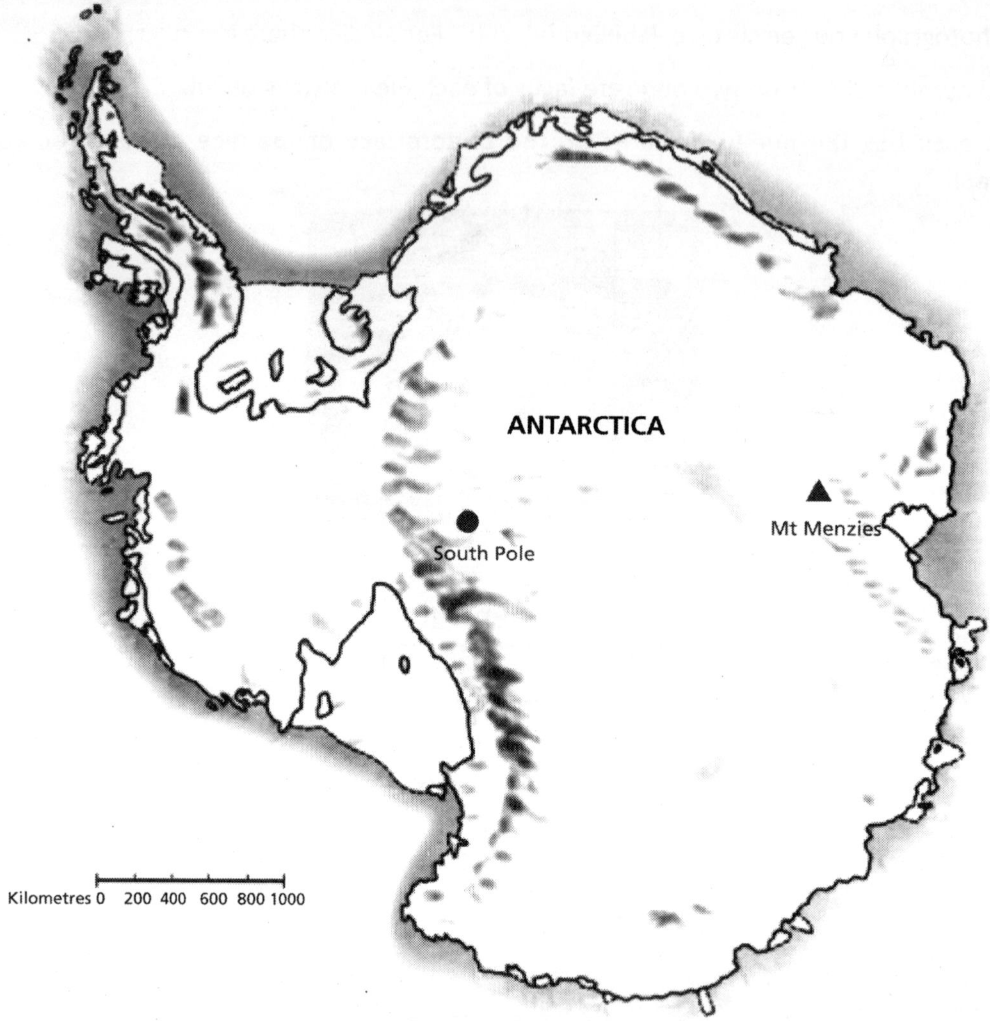

QUESTION 5.1

Estimate the area of Antarctica using the map scale.

Show your working out and explain how you made your estimate. (You can draw over the map if it helps you with your estimation)

....

....

....

MATHEMATICS UNIT 6 : GROWING UP

Youth grows taller

In 1998 the average height of both young males and young females in the Netherlands is represented in this graph.

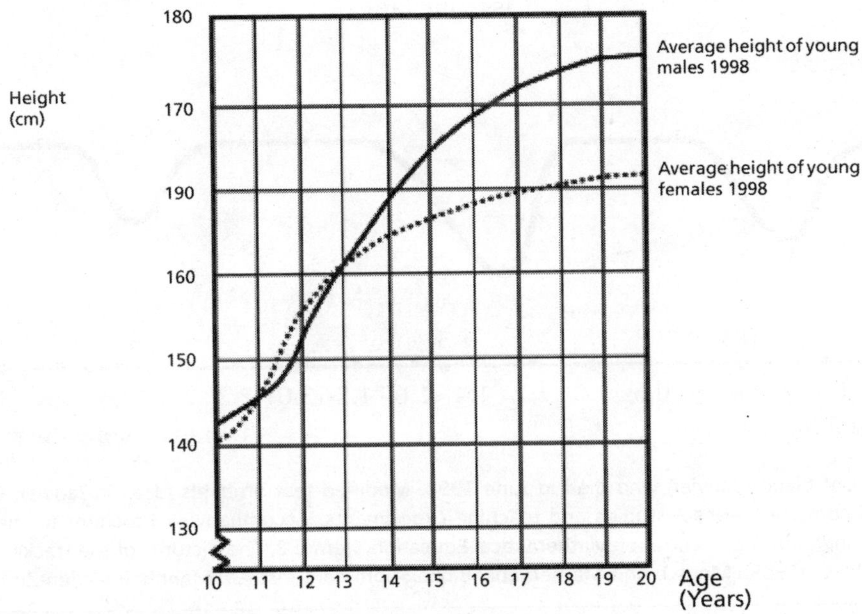

QUESTION 6.1

Since 1980 the average height of 20-year-old females has increased by 2.3 cm, to 170.6 cm. What was the average height of a 20-year-old female in 1980?

Answer: ____________________ cm

QUESTION 6.2

Explain how the graph shows that on average the growth rate for girls slows down after 12 years of age.

....

....

QUESTION 6.3

According to this graph, on average, during which period in their life are females taller than males of the same age?

....

....

MATHEMATICS UNIT 7 : SPEED OF RACING CAR

This graph shows how the speed of a racing car varies along a flat 3 kilometre track during its second lap.

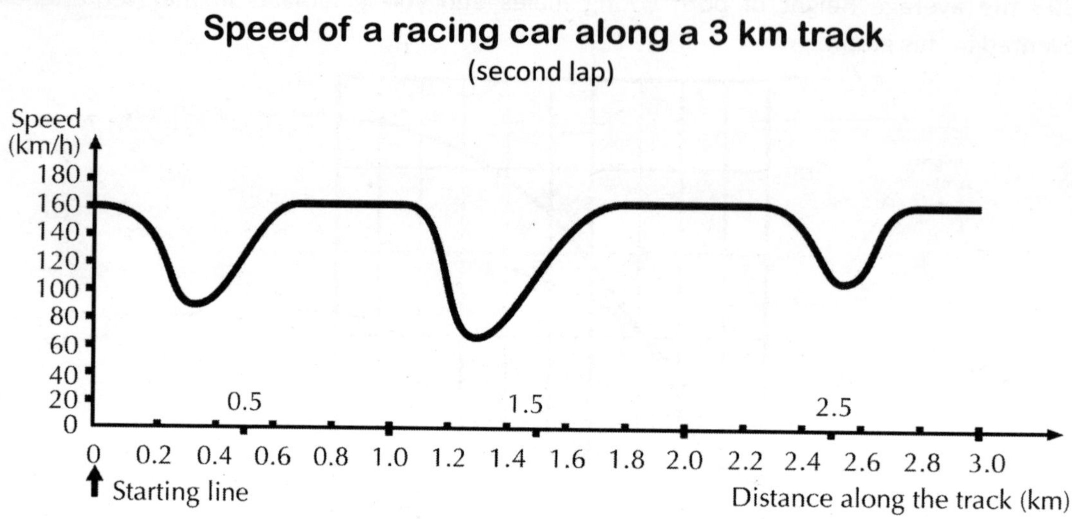

Note: In memory of Claude Janvier, who died in June 1998. Modified task after his ideas in Janvier, C. (1978): The interpretation of complex graphs – studies and teaching experiments. Accompanying brochure to the Dissertation. University of Nottingham, Shell Centre for Mathematical Education, Item C-2. The pictures of the tracks are taken from Fischer, R. & Malle, G. (1985): Mensch und Mathematik. Bibliographisches Institut: Mannheim-Wien-Zurich, 234-238.

QUESTION 7.1

What is the approximate distance from the starting line to the beginning of the longest straight section of the track?

A. 0.5 km

B. 1.5 km

C. 2.3 km

D. 2.6 km

QUESTION 7.2

Where was the lowest speed recorded during the second lap?

A. at the starting line.

B. at about 0.8 km.

C. at about 1.3 km.

D. halfway around the track.

QUESTION 7.3

What can you say about the speed of the car between the 2.6 km and 2.8 km marks?

A. The speed of the car remains constant.

B. The speed of the car is increasing.

C. The speed of the car is decreasing.

D. The speed of the car cannot be determined from the graph.

QUESTION 7.4

Here are pictures of five tracks:

Along which one of these tracks was the car driven to produce the speed graph shown earlier?

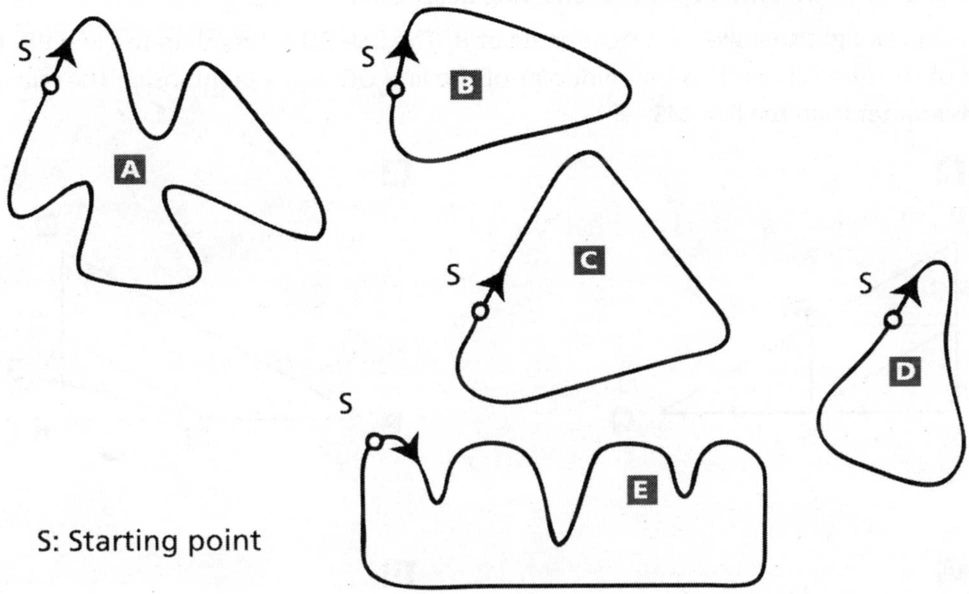

S: Starting point

MATHEMATICS UNIT 8 : TRIANGLES

QUESTION 8.1

Circle the one figure below that fits the following description.

Triangle PQR is a right triangle with right angle at R. The line RQ is less than the line PR. M is the midpoint of the line PQ and N is the midpoint of the line QR. S is a point inside the triangle. The line MN is greater than the line MS.

A

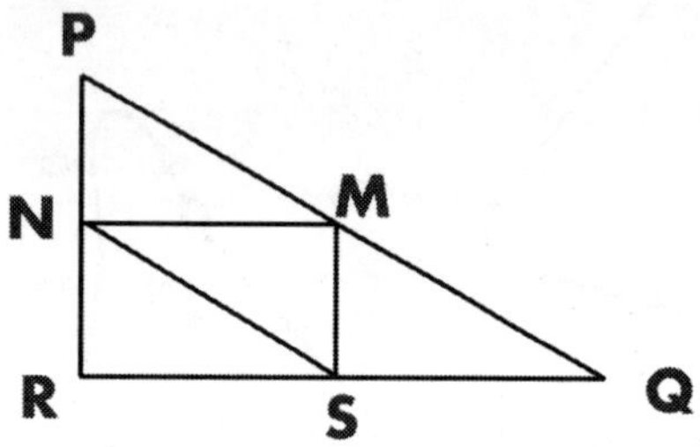

B

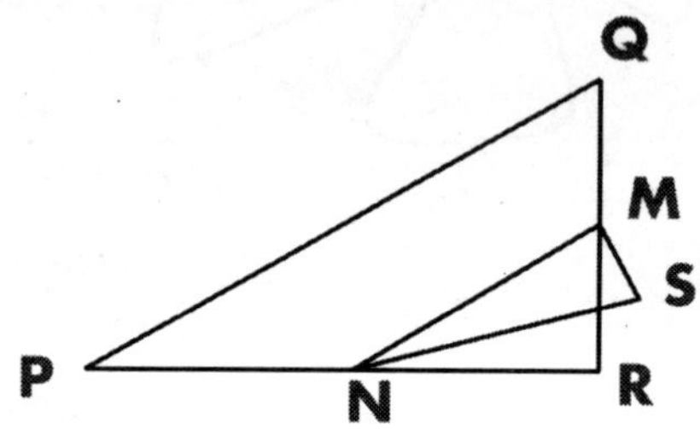

C

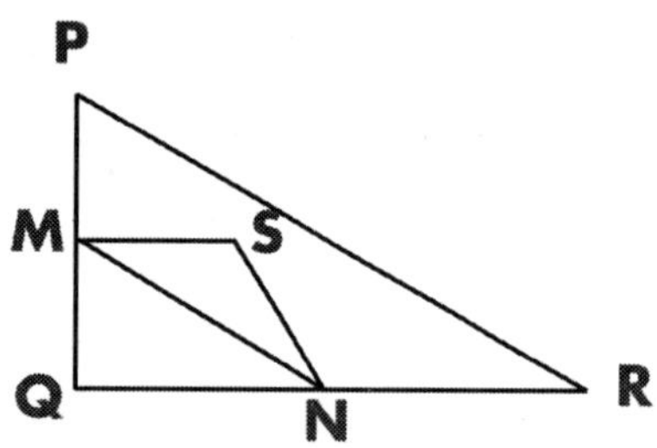

D

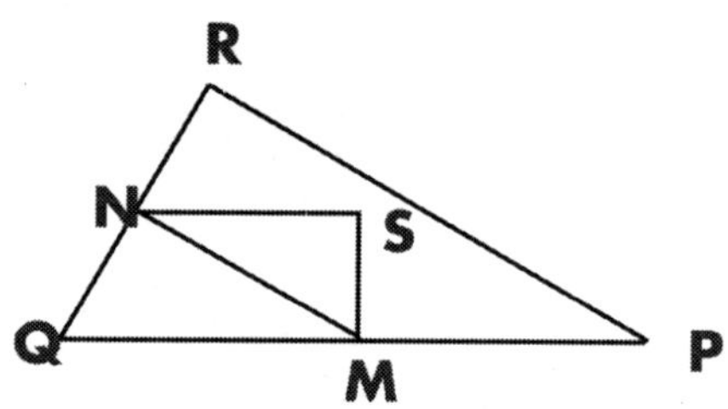

E

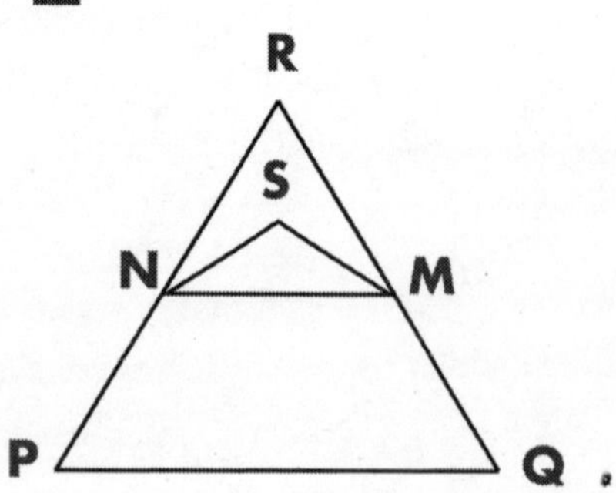

MATHEMATICS UNIT 9 : ROBBERIES

QUESTION 9.1

A TV reporter showed this graph and said:

"The graph shows that there is a huge increase in the number of robberies from 1998 to 1999."

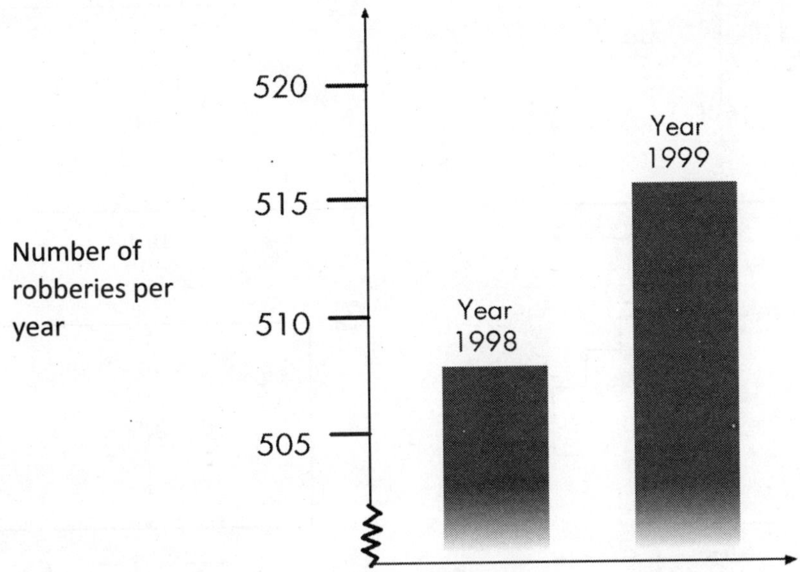

Do you consider the reporter's statement to be a reasonable interpretation of the graph? Give an explanation to support your answer.

....

....

....

....

....

MATHEMATICS UNIT 10 : CARPENTER

QUESTION 10.1

A carpenter has 32 metres of timber and wants to make a border around a garden bed. He is considering the following designs for the garden bed.

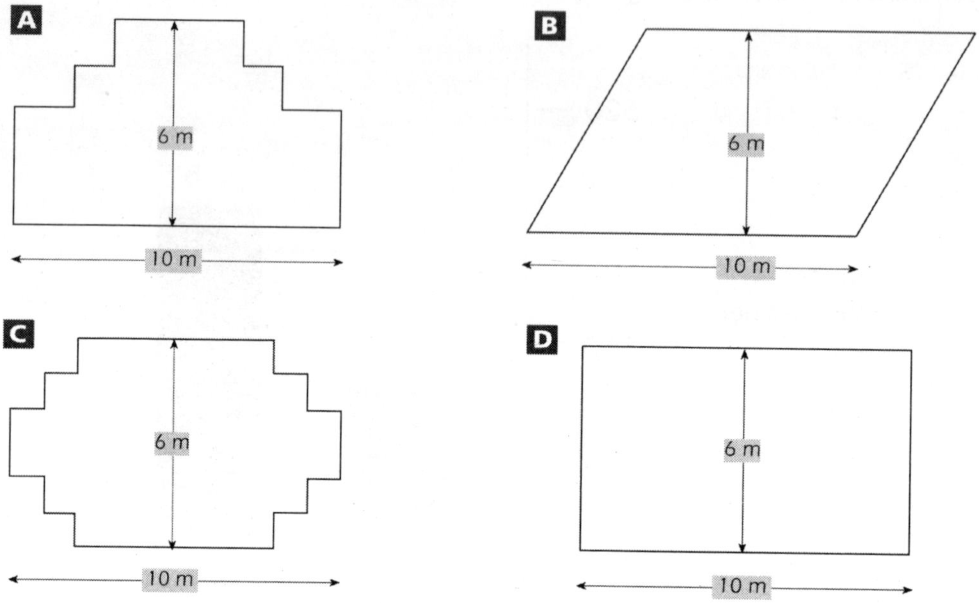

Circle either "Yes" or "No" for each design to indicate whether the garden bed can be made with 32 metres of timber.

Garden bed design	Using this design, can the garden bed be made with 32 metres of timber?
Design A	Yes / No
Design B	Yes / No
Design C	Yes / No
Design D	Yes / No

MATHEMATICS UNIT 11 : INTERNET RELAY CHAT

Mark (from Sydney, Australia) and Hans (from Berlin, Germany) often communicate with each other using "chat" on the Internet. They have to log on to the Internet at the same time to be able to chat.

To find a suitable time to chat, Mark looked up a chart of world times and found the following:

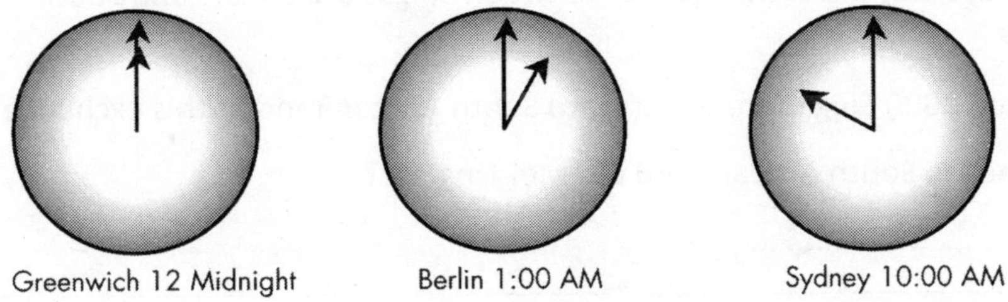

QUESTION 11.1

At 7:00 PM in Sydney, what time is it in Berlin?

Answer: ....

QUESTION 11.2

Mark and Hans are not able to chat between 9:00 AM and 4:30 PM their local time, as they have to go to school. Also, from 11:00 PM till 7:00 AM their local time they won't be able to chat because they will be sleeping.

When would be a good time for Mark and Hans to chat? Write the local times in the table.

Place	Time
Sydney	
Berlin	

MATHEMATICS UNIT 12 : EXCHANGE RATE

Mei-Ling from Singapore was preparing to go to South Africa for 3 months as an exchange student. She needed to change some Singapore dollars (SGD) into South African rand (ZAR).

QUESTION 12.1

Mei-Ling found out that the exchange rate between Singapore dollars and South African rand was:
1 SGD = 4.2 ZAR

Mei-Ling changed 3000 Singapore dollars into South African rand at this exchange rate.

How much money in South African rand did Mei-Ling get?

Answer: ....

QUESTION 12.2

On returning to Singapore after 3 months, Mei-Ling had 3 900 ZAR left. She changed this back to Singapore dollars, noting that the exchange rate had changed to:

1 SGD = 4.0 ZAR

How much money in Singapore dollars did Mei-Ling get?

Answer: ....

QUESTION 12.3

During these 3 months the exchange rate had changed from 4.2 to 4.0 ZAR per SGD.

Was it in Mei-Ling's favour that the exchange rate now was 4.0 ZAR instead of 4.2 ZAR, when she changed her South African rand back to Singapore dollars? Give an explanation to support your answer.

MATHEMATICS UNIT 13: EXPORTS

The graphics below show information about exports from Zedland, a country that uses zeds as its currency.

Total annual exports from Zedland in millions of zeds, 1996 to 2000

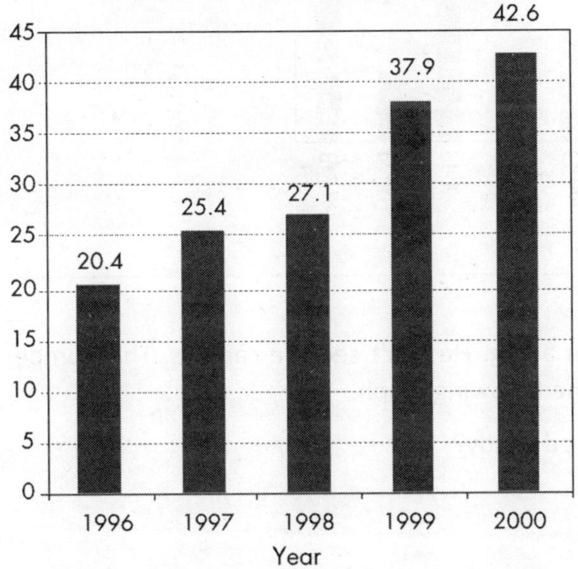

Distribution of exports from Zedland in 2000

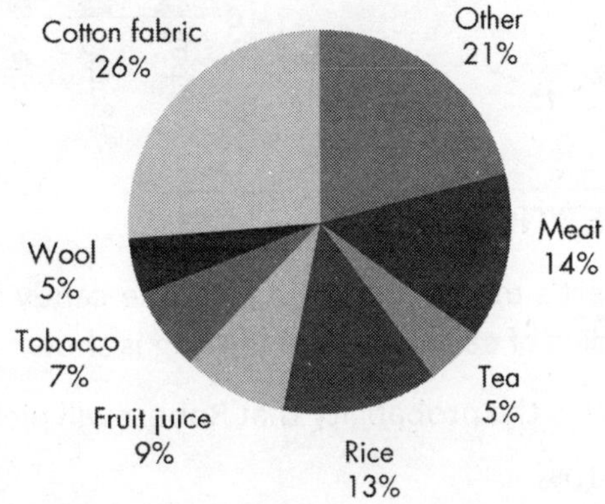

QUESTION 13.1

What was the total value (in millions of zeds) of exports from Zedland in 1998?

Answer: ....

QUESTION 13.2

What was the value of fruit juice exported from Zedland in 2000?

A. 1.8 million zeds.

B. 2.3 million zeds.

C. 2.4 million zeds.

D. 3.4 million zeds.

E. 3.8 million zeds.

MATHEMATICS UNIT 14 : COLOURED CANDIES

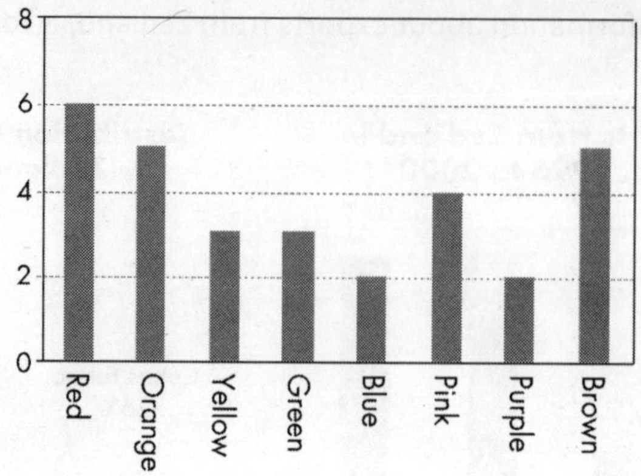

QUESTION 14.1

Robert's mother lets him pick one candy from a bag. He can't see the candies. The number of candies of each colour in the bag is shown in the following graph.

What is the probability that Robert will pick a red candy?

A. 10%

B. 20%

C. 25%

D. 50%

MATHEMATICS UNIT 15 : SCIENCE TESTS

QUESTION 15.1

In Mei Lin's school, her science teacher gives tests that are marked out of 100. Mei Lin has an average of 60 marks on her first four Science tests. On the fifth test she got 80 marks.

What is the average of Mei Lin's marks in Science after all five tests?

Answer: ....

MATHEMATICS UNIT 16 : BOOKSHELVES

QUESTION 16.1

To complete one set of bookshelves a carpenter needs the following components:

4 long wooden panels,

6 short wooden panels,

12 small clips,

2 large clips and

14 screws.

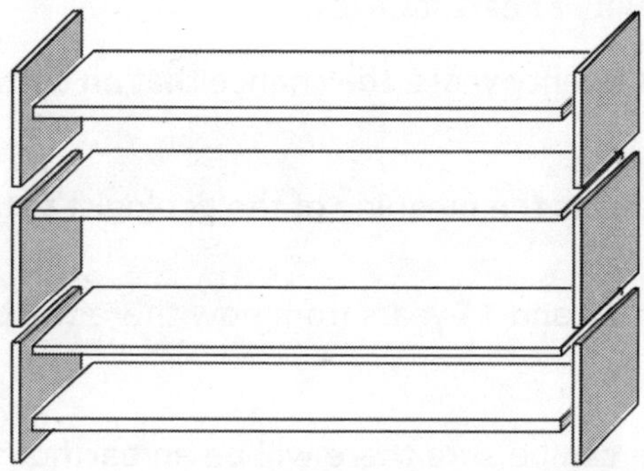

The carpenter has in stock 26 long wooden panels, 33 short wooden panels, 200 small clips, 20 large clips and 510 screws.

How many sets of bookshelves can the carpenter make?

Answer: ....

MATHEMATICS UNIT 17 : LITTER

QUESTION 17.1

For a homework assignment on the environment, students collected information on the decomposition time of several types of litter that people throw away:

Type of Litter	Decomposition time
Banana peel	1–3 years
Orange peel	1–3 years
Cardboard boxes	0.5 year
Chewing gum	20–25 years
Newspapers	A few days
Polystyrene cups	Over 100 years

A student thinks of displaying the results in a bar graph.

Give one reason why a bar graph is unsuitable for displaying these data.

....

....

MATHEMATICS UNIT 18 : EARTHQUAKE

QUESTION 18.1

A documentary was broadcast about earthquakes and how often earthquakes occur. It included a discussion about the predictability of earthquakes.

A geologist stated: "In the next twenty years, the chance that an earthquake will occur in Zed City is two out of three".

Which of the following best reflects the meaning of the geologist's statement?

A. $\frac{2}{3} \times 20 = 13.3$, so between 13 and 14 years from now there will be an earthquake in Zed City.

B. $\frac{2}{3}$ is more than $\frac{1}{2}$, so you can be sure there will be an earthquake in Zed City at some time during the next 20 years.

C. The likelihood that there will be an earthquake in Zed City at some time during the next 20 years is higher than the likelihood of no earthquake.

D. You cannot tell what will happen, because nobody can be sure when an earthquake will occur.

MATHEMATICS UNIT 19 : CHOICES

QUESTION 19.1

In a pizza restaurant, you can get a basic pizza with two toppings: cheese and tomato. You can also make up your own pizza with extra toppings. You can choose from four different extra toppings: olives, ham, mushrooms and salami.

Ross wants to order a pizza with two different extra toppings.

How many different combinations can Ross choose from?

Answer: .... combinations.

MATHEMATICS UNIT 20 : TEST SCORES

QUESTION 20.1

The diagram below shows the results on a Science test for two groups, labelled as Group A and Group B.

The mean score for Group A is 62.0 and the mean for Group B is 64.5. Students pass this test when their score is 50 or above.

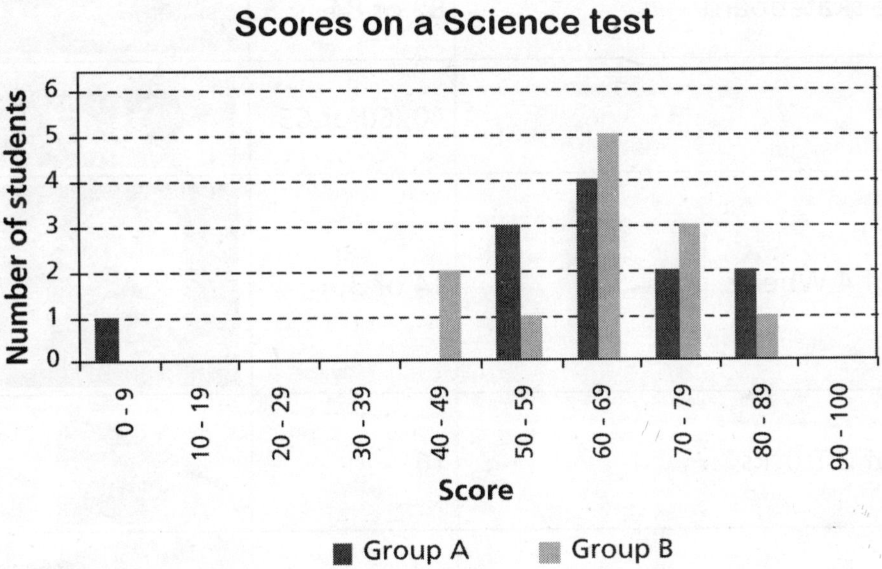

Looking at the diagram, the teacher claims that Group B did better than Group A in this test.

The students in Group A don't agree with their teacher. They try to convince the teacher that Group B may not necessarily have done better.

Give one mathematical argument, using the graph, that the students in Group A could use.

....

....

....

MATHEMATICS UNIT 21 : SKATEBOARD

Eric is a great skateboard fan. He visits a shop named SKATERS to check some prices.

At this shop you can buy a complete board. Or you can buy a deck, a set of 4 wheels, a set of 2 trucks and a set of hardware, and assemble your own board.

The prices for the shop's products are:

Product	Price in zeds	
Complete skateboard	82 or 84	
Deck	40, 60 or 65	
One set of 4 Wheels	14 or 36	
One set of 2 Trucks	16	
One set of hardware (bearings, rubber pads, bolts and nuts)	10 or 20	

QUESTION 21.1

Eric wants to assemble his own skateboard. What is the minimum price and the maximum price in this shop for self-assembled skateboards?

(a) Minimum price: .... zeds.

(b) Maximum price: .... zeds.

QUESTION 21.2

The shop offers three different decks, two different sets of wheels and two different sets of hardware. There is only one choice for a set of trucks.

How many different skateboards can Eric construct?

A. 6

B. 8

C. 10

D. 12

QUESTION 21.3

Eric has 120 zeds to spend and wants to buy the most expensive skateboard he can afford.

How much money can Eric afford to spend on each of the 4 parts? Put your answer in the table below.

Part	Amount (zeds)
Deck	
Wheels	
Trucks	
Hardware	

MATHEMATICS UNIT 22 : STAIRCASE

QUESTION 22.1

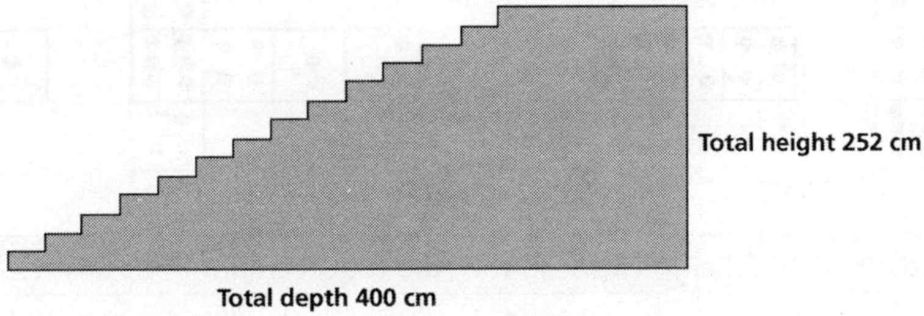

The diagram above illustrates a staircase with 14 steps and a total height of 252 cm:

What is the height of each of the 14 steps?

Height: .... cm.

MATHEMATICS UNIT 23: NUMBER CUBES

QUESTION 23.1

On the right, there is a picture of two dice.

Dice are special number cubes for which the following rule applies:

The total number of dots on two opposite faces is always seven.

You can make a simple number cube by cutting, folding and gluing cardboard. This can be done in many ways. In the figure below you can see four cuttings that can be used to make cubes, with dots on the sides.

Which of the following shapes can be folded together to form a cube that obeys the rule that the sum of opposite faces is 7? For each shape, circle either "Yes" or "No" in the table below.

I

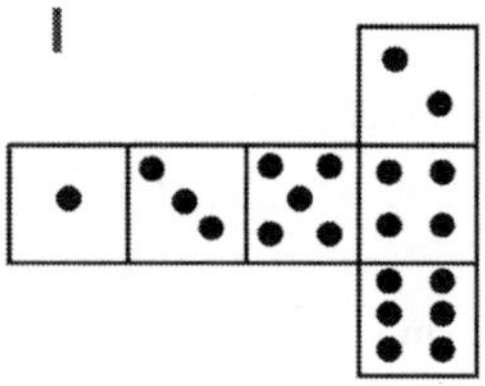

II

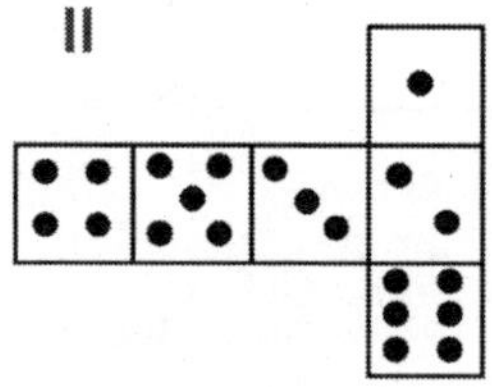

III

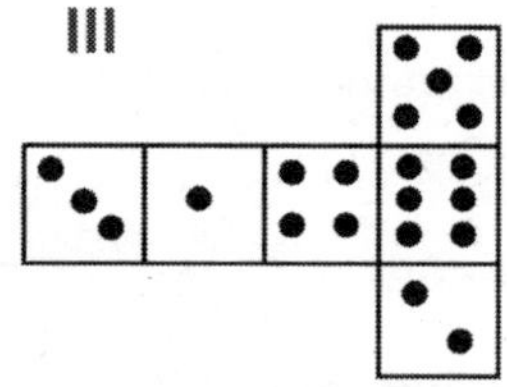

IV

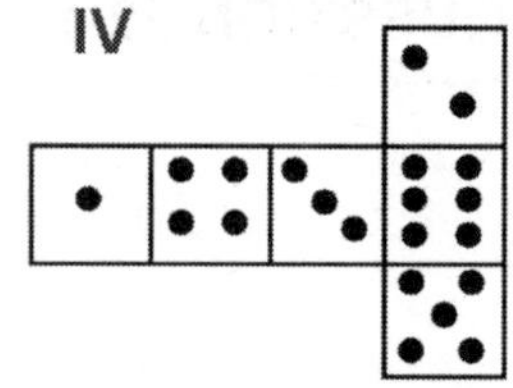

Shape	Obeys the rule that the sum of opposite faces is 7?
I	Yes / No
II	Yes / No
III	Yes / No
IV	Yes / No

MATHEMATICS UNIT 24 : SUPPORT FOR THE PRESIDENT

QUESTION 24.1

In Zedland, opinion polls were conducted to find out the level of support for the President in the forthcoming election. Four newspaper publishers did separate nationwide polls. The results for the four newspaper polls are shown below:

Newspaper 1: 36.5% (poll conducted on January 6, with a sample of 500 randomly selected citizens with voting rights)

Newspaper 2: 41.0% (poll conducted on January 20, with a sample of 500 randomly selected citizens with voting rights)

Newspaper 3: 39.0% (poll conducted on January 20, with a sample of 1000 randomly selected citizens with voting rights)

Newspaper 4: 44.5% (poll conducted on January 20, with 1000 readers phoning in to vote).

Which newspaper's result is likely to be the best for predicting the level of support for the President if the election is held on January 25? Give two reasons to support your answer.

....

....

....

....

MATHEMATICS UNIT 25 : THE BEST CAR

A car magazine uses a rating system to evaluate new cars, and gives the award of "The Car of the Year" to the car with the highest total score. Five new cars are being evaluated, and their ratings are shown in the table.

Car	Safety Features (S)	Fuel Efficiency (F)	External Appearance (E)	Internal Fittings (T)
Ca	3	1	2	3
M2	2	2	2	2
Sp	3	1	3	2
N1	1	3	3	3
KK	3	2	3	2

The ratings are interpreted as follows:

3 points = Excellent

2 points = Good

1 point = Fair

QUESTION 25.1

To calculate the total score for a car, the car magazine uses the following rule, which is a weighted sum of the individual score points:

Total Score = (3 × S) + F + E + T

Calculate the total score for Car "Ca". Write your answer in the space below.

Total score for "Ca": ....

QUESTION 25.2

The manufacturer of car "Ca" thought the rule for the total score was unfair.

Write down a rule for calculating the total score so that Car "Ca" will be the winner.

Your rule should include all four of the variables, and you should write down your rule by filling in positive numbers in the four spaces in the equation below.

Total score = ...× S + ... × F + ... × E + ... × T.

MATHEMATICS UNIT 26 : STEP PATTERN

QUESTION 26.1

Robert builds a step pattern using squares. Here are the stages he follows.

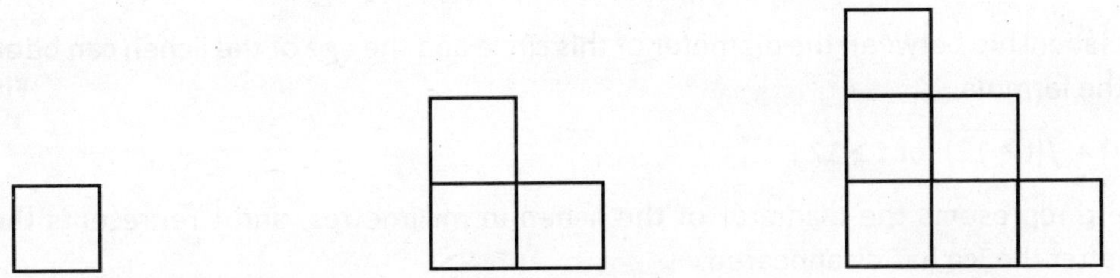

Stage 1 Stage 2 Stage 3

As you can see, he uses one square for Stage 1, three squares for Stage 2 and six for Stage 3.

How many squares should he use for the fourth stage?

Answer: .... squares.

MATHEMATICS UNIT 27 : LICHEN

A result of global warming is that the ice of some glaciers is melting. Twelve years after the ice disappears, tiny plants, called lichen, start to grow on the rocks.

Each lichen grows approximately in the shape of a circle.

The relationship between the diameter of this circle and the age of the lichen can be approximated with the formula:

$d = 7.0 \times \sqrt{(t - 12)}$ for $t \geq 12$

where d represents the diameter of the lichen in millimetres, and t represents the number of years after the ice has disappeared.

QUESTION 27.1

Using the formula, calculate the diameter of the lichen, 16 years after the ice disappeared.

Show your calculation.

....

....

QUESTION 27.2

Ann measured the diameter of some lichen and found it was 35 millimetres.

How many years ago did the ice disappear at this spot?

Show your calculation.

....

....

MATHEMATICS UNIT 28 : COINS

You are asked to design a new set of coins. All coins will be circular and coloured silver, but of different diameters.

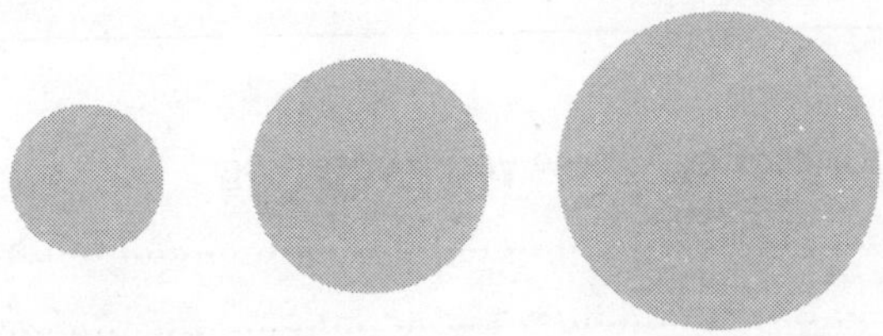

Researchers have found out that an ideal coin system meets the following requirements:

- diameters of coins should not be smaller than 15 mm and not be larger than 45 mm.
- given a coin, the diameter of the next coin must be at least 30% larger.
- the minting machinery can only produce coins with diameters of a whole number of millimetres (e.g. 17 mm is allowed, 17.3 mm is not).

QUESTION 28.1

You are asked to design a set of coins that satisfy the above requirements.

You should start with a 15 mm coin and your set should contain as many coins as possible. What would be the diameters of the coins in your set?

....

....

MATHEMATICS UNIT 29 : PIZZAS

A pizzeria serves two round pizzas of the same thickness in different sizes. The smaller one has a diameter of 30 cm and costs 30 zeds. The larger one has a diameter of 40 cm and costs 40 zeds.

QUESTION 29.1

Which pizza is better value for money? Show your reasoning.

MATHEMATICS UNIT 30: SHAPES

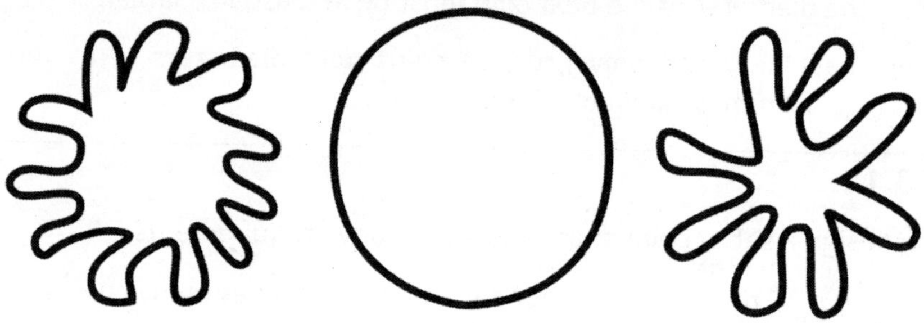

A B C

QUESTION 30.1

Which of the figures has the largest area? Explain your reasoning.

QUESTION 30.2

Describe a method for estimating the area of figure C.

QUESTION 30.3

Describe a method for estimating the perimeter of figure C.

MATHEMATICS UNIT 31 : BRAKING

The approximate distance to stop a moving vehicle is the sum of:

- the distance covered during the time the driver takes to begin to apply the brakes (reaction-time distance)
- the distance travelled while the brakes are applied (braking distance)

The 'snail' diagram below gives the theoretical stopping distance for a vehicle in good braking conditions (a particularly alert driver, brakes and tyres in perfect condition, a dry road with a good surface) and how much the stopping distance depends on speed.

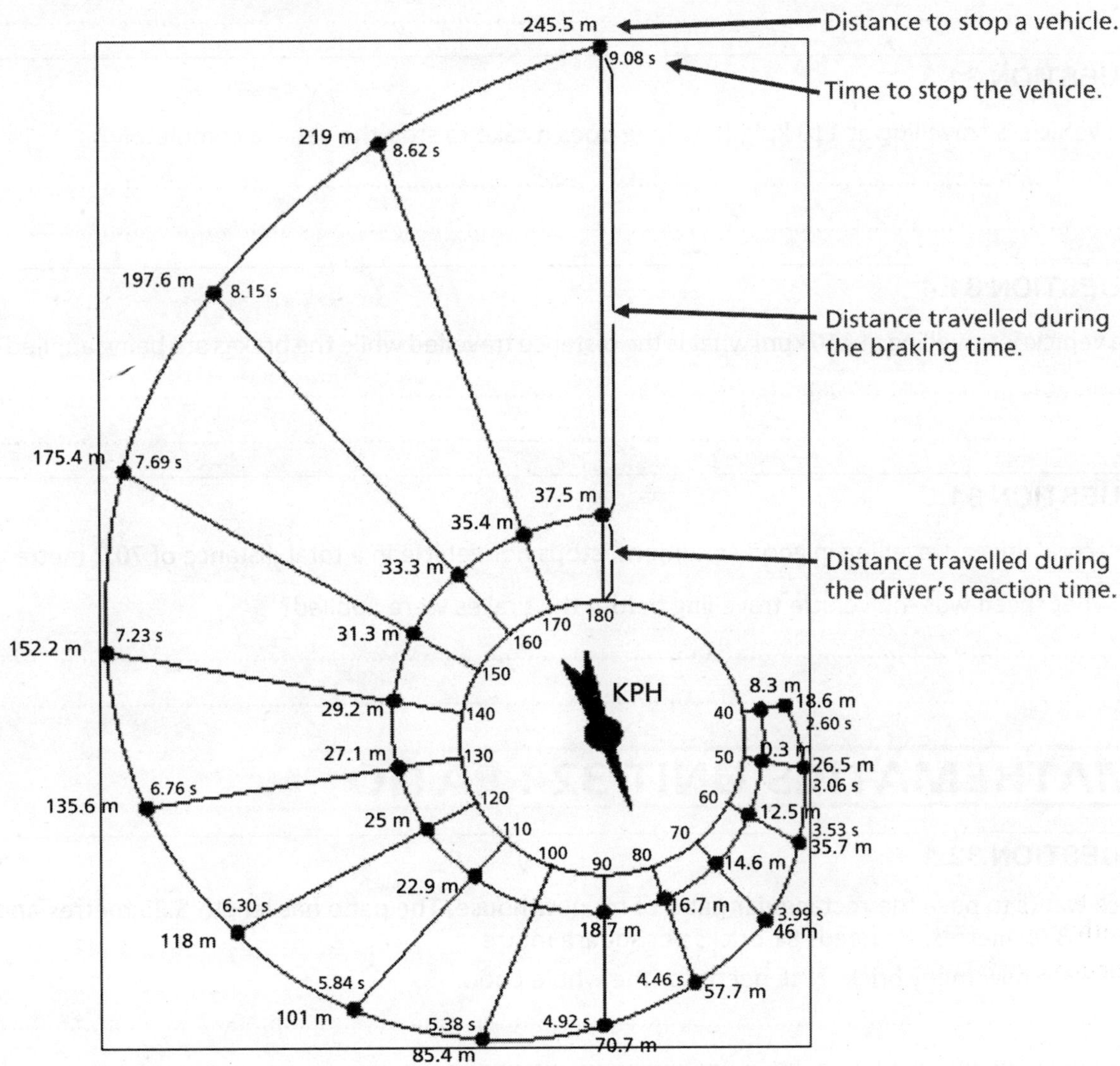

Source: La Prévention Routière, Ministère de l'Education nationale, de la Recherche et de la Technologie, France.

QUESTION 31.1

If a vehicle is travelling at 110 kph, what distance does the vehicle travel during the driver's reaction time?

....

....

QUESTION 31.2

If a vehicle is travelling at 110 kph, what is the total distance travelled before the vehicle stops?

....

....

QUESTION 31.3

If a vehicle is travelling at 110 kph, how long does it take to stop the vehicle completely?

....

....

QUESTION 31.4

If a vehicle is travelling at 110 kph, what is the distance travelled while the brakes are being applied?

....

....

QUESTION 31.5

A second driver, travelling in good conditions, stops her vehicle in a total distance of 70.7 metres.

At what speed was the vehicle travelling before the brakes were applied?

....

....

MATHEMATICS UNIT 32 : PATIO

QUESTION 32.1

Nick wants to pave the rectangular patio of his new house. The patio has length 5.25 metres and width 3.00 metres. He needs 81 bricks per square metre.
Calculate how many bricks Nick needs for the whole patio.

....

....

....

MATHEMATICS UNIT 33: DRUG CONCENTRATIONS

QUESTION 33.1

A woman in hospital receives an injection of penicillin. Her body gradually breaks the penicillin down so that one hour after the injection only 60% of the penicillin will remain active.

This pattern continues: at the end of each hour only 60% of the penicillin that was present at the end of the previous hour remains active.

Suppose the woman is given a dose of 300 milligrams of penicillin at 8 o'clock in the morning.

Complete this table showing the amount of penicillin that will remain active in the woman's blood at intervals of one hour from 0800 until 1100 hours.

Time	0800	0900	1000	1100
Penicillin (mg)	300			

QUESTION 33.2

Peter has to take 80 mg of a drug to control his blood pressure. The following graph shows the initial amount of the drug, and the amount that remains active in Peter's blood after one, two, three and four days.

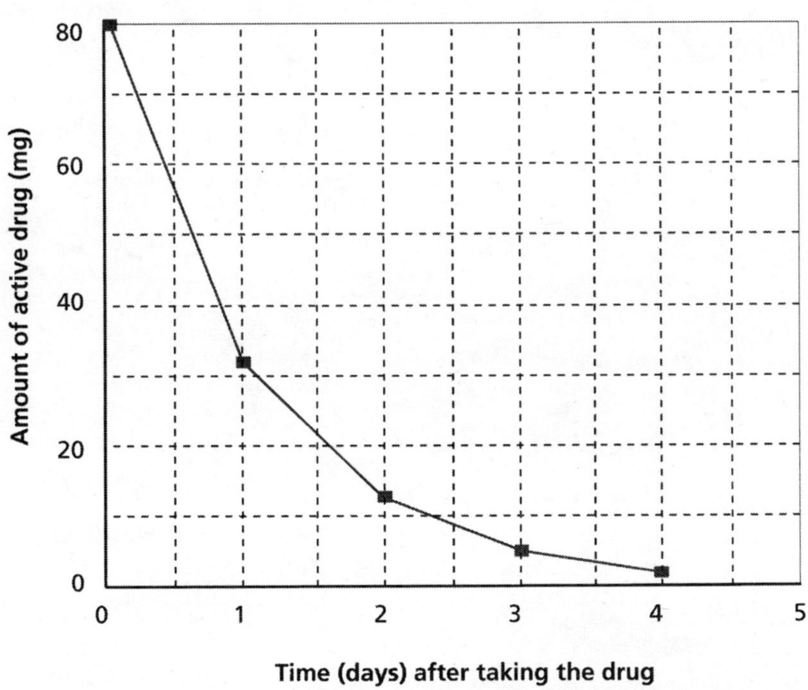

How much of the drug remains active at the end of the first day?

A. 6 mg.

B. 12 mg.

C. 26 mg.

D. 32 mg.

QUESTION 33.3

From the graph for the previous question it can be seen that each day, about the same proportion of the previous day's drug remains active in Peter's blood.

At the end of each day which of the following is the approximate percentage of the previous day's drug that remains active?

A. 20%.

B. 30%.

C. 40%.

D. 80%.

MATHEMATICS UNIT 34 : BUILDING BLOCKS

Susan likes to build blocks from small cubes like the one shown in the following diagram:

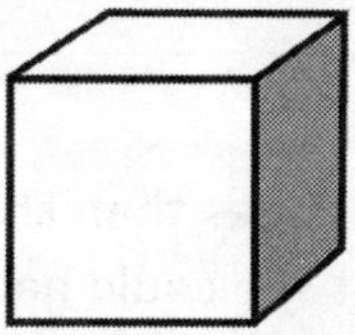

Small cube

Susan has lots of small cubes like this one. She uses glue to join cubes together to make other blocks.

First, Susan glues eight of the cubes together to make the block shown in Diagram A:

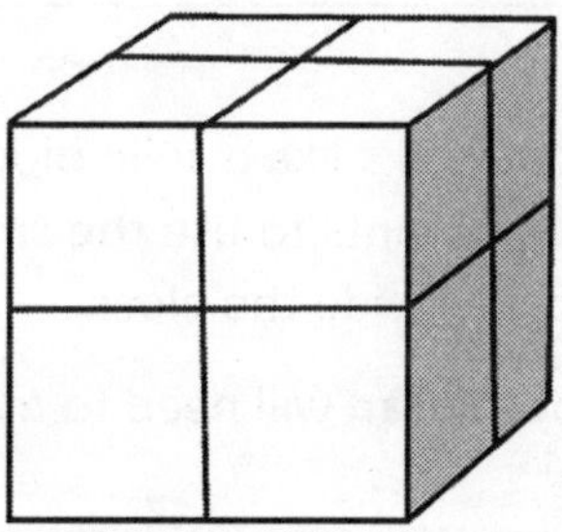

Diagram A

Then Susan makes the solid blocks shown in Diagram B and Diagram C below:

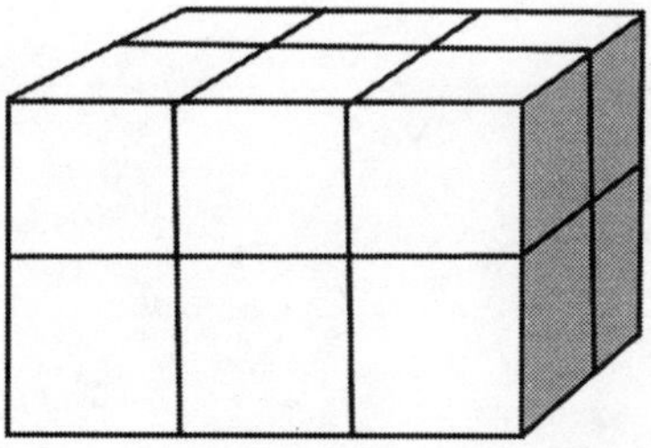

Diagram B

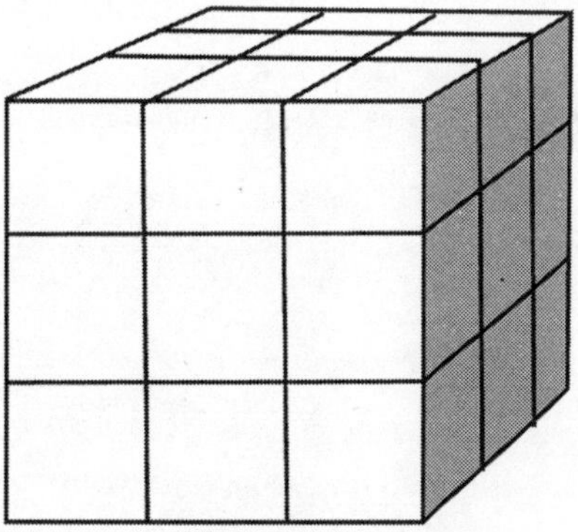

Diagram C

Diagram B and Diagram C

QUESTION 34.1

How many small cubes will Susan need to make the block shown in Diagram B?

Answer: .... cubes.

QUESTION 34.2

How many small cubes will Susan need to make the solid block shown in Diagram C?

Answer: .... cubes.

QUESTION 34.3

Susan realises that she used more small cubes than she really needed to make a block like the one shown in Diagram C. She realises that she could have glued small cubes together to look like Diagram C, but the block could have been hollow on the inside.

What is the minimum number of cubes she needs to make a block that looks like the one shown in Diagram C, but is hollow?

Answer: .... cubes.

QUESTION 34.4

Now Susan wants to make a block that looks like a solid block that is 6 small cubes long, 5 small cubes wide and 4 small cubes high. She wants to use the smallest number of cubes possible, by leaving the largest possible hollow space inside the block.

What is the minimum number of cubes Susan will need to make this block?

Answer: .... cubes.

MATHEMATICS UNIT 35 : REACTION TIME

In a Sprinting event, the 'reaction time' is the time interval between the starter's gun firing and the athlete leaving the starting block. The 'final time' includes both this reaction time, and the running time.

The following table gives the reaction time and the final time of 8 runners in a 100 metre sprint race.

Lane	Reaction time (sec)	Final time (sec)
1.	0.147	10.09
2.	0.136	9.99
3.	0.197	9.87
4.	0.180	Did not finish the race
5.	0.210	10.17
6.	0.216	10.04
7.	0.174	10.08
8.	0.193	10.13

QUESTION 35.1

Identify the Gold, Silver and Bronze medallists from this race. Fill in the table below with the medallists' lane number, reaction time and final time.

Medal	Lane	Reaction time (secs)	Final time (secs)
GOLD			
SILVER			
BRONZE			

QUESTION 35.2

To date, no humans have been able to react to a starter's gun in less than 0.110 second.

If the recorded reaction time for a runner is less than 0.110 second, then a false start is considered to have occurred because the runner must have left before hearing the gun.

If the Bronze medallist had a faster reaction time, would he have had a chance to win the Silver medal?

Give an explanation to support your answer.

....

....

MATHEMATICS UNIT 36 : WATER TANK

QUESTION 36.1

A water tank has shape and dimensions as shown in the diagram.

At the beginning the tank is empty. Then it is filled with water at the rate of one litre per second.

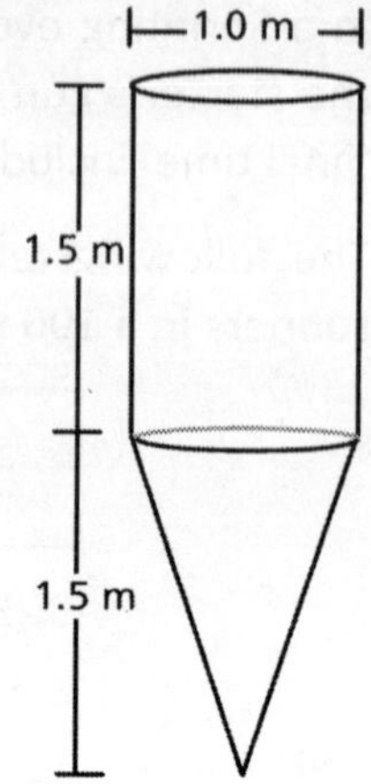

Water tank

Which of the following graphs shows how the height of the water surface changes over time?

A

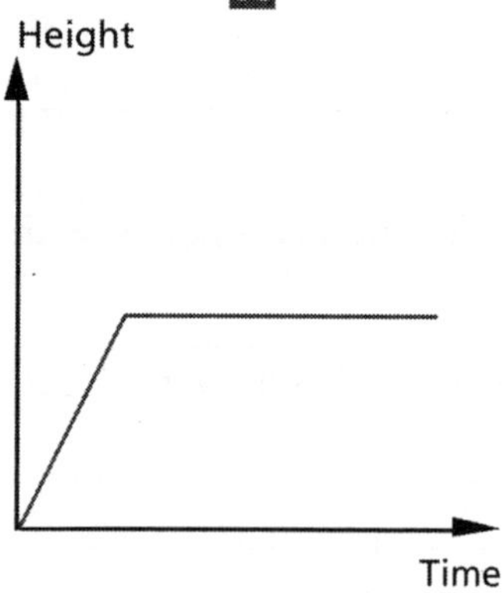

B

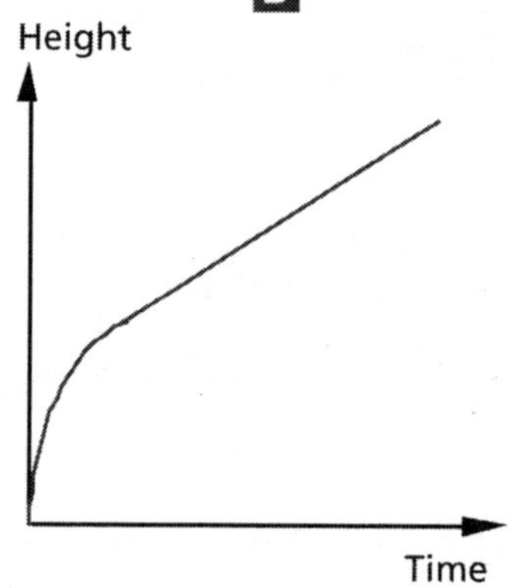

C

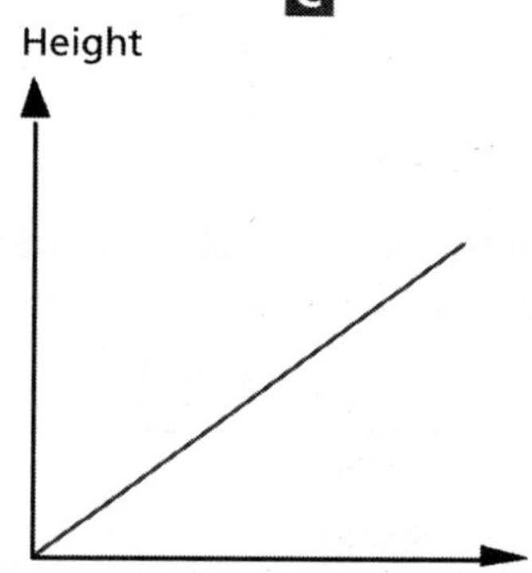

D

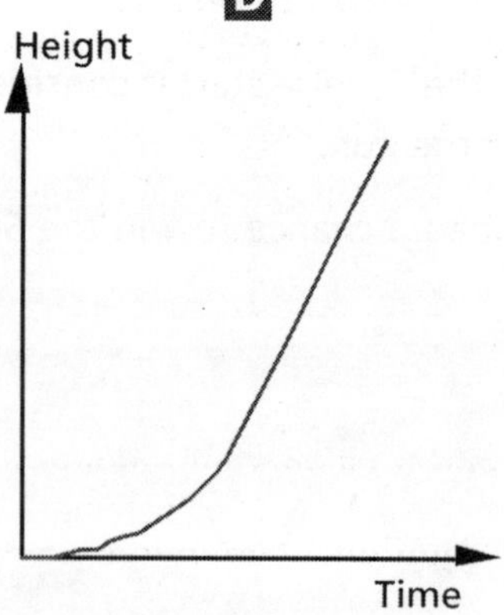

E

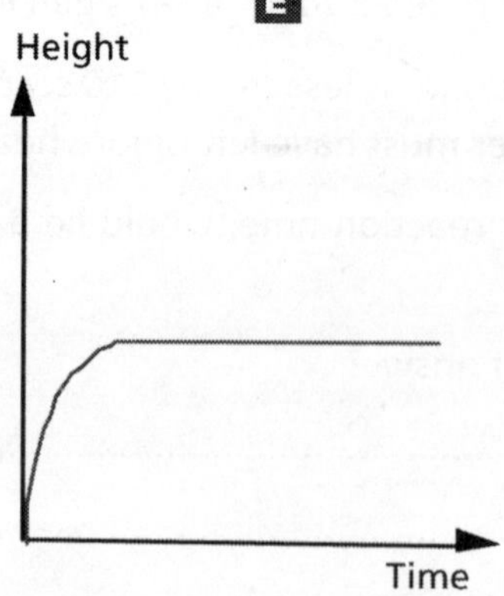

MATHEMATICS UNIT 37 : SPRING FAIR

QUESTION 37.1

A game in a booth at a spring fair involves using a spinner first. Then, if the spinner stops on an even number, the player is allowed to pick a marble from a bag. The spinner and the marbles in the bag are represented in the diagram below.

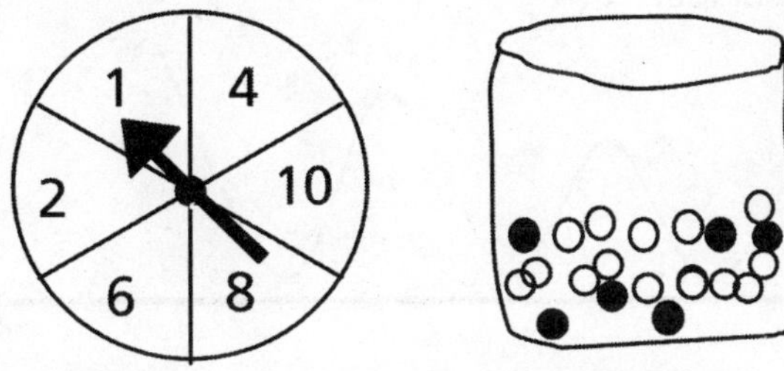

Prizes are given when a black marble is picked. Sue plays the game once.

How likely is it that Sue will win a prize?

A. Impossible.

B. Not very likely.

C. About 50% likely.

D. Very likely.

E. Certain.

MATHEMATICS UNIT 38 : SWING

QUESTION 38.1

Mohammed is sitting on a swing. He starts to swing. He is trying to go as high as possible.

Which diagram best represents the height of his feet above the ground as he swings?

A

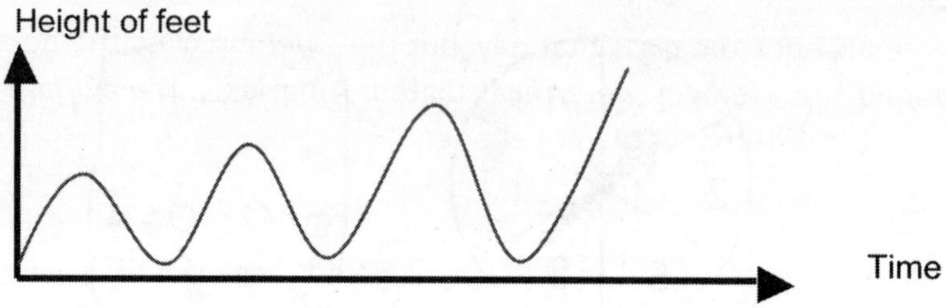

B

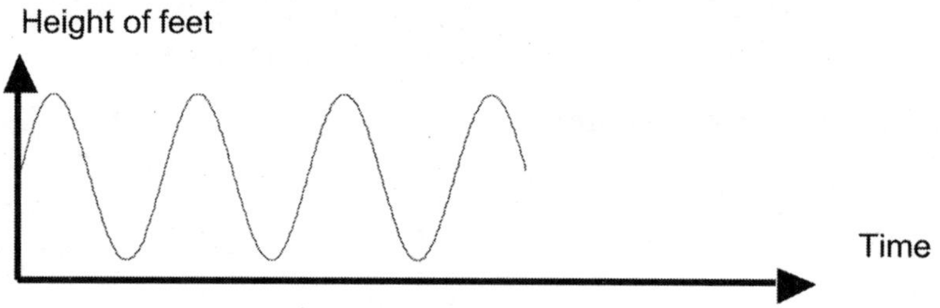

C

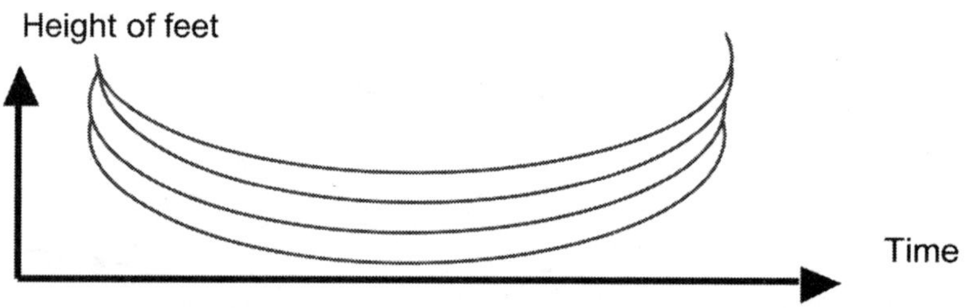

D

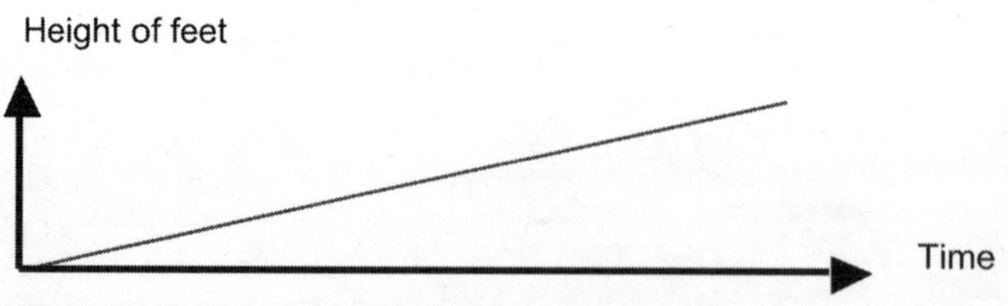

MATHEMATICS UNIT 39 : STUDENT HEIGHTS

QUESTION 39.1

In a mathematics class one day, the heights of all students were measured. The average height of boys was 160 cm, and the average height of girls was 150 cm. Alena was the tallest – her height was 180 cm. Zdenek was the shortest – his height was 130 cm.

Two students were absent from class that day, but they were in class the next day. Their heights were measured, and the averages were recalculated. Amazingly, the average height of the girls and the average height of the boys did not change.

Which of the following conclusions can be drawn from this information?

Circle 'Yes' or 'No' for each conclusion.

Conclusion	Can this conclusion be drawn?
Both students are girls.	Yes / No
One of the students is a boy and the other is a girl.	Yes / No
Both students have the same height.	Yes / No
The average height of all students did not change.	Yes / No
Zdenek is still the shortest.	Yes / No

MATHEMATICS UNIT 40 : PAYMENTS BY AREA

People living in an apartment building decide to buy the building. They will put their money together in such a way that each will pay an amount that is proportional to the size of their apartment.

For example, a man living in an apartment that occupies one fifth of the floor area of all apartments will pay one fifth of the total price of the building.

QUESTION 40.1

Circle Correct or Incorrect for each of the following statements.

Statement	Correct / Incorrect
A person living in the largest apartment will pay more money for each square metre of his apartment than the person living in the smallest apartment.	Correct / Incorrect
If we know the areas of two apartments and the price of one of them we can calculate the price of the second.	Correct / Incorrect
If we know the price of the building and how much each owner will pay, then the total area of all apartments can be calculated.	Correct / Incorrect
If the total price of the building were reduced by 10%, each of the owners would pay 10% less.	Correct / Incorrect

QUESTION 40.2

There are three apartments in the building. The largest, apartment 1, has a total area of 95 m^2.

Apartments 2 and 3 have areas of 85 m^2 and 70 m^2 respectively. The selling price for the building is 300 000 zeds.

How much should the owner of apartment 2 pay? Show your work.

....

....

MATHEMATICS UNIT 41 : SHOES FOR KIDS

The following table shows the recommended Zedland shoe sizes corresponding to various foot lengths.

Conversion table for kids shoe sizes in Zedland

From (in mm)	To (in mm)	Shoe size
107	115	18
116	122	19
123	128	20
129	134	21
135	139	22
140	146	23
147	152	24
153	159	25
160	166	26
167	172	27
173	179	28
180	186	29
187	192	30
193	199	31
200	206	32
207	212	33
213	219	34
220	226	35

QUESTION 41.1

Marina's feet are 163 mm long. Use the table to determine which Zedland shoe size Marina should try on.

Answer: ....

MATHEMATICS UNIT 42 : TABLE TENNIS TOURNAMENT

QUESTION 42.1

Teun, Riek, Bep and Dirk have formed a practice group in a table tennis club. Each player wishes to play against each other player once. They have reserved two practice tables for these matches.

Complete the following match schedule; by writing the names of the players playing in each match.

	Practice Table 1	Practice Table 2
Round 1	Teun - Riek	Bep - Dirk
Round 2	.... -	.... - ....
Round 3	.... -	.... - ....

MATHEMATICS UNIT 43: LIGHTHOUSE

Lighthouses are towers with a light beacon on top. Lighthouses assist sea ships in finding their way at night when they are sailing close to the shore.

A lighthouse beacon sends out light flashes with a regular fixed pattern. Every lighthouse has its own pattern.

In the diagram below you see the pattern of a certain lighthouse. The light flashes alternate with dark periods.

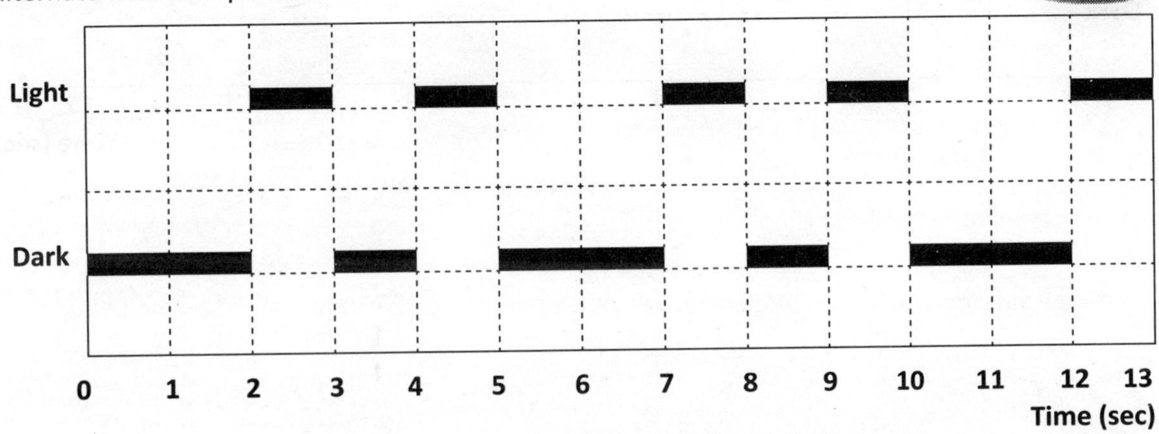

It is a regular pattern. After some time the pattern repeats itself. The time taken by one complete cycle of a pattern, before it starts to repeat, is called the period. When you find the period of a pattern, it is easy to extend the diagram for the next seconds or minutes or even hours.

QUESTION 43.1

Which of the following could be the period of the pattern of this lighthouse?

A. 2 seconds.

B. 3 seconds.

C. 5 seconds.

D. 12 seconds.

QUESTION 43.2

For how many seconds does the lighthouse send out light flashes in 1 minute?

A. 4

B. 12

C. 20

D. 24

QUESTION 43.3

In the diagram below, make a graph of a possible pattern of light flashes of a lighthouse that sends out light flashes for 30 seconds per minute. The period of this pattern must be equal to 6 seconds.

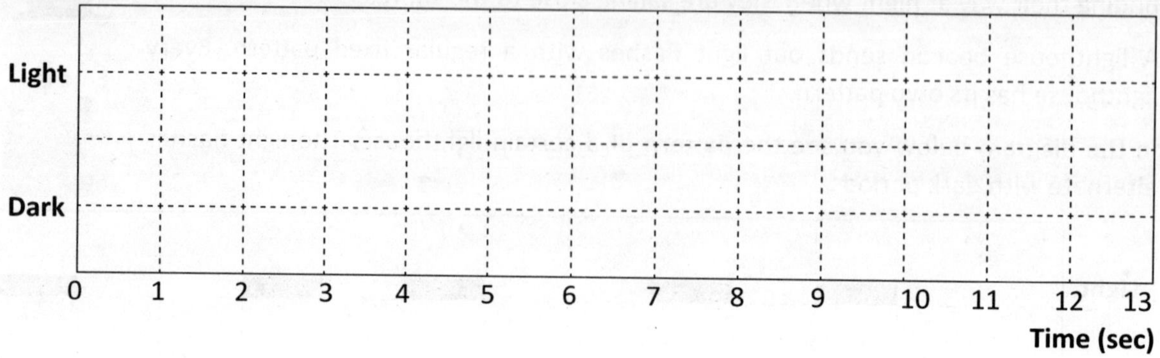

MATHEMATICS UNIT 44 : DECREASING CO_2 LEVELS

Many scientists fear that the increasing level of CO_2 gas in our atmosphere is causing climate change.

The diagram below shows the CO_2 emission levels in 1990 (the light bars) for several countries (or regions), the emission levels in 1998 (the dark bars), and the percentage change in emission levels between 1990 and 1998 (the arrows with percentages).

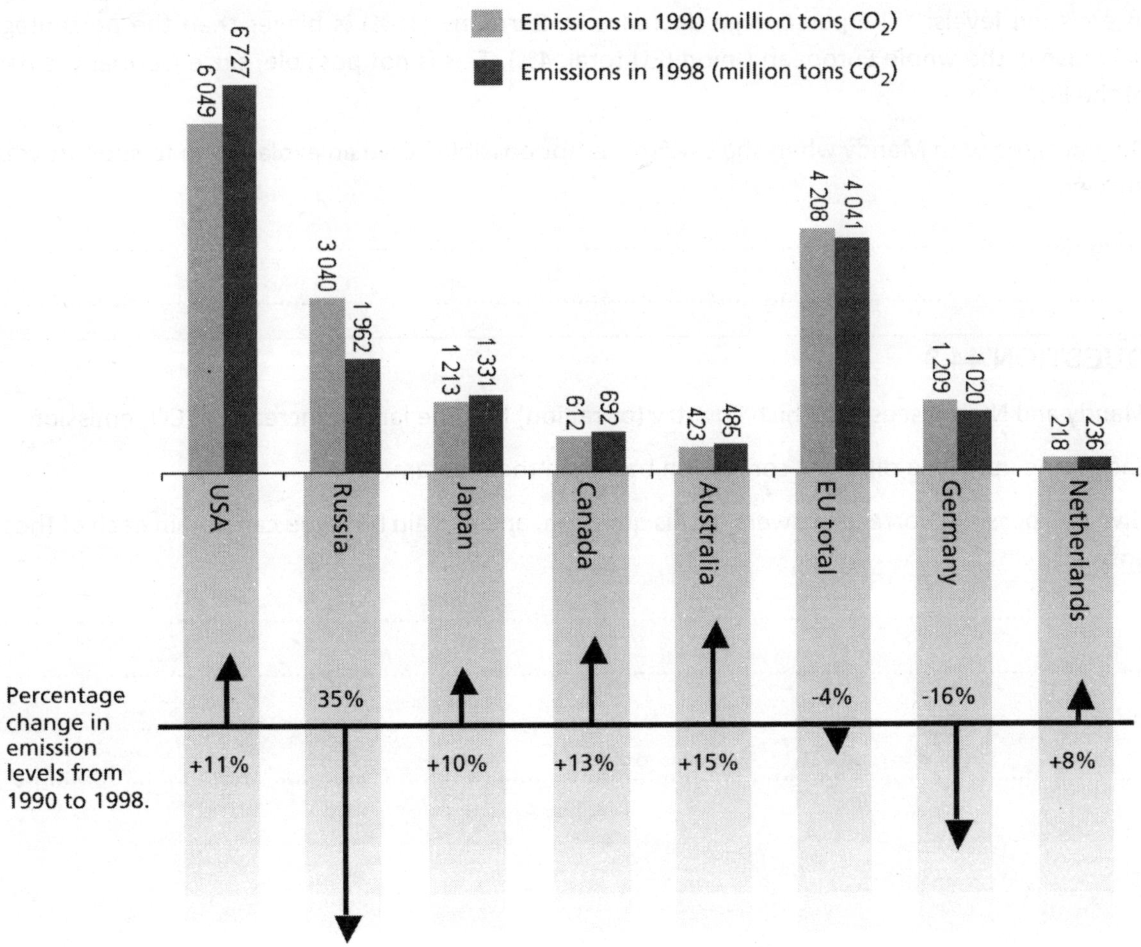

QUESTION 44.1

In the diagram you can read that in the USA, the increase in CO_2 emission level from 1990 to 1998 was 11%.

Show the calculation to demonstrate how the 11% is obtained.

....

....

QUESTION 44.2

Mandy analysed the diagram and claimed she discovered a mistake in the percentage change in emission levels: "The percentage decrease in Germany (16%) is bigger than the percentage decrease in the whole European Union (EU total, 4%). This is not possible, since Germany is part of the EU."

Do you agree with Mandy when she says this is not possible? Give an explanation to support your answer.

....

....

QUESTION 44.3

Mandy and Niels discussed which country (or region) had the largest increase of CO_2 emissions.

Each came up with a different conclusion based on the diagram.

Give two possible 'correct' answers to this question, and explain how you can obtain each of these answers.

....

....

....

....

MATHEMATICS UNIT 45 : TWISTED BUILDING

In modern architecture, buildings often have unusual shapes. The picture below shows a computer model of a 'twisted building' and a plan of the ground floor. The compass points show the orientation of the building.

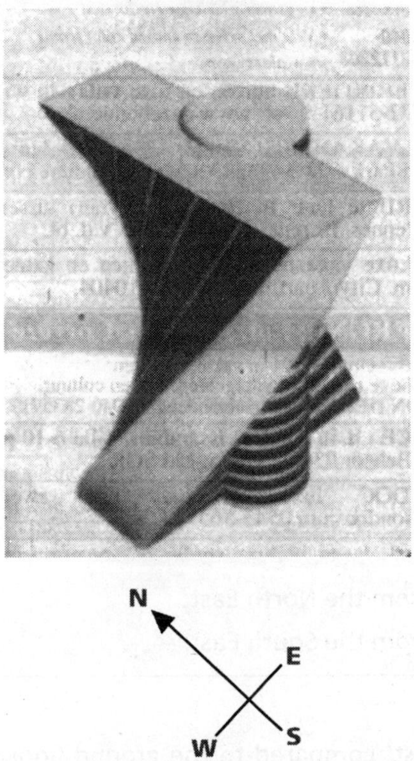

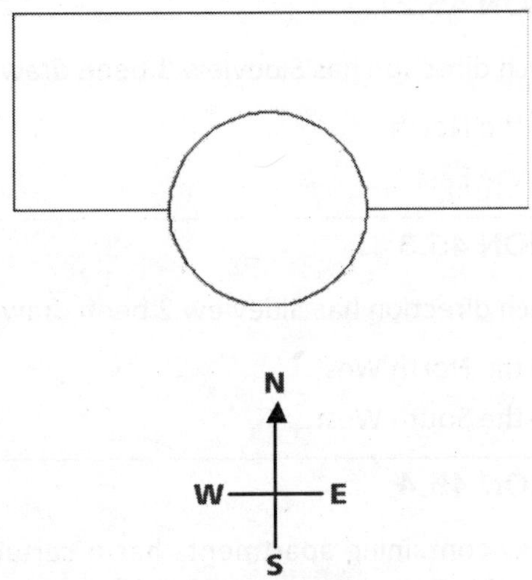

The ground floor of the building contains the main entrance and has room for shops. Above the ground floor there are 20 storeys containing apartments.

The plan of each storey is similar to the plan of the ground floor, but each has a slightly different orientation from the storey below. The cylinder contains the elevator shaft and a landing on each floor.

QUESTION 45.1

Estimate the total height of the building, in metres. Explain how you found your answer.

....

....

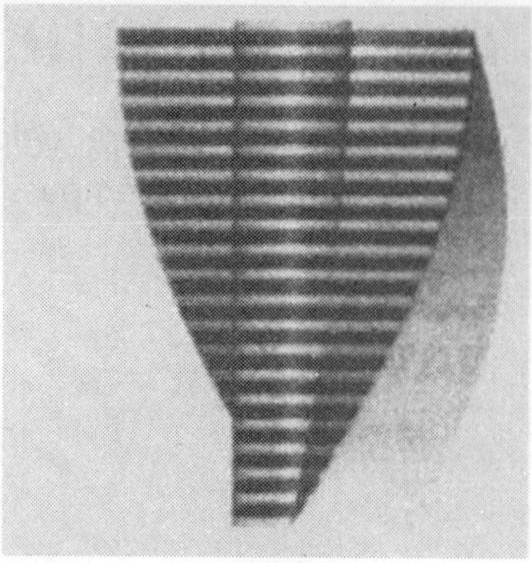

Sideview 1

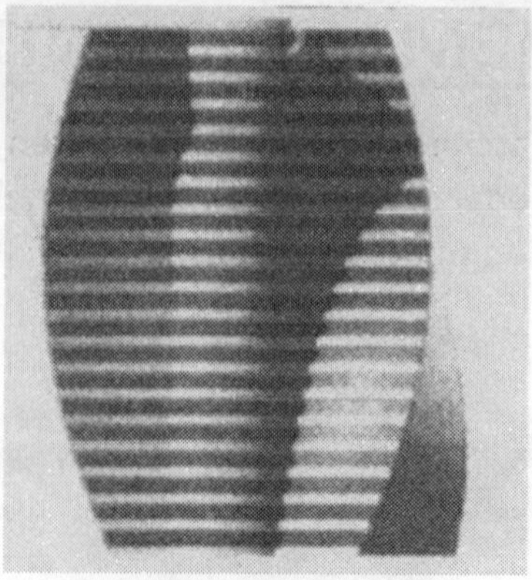

Sideview 2

QUESTION 45.2

From which direction has Sideview 1 been drawn?

A. From the North.

B. From the West.

C. From the East.

D. From the South.

QUESTION 45.3

From which direction has Sideview 2 been drawn?

A. From the North West.

B. From the North East.

C. From the South West.

D. From the South East.

QUESTION 45.4

Each storey containing apartments has a certain 'twist' compared to the ground floor. The top floor (the 20th floor above the ground floor) is at right angles to the ground floor.

The drawing below represents the ground floor.

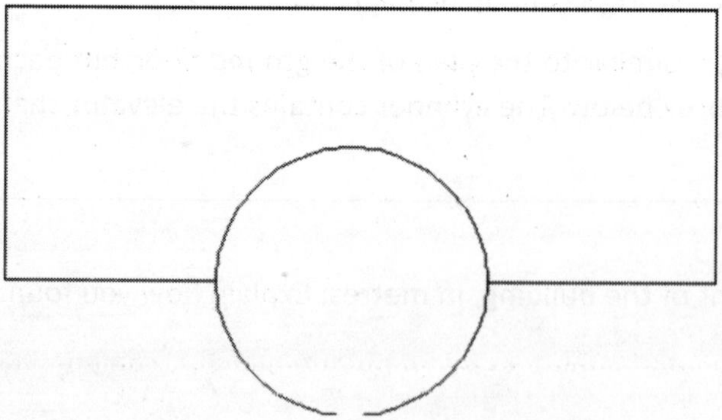

Draw in this diagram the plan of the 10th floor above the ground floor, showing how this floor is situated compared to the ground floor.

MATHEMATICS UNIT 46 : HEARTBEAT

For health reasons people should limit their efforts, for instance during sports, in order not to exceed a certain heartbeat frequency.

For years the relationship between a person's recommended maximum heart rate and the person's age was described by the following formula:

Recommended maximum heart rate = 220 - age

Recent research showed that this formula should be modified slightly. The new formula is as follows:

Recommended maximum heart rate = 208 – (0.7 × age)

QUESTION 46.1

A newspaper article stated: "A result of using the new formula instead of the old one is that the recommended maximum number of heartbeats per minute for young people decreases slightly and for old people it increases slightly."

From which age onwards does the recommended maximum heart rate increase as a result of the introduction of the new formula? Show your work.

....

....

QUESTION 46.2

The formula *recommended maximum heart rate* = 208 – (0.7 x age) is also used to determine when physical training is most effective. Research has shown that physical training is most effective when the heartbeat is at 80% of the recommended maximum heart rate.

Write down a formula for calculating the heart rate for most effective physical training, expressed in terms of age.

....

....

MATHEMATICS UNIT 47 : SPACE FLIGHT

Space station Mir remained in orbit for 15 years and circled Earth some 86 500 times during its time in space.

The longest stay of one cosmonaut in the Mir was around 680 days.

QUESTION 47.1

Approximately how many times did this cosmonaut fly around Earth?

A. 110

B. 1 100

C. 11 000

D. 110 000

MATHEMATICS UNIT 48 : ROCK CONCERT

QUESTION 48.1

For a rock concert a rectangular field of size 100 m by 50 m was reserved for the audience. The concert was completely sold out and the field was full with all the fans standing.

Which one of the following is likely to be the best estimate of the total number of people attending the concert?

A. 2 000

B. 5 000

C. 20 000

D. 50 000

E. 100 000

MATHEMATICS UNIT 49 : MOVING WALKWAYS

QUESTION 49.1

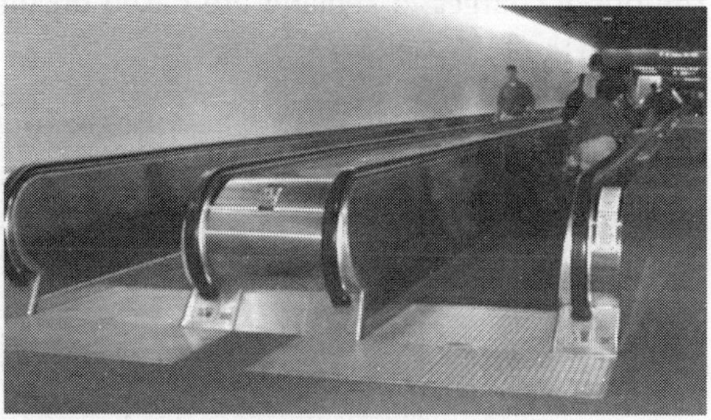

On the right is a photograph of moving walkways.

The following Distance-Time graph shows a comparison between "walking on the moving walkway" and "walking on the ground next to the moving walkway."

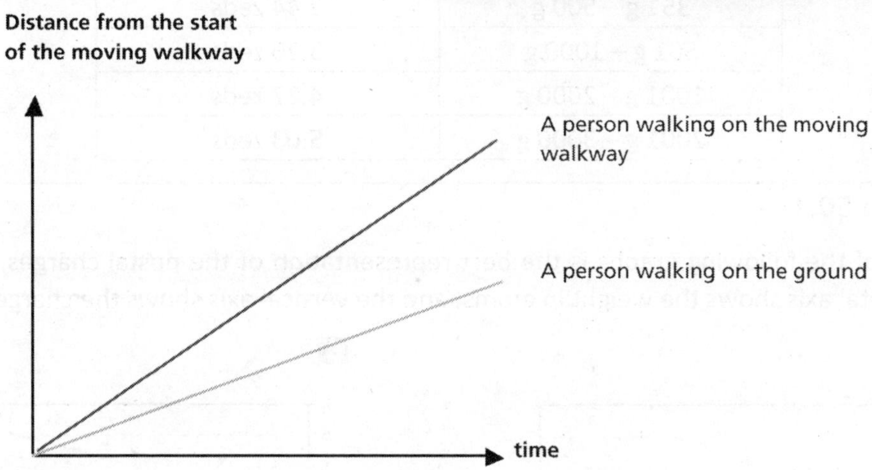

Assuming that, in the above graph, the walking pace is about the same for both persons, add a line to the graph that would represent the distance versus time for a person who is standing still on the moving walkway.

MATHEMATICS UNIT 50 : POSTAL CHARGES

The postal charges in Zedland are based on the weight of the items (to the nearest gram), as shown in the table below:

Weight (to nearest gram)	Charge
Up to 20 g	0.46 zeds
21 g – 50 g	0.69 zeds
51 g – 100 g	1.02 zeds
101 g – 200 g	1.75 zeds
201 g – 350 g	2.13 zeds
351 g – 500 g	2.44 zeds
501 g – 1000 g	3.20 zeds
1001 g – 2000 g	4.27 zeds
2001 g – 3000 g	5.03 zeds

QUESTION 50.1

Which one of the following graphs is the best representation of the postal charges in Zedland? (The horizontal axis shows the weight in grams, and the vertical axis shows the charge in zeds.)

A

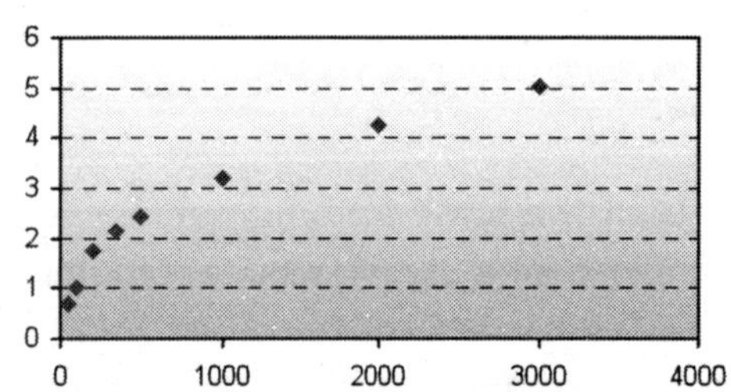

B

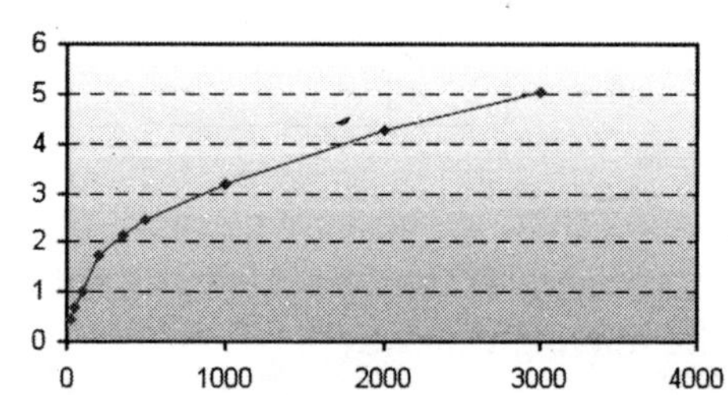

C

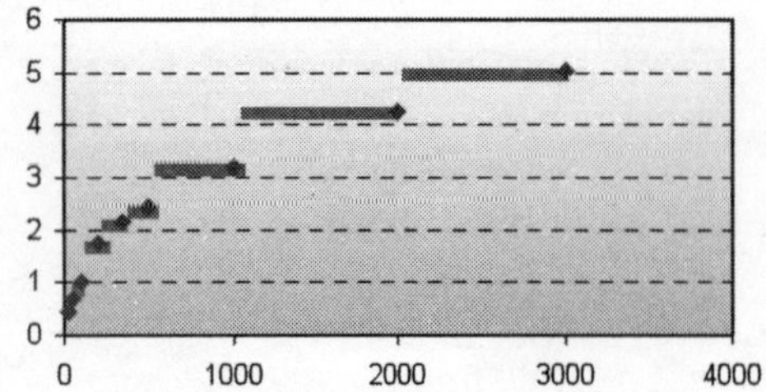

D

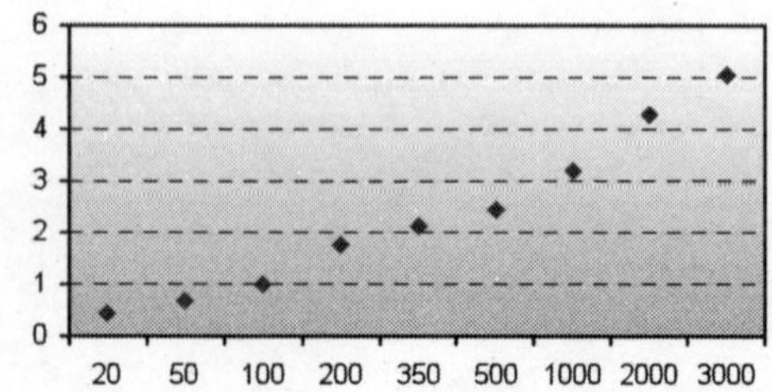

QUESTION 50.2

Jan wants to send two items, weighing 40 grams and 80 grams respectively, to a friend.

According to the postal charges in Zedland, decide whether it is cheaper to send the two items as one parcel, or send the items as two separate parcels. Show your calculations of the cost in each case.

....

....

....

....

CHAPTER 4

Science Sample Tasks

Science questions in PISA aim at evaluating how well students apply scientific ways of thinking to situations they could encounter in their everyday lives. This allows PISA to include scientific knowledge relevant to the science curricula of participating countries without being constrained by the common denominator of national curricula. To capture this idea, PISA uses the concept of *scientific literacy*.

In 2000 and 2003, scientific literacy was defined as:

> the capacity to use scientific knowledge, to identify questions and to draw evidence-based conclusions in order to understand and help make decisions about the natural world and the changes made to it through human activity.

To assess the students in science, three interconnected dimensions were distinguished: scientific *concepts*, scientific *processes* and scientific *situations*.

Scientific concepts are drawn from physics, chemistry and biology. More specifically, PISA used themes such as "forces and movement" or "the earth and its place in the universe". The selection of topics is based on their relevance to everyday situations, their enduring relevance as well as the possibility to combine the topic with scientific processes (so for example more than just recalling a name or a definition). The knowledge thus refers to the scientific concepts which students need to grasp.

Students and people in general need to use and apply their scientific knowledge and understanding via scientific processes. In PISA the focus lies on processes which citizens will need, such as: distinguishing between questions which science can and cannot answer, deciding when scientific evidence is and is not valid and weighing evidence for and against a particular course of action that affects life at the personal, social or global level. In PISA 2000, a distinction was made between the following five scientific processes:

1. Recognising scientifically investigable questions.
2. Identifying evidence needed in a scientific investigation.
3. Drawing or evaluating conclusions.
4. Communicating valid conclusions.
5. Demonstrating understanding of scientific concepts.

In PISA 2003, three processes were distinguished:

1. Describing, explaining and predicting scientific phenomena.
2. Understanding scientific investigation.
3. Interpreting scientific evidence and conclusions.

The third of the three interrelated dimensions are scientific situations (sometimes referred to as areas of applications or as contexts). The situation can be science in life and health, science in earth and the environment or science in technology.

In PISA 2006, science was assessed more comprehensively. As a result, some changes were made to the assessment. A major difference between the definition of scientific literacy used in PISA 2000 and 2003 and the PISA 2006 definition is the distinction between knowledge of science and knowledge about science in the 2006 assessment. The former means an understanding of scientific concepts and theories whereas the latter refers to an understanding of the nature, power and limitations of science as a human activity.

In addition, the 2006 definition draws attention to the relationship between science and technology. PISA 2006 defines scientific literacy in terms of an individual's:

- Scientific knowledge and use of that knowledge to identify questions, to acquire new knowledge, to explain phenomena, and to draw evidence-based conclusions about science-related issues.
- Understanding of the characteristic features of science as a form of human knowledge and enquiry.
- Awareness of how science and technology shape our material, intellectual and cultural environments.
- Willingness to engage with science-related issues, and with the ideas of science, as a reflective citizen.

Instead of the three interconnected dimensions which were distinguished in PISA 2000 and 2003 (concepts, processes and situations), PISA 2006 differentiates between four interrelated aspects: *knowledge, competencies, contexts* and *attitudes*. The first three bear some resemblance to the earlier dimensions, but have been altered in fundamental ways. The attitudinal aspect is new.

Knowledge is subdivided into knowledge of science and knowledge about science. Knowledge of science includes four sub-categories (physical systems; living systems; earth and space systems; technology systems) and knowledge about science encompasses two sub-categories (scientific enquiry and scientific explanations).

The three competencies which are assessed are:

1. Identifying scientific issues.
2. Explaining phenomena scientifically.
3. Using scientific evidence.

The context can be personal, social or global, as well as - in some cases - historical. Each question used in a PISA survey falls into one category of each of the three aspects. For example, Question 10.1 from the unit Acid Rain (used in the PISA 2006 survey) is classified into the competency explaining phenomena scientifically, into the knowledge of science sub-category living systems and into a global context. As the last two categorisations are generally fairly obvious, they will not be explicitly mentioned for the questions presented here.

The fourth dimension is student attitudes. These questions are different from the rest, because they have no right or wrong answer. They relate to the same scientific issue as the other questions in that unit, but they ask about students' attitudes towards that issue. The attitude dimension is divided into the following four sub-categories: a) interest in science, b) support for scientific enquiry, c) self-belief as science learners and d) responsibility towards resources and environments.

To report the results of PISA 2000 and PISA 2003, a single science scale was used. The average score on this scale is 500 with two-thirds of students scoring between 400 and 600. In 2006, when science was assessed more comprehensively, separate scales for each of the competencies and knowledge domains were created in addition to an overall science scale. Like the science scales in PISA 2000 and 2003, each of these scales has a mean score of 500 points with two-thirds of students scoring between 400 and 600. More information on PISA proficiency scales can be found in Annex A.

This chapter presents 40 units. The first 12 units were used in the PISA surveys. Units 13 to 40 were used in developing and testing out the surveys. While it was decided not to include these units in the PISA surveys, they are nevertheless illustrative of the kinds of questions asked in PISA. The questions presented in this chapter are all publicly released PISA science questions. Following the section with questions, answers for all questions are given. For units 1 to 12, a comment box includes score points, percentage of students who answered correctly across OECD countries and the question category. For country results, refer to Annex B. For units 13 to 40, a comment box lists the question category. Because these units were not used in the PISA surveys, the information regarding score points and percentage of students who answered correctly is not known or it not sufficiently reliable to be presented here.

SCIENCE UNIT 1 : SEMMELWEIS DIARY

Semmelweis' Diary Text 1

'July 1846. Next week I will take up a position as "Herr Doktor" at the First Ward of the maternity clinic of the Vienna General Hospital. I was frightened when I heard about the percentage of patients who die in this clinic. This month not less than 36 of the 208 mothers died there, all from puerperal fever. Giving birth to a child is as dangerous as first-degree pneumonia.'

These line from the diary of Ignaz Semmelweis (1818-1865) illustrate the devastating effects of puerperal fever, a contagious disease that killed many women after childbirth. Semmelweis collected data about the number of deaths from puerperal fever in both the First and the Second Wards (see diagram).

Number of Deaths per 100 deliveries from puerperal fever

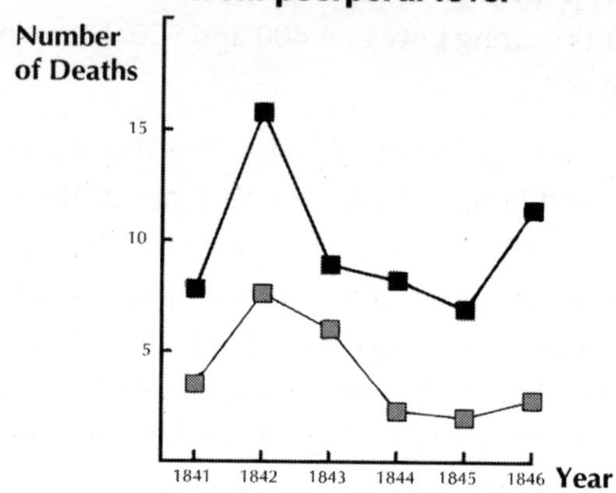

Physicians, among them Semmelweis, were completely in the dark about the cause of puerperal fever. Semmelweis' diary again:

'December 1846. Why do so many women die from this fever after giving birth without any problems? For centuries science has told us that it is an invisible epidemic that kills mothers. Causes may be changes in the air or some extraterrestrial influence or a movement of the earth itself, an earthquake.'

Nowadays not many people would consider extraterrestrial influence or an earthquake as possible causes of fever. We now know it has to do with hygienic conditions. But in the time Semmelweis lived, many people, even scientists, did! However, Semmelweis knew that it was unlikely that fever could be caused by extraterrestrial influence or an earthquake. He pointed at the data he collected (see diagram) and used this to try to persuade his colleagues.

QUESTION 1.1

Suppose you were Semmelweis. Give a reason (based on the data Semmelweis collected) why puerperal fever is unlikely to be caused by earthquakes.

....

....

....

....

Semmelweis' Diary Text 2

Part of the research in the hospital was dissection. The body of a deceased person was cut open to find a cause of death. Semmelweis recorded that the students working on the First ward usually took part in dissections on women who died the previous day, before they examined women who had just given birth. They did not pay much attention to cleaning themselves after the dissections. Some were even proud of the fact that you could tell by their smell that they had been working in the mortuary, as this showed how industrious they were! One of Semmelweis' friends died after having cut himself during such a dissection. Dissection of his body showed he had the same symptoms as mothers who died from puerperal fever. This gave Semmelweis a new idea.

QUESTION 1.2

Semmelweis' new idea had to do with the high percentage of women dying in the maternity wards and the students' behaviour.

What was this idea?

A. Having students clean themselves after dissections should lead to a decrease of puerperal fever.

B. Students should not take part in dissections because they may cut themselves.

C. Students smell because they do not clean themselves after a dissection.

D. Students want to show that they are industrious, which makes them careless when they examine the women.

QUESTION 1.3

Semmelweis succeeded in his attempts to reduce the number of deaths due to puerperal fever. But puerperal fever even today remains a disease that is difficult to eliminate.

Fevers that are difficult to cure are still a problem in hospitals. Many routine measures serve to control this problem. Among those measures are washing sheets at high temperatures.

Explain why high temperature (while washing sheets) helps to reduce the risk that patients will contract a fever.

....

....

QUESTION 1.4

Many diseases may be cured by using antibiotics. However, the success of some antibiotics against puerperal fever has diminished in recent years.

What is the reason for this?

A. Once produced, antibiotics gradually lose their activity.

B. Bacteria become resistant to antibiotics.

C. These antibiotics only help against puerperal fever, but not against other diseases.

D. The need for these antibiotics has been reduced because public health conditions have improved considerably in recent years.

SCIENCE UNIT 2 : OZONE

Read the following section of an article about the ozone layer.

The atmosphere is an ocean of air and a precious natural resource for sustaining life on the Earth. Unfortunately, human activities based on national/personal interests are causing harm to this common resource, notably by depleting the fragile ozone layer, which acts as a protective shield for life on the Earth.

Ozone molecules consist of three oxygen atoms, as opposed to oxygen molecules which consist of two oxygen atoms. Ozone molecules are exceedingly rare: fewer than ten in every million molecules of air. However, for nearly a billion years, their presence in the atmosphere has played a vital role in safeguarding life on Earth. Depending on where it is located, ozone can either protect or harm life on Earth. The ozone in the troposphere (up to 10 kilometres above the Earth's surface) is "bad" ozone which can damage lung tissues and plants. But about 90 percent of ozone found in the stratosphere (between 10 and 40 kilometres above the Earth's surface) is "good" ozone which plays a beneficial role by absorbing dangerous ultraviolet (UV-B) radiation from the Sun.

Without this beneficial ozone layer, humans would be more susceptible to certain diseases due to the increased incidence of ultra-violet rays from the Sun. In the last decades the amount of ozone has decreased. In 1974 it was hypothesised that chlorofluorocarbons (CFCs) could be a cause for this. Until 1987, scientific assessment of the cause-effect relationship was not convincing enough to implicate CFCs. However, in September 1987, diplomats from around the world met in Montreal (Canada) and agreed to set sharp limits to the use of CFCs.

Source: Connect, UNESCO International Science, Technology & Environmental Education Newsletter, Section from an article entitled 'The Chemistry of Atmospheric policy', Vol. XXII, No. 2, 1997 (spelling adapted)

QUESTION 2.1

In the text above nothing is mentioned about the way ozone is formed in the atmosphere. In fact each day some ozone is formed and some other ozone disappears. The way ozone is formed is illustrated in the following comic strip.

Suppose you have an uncle who tries to understand the meaning of this strip. However, he did not get any science education at school and he doesn't understand what the author of the strip is explaining. He knows that there are no little fellows in the atmosphere but he wonders what those little fellows in the strip stand for, what those strange notations O, O2 and O3 mean and which processes the strip represents. He asks you to explain the strip. Assume that your uncle knows:

that O is the symbol for oxygen;

what atoms and molecules are.

Write an explanation of the comic strip for your uncle.

In your explanation, use the words atoms and molecules in the way they are used in lines 5 and 6.

....

....

QUESTION 2.2

Ozone is also formed during thunderstorms. It causes the typical smell after such a storm. In lines 9–13 the author of the text distinguishes between "bad ozone" and "good ozone".

In terms of the article, is the ozone that is formed during thunderstorms "bad ozone" or "good ozone"?

Choose the answer and the explanation that is supported by the text.

	Bad ozone or good ozone?	Explanation
A	Bad	It is formed during bad weather.
B	Bad	It is formed in the tropospheres.
C	Good	It is formed in the tropospheres.
D	Good	It is smells good.

QUESTION 2.3

Lines 14 and 15 state: "Without this beneficial ozone layer, humans would be more susceptible to certain diseases due to the increased incidence of ultra-violet rays from the Sun."

Name one of these specific diseases.

....

SCIENCE UNIT 3: DAYLIGHT

Read the following information and answer the questions that follow.

Daylight on 22 June 2022

> Today, as the Northern Hemisphere celebrates its longest day, Australians will experience their shortest. In Melbourne*, Australia, the Sun will rise at 7:36 am and set at 5:08 pm, giving nine hours and 32 minutes of daylight. Compare today to the year's longest day in the Southern Hemisphere, expected on 22 December, when the Sun will rise at 5:55 am and set at 8:42 pm, giving 14 hours and 47 minutes of daylight. The President of the Astronomical Society, Mr Perry Vlahos, said the existence of changing seasons in the Northern and Southern Hemispheres was linked to the Earth's 23-degree tilt.

*Melbourne is a city in Australia at a latitude of about 38 degrees South of the equator.

Source: The Age newspaper, Melbourne, Australia, 22nd June 1998 (adapted).

QUESTION 3.1

Which statement explains why daylight and darkness occur on Earth?

A. The Earth rotates on its axis.

B. The Sun rotates on its axis.

C. The Earth's axis is tilted.

D. The Earth revolves around the Sun.

QUESTION 3.2

In the Figure light rays from the Sun are shown shining on the Earth

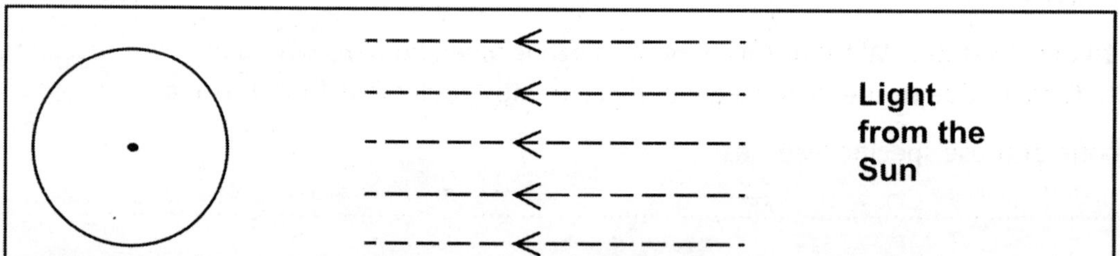

Figure: light rays from Sun

Suppose it is the shortest day in Melbourne.

Show the Earth's axis, the Northern Hemisphere, the Southern Hemisphere and the Equator on the Figure. Label all parts of your answer.

SCIENCE UNIT 4 : CLONING

Read the newspaper article and answer the questions that follow.

A copying machine for living beings?

Without any doubt, if there had been elections for the animal of the year 1997, Dolly would have been the winner! Dolly is a Scottish sheep that you see in the photo. But Dolly is not just a simple sheep. She is a clone of another sheep. A clone means: a copy. Cloning means copying 'from a single master copy'. Scientists succeeded in creating a sheep (Dolly) that is identical to a sheep that functioned as a 'master copy'. It was the Scottish scientist Ian Wilmut who designed the 'copying machine' for sheep. He took a very small piece from the udder of an adult sheep (sheep 1). From that small piece he removed the nucleus, then he transferred the nucleus into the egg-cell of another (female) sheep (sheep 2). But first he removed from that egg-cell all the material that would have determined sheep 2 characteristics in a lamb produced from that egg-cell. Ian Wilmut implanted the manipulated egg-cell of sheep 2 into yet another (female) sheep (sheep 3). Sheep 3 became pregnant and had a lamb: Dolly.

Some scientists think that within a few years it will be possible to clone people as well. But many governments have already decided to forbid cloning of people by law.

Source: Tijdschrift van de Eenhoorn Educatief (Brussels Onderwijs Punt): March 1997.

QUESTION 4.1

Which sheep is Dolly identical to?

A. Sheep 1
B. Sheep 2
C. Sheep 3
D. Dolly's father

QUESTION 4.2

In line 14 the part of the udder that was used is described as "a very small piece". From the article text you can work out what is meant by "a very small piece".

That "very small piece" is

A. a cell.
B. a gene.
C. a cell nucleus.
D. a chromosome.

QUESTION 4.3

In the last sentence of the article it is stated that many governments have already decided to forbid cloning of people by law.

Two possible reasons for this decision are mentioned below.

Are these reasons scientific reasons?

Circle either "Yes" or "No" for each.

Reason:	Scientific?
Cloned people could be more sensitive to certain diseases than normal people.	Yes / No
People should not take over the role of a Creator.	Yes / No

SCIENCE UNIT 5 : GREENHOUSE

Read the texts and answer the questions that follow.

The greenhouse effect: fact or fiction?

Living things need energy to survive. The energy that sustains life on the Earth comes from the Sun, which radiates energy into space because it is so hot. A tiny proportion of this energy reaches the Earth.

The Earth's atmosphere acts like a protective blanket over the surface of our planet, preventing the variations in temperature that would exist in an airless world.

Most of the radiated energy coming from the Sun passes through the Earth's atmosphere. The Earth absorbs some of this energy, and some is reflected back from the Earth's surface. Part of this reflected energy is absorbed by the atmosphere.

As a result of this the average temperature above the Earth's surface is higher than it would be if there were no atmosphere. The Earth's atmosphere has the same effect as a greenhouse, hence the term *greenhouse effect*.

The greenhouse effect is said to have become more pronounced during the twentieth century.

It is a fact that the average temperature of the Earth's atmosphere has increased. In newspapers and periodicals the increased carbon dioxide emission is often stated as the main source of the temperature rise in the twentieth century.

A student named André becomes interested in the possible relationship between the average temperature of the Earth's atmosphere and the carbon dioxide emission on the Earth.

In a library he comes across the following two graphs.

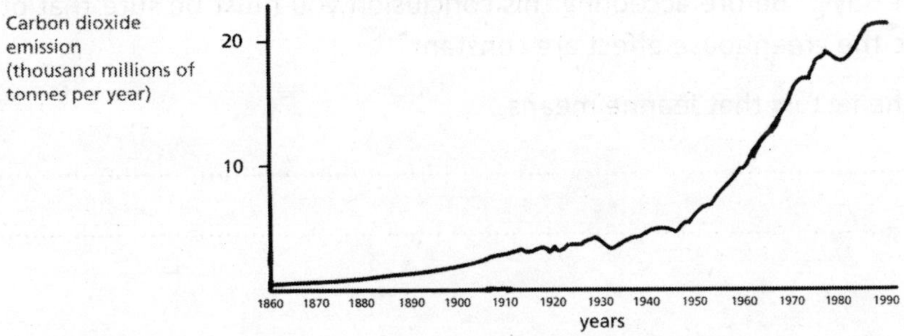

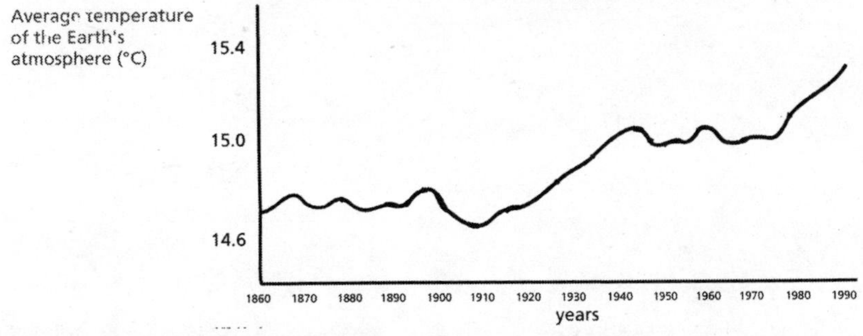

Source: CSTI Environmental Information Paper 1, 1992.

André concludes from these two graphs that it is certain that the increase in the average temperature of the Earth's atmosphere is due to the increase in the carbon dioxide emission.

QUESTION 5.1

What is it about the graphs that supports André's conclusion?

....

....

QUESTION 5.2

Another student, Jeanne, disagrees with André's conclusion. She compares the two graphs and says that some parts of the graphs do not support his conclusion.

Give an example of a part of the graphs that does not support André's conclusion. Explain your answer.

....

....

....

QUESTION 5.3

André persists in his conclusion that the average temperature rise of the Earth's atmosphere is caused by the increase in the carbon dioxide emission. But Jeanne thinks that his conclusion is premature. She says: "Before accepting this conclusion you must be sure that other factors that could influence the greenhouse effect are constant".

Name one of the factors that Jeanne means.

....

....

SCIENCE UNIT 6 : CLOTHES

Read the text and answer the questions that follow.

CLOTHES TEXT

A team of British scientists is developing "intelligent" clothes that will give disabled children the power of "speech". Children wearing waistcoats made of a unique electrotextile, linked to a speech synthesiser, will be able to make themselves understood simply by tapping on the touch-sensitive material.

The material is made up of normal cloth and an ingenious mesh of carbon impregnated fibres that can conduct electricity. When pressure is applied to the fabric, the pattern of signals that passes through the conducting fibres is altered and a computer chip can work out where the cloth has been touched. It then can trigger whatever electronic device is attached to it, which could be no bigger than two boxes of matches.

"The smart bit is in how we weave the fabric and how we send signals through it – and we can weave it into existing fabric designs so you cannot see it's in there," says one of the scientists.

Without being damaged, the material can be washed, wrapped around objects or scrunched up. The scientist also claims it can be mass-produced cheaply.

Source: Steve Farrer, `Interactive fabric promises a material gift of the garb', The Australian, 10 August 1998.

QUESTION 6.1

Can these claims made in the article be tested through scientific investigation in the laboratory?

Circle either "Yes" or "No" for each.

The material can be	Can the claim be tested through scientific investigation in the laboratory?
washed without being damaged.	Yes / No
wrapped around objects without being damaged.	Yes / No
scrunched up without being damaged.	Yes / No
mass-produced cheaply.	Yes / No

QUESTION 6.2

Which piece of laboratory equipment would be among the equipment you would need to check that the fabric is conducting electricity?

A. Voltmeter

B. Light box

C. Micrometer

D. Sound meter

SCIENCE UNIT 7 : THE GRAND CANYON

The Grand Canyon is located in a desert in the USA. It is a very large and deep canyon containing many layers of rock. Sometime in the past, movements in the Earth's crust lifted these layers up. The Grand Canyon is now 1.6 km deep in parts. The Colorado River runs through the bottom of the canyon.

See the picture below of the Grand Canyon taken from its south rim. Several different layers of rock can be seen in the walls of the canyon.

QUESTION 7.1

The temperature in the Grand Canyon ranges from below 0°C to over 40°C. Although it is a desert area, cracks in the rocks sometimes contain water. How do these temperature changes and the water in rock cracks help to speed up the breakdown of rocks?

A. Freezing water dissolves warm rocks.
B. Water cements rocks together.
C. Ice smoothes the surface of rocks.
D. Freezing water expands in the rock cracks.

QUESTION 7.2

There are many fossils of marine animals, such as clams, fish and corals, in the Limestone A layer of the Grand Canyon. What happened millions of years ago that explains why such fossils are found there?

A. In ancient times, people brought seafood to the area from the ocean.
B. Oceans were once much rougher and sea life washed inland on giant waves.
C. An ocean covered this area at that time and then receded later.
D. Some sea animals once lived on land before migrating to the sea.

QUESTION 7.3

About five million people visit the Grand Canyon national park every year. There is concern about the damage that is being caused to the park by so many visitors.

Can the following questions be answered by scientific investigation? Circle "Yes" or "No" for each question.

Can this question be answered by scientific investigation?	Yes or No?
How much erosion is caused by use of the walking tracks?	Yes / No
Is the park area as beautiful as it was 100 years ago?	Yes / No

QUESTION 7.4 (ATTITUDE)

How much do you agree with the following statements?
Tick only one box in each row.

	Strongly Agree	Agree	Disagree	Strongly Disagree
The systematic study of fossils is important.	☐ 1	☐ 2	☐ 3	☐ 4
Action to protect National Parks from damage should be based on scientific evidence.	☐ 1	☐ 2	☐ 3	☐ 4
Scientific investigation of geological layers is important.	☐ 1	☐ 2	☐ 3	☐ 4

SCIENCE UNIT 8 : SUNSCREENS

Mimi and Dean wondered which sunscreen product provides the best protection for their skin. Sunscreen products have a Sun Protection Factor (SPF) that shows how well each product absorbs the ultraviolet radiation component of sunlight. A high SPF sunscreen protects skin for longer than a low SPF sunscreen.

Mimi thought of a way to compare some different sunscreen products. She and Dean collected the following:

- two sheets of clear plastic that do not absorb sunlight;
- one sheet of light-sensitive paper;
- mineral oil (M) and a cream containing zinc oxide (ZnO); and
- four different sunscreens that they called S1, S2, S3, and S4.

Mimi and Dean included mineral oil because it lets most of the sunlight through, and zinc oxide because it almost completely blocks sunlight.

Dean placed a drop of each substance inside a circle marked on one sheet of plastic, then put the second plastic sheet over the top. He placed a large book on top of both sheets and pressed down.

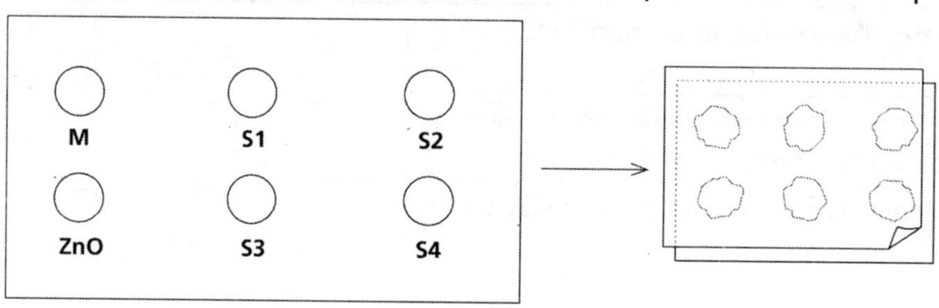

Mimi then put the plastic sheets on top of the sheet of light-sensitive paper. Light-sensitive paper changes from dark grey to white (or very light grey), depending on how long it is exposed to sunlight. Finally, Dean placed the sheets in a sunny place.

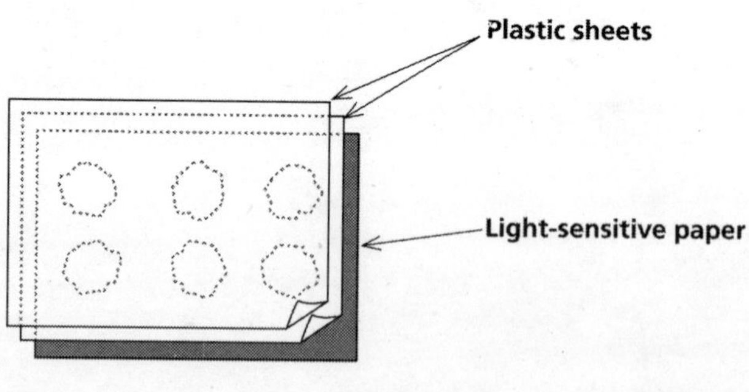

QUESTION 8.1

Which one of these statements is a scientific description of the role of the mineral oil and the zinc oxide in comparing the effectiveness of the sunscreens?

A. Mineral oil and zinc oxide are both factors being tested.
B. Mineral oil is a factor being tested and zinc oxide is a reference substance.
C. Mineral oil is a reference substance and zinc oxide is a factor being tested.
D. Mineral oil and zinc oxide are both reference substances.

QUESTION 8.2

Which one of these questions were Mimi and Dean trying to answer?

A. How does the protection for each sunscreen compare with the others?
B. How do sunscreens protect your skin from ultraviolet radiation?
C. Is there any sunscreen that gives less protection than mineral oil?
D. Is there any sunscreen that gives more protection than zinc oxide?

QUESTION 8.3

Why was the second sheet of plastic pressed down?

A. To stop the drops from drying out.
B. To spread the drops out as far as possible.
C. To keep the drops inside the marked circles.
D. To make the drops the same thickness.

QUESTION 8.4

The light-sensitive paper is a dark grey and fades to a lighter grey when it is exposed to some sunlight, and to white when exposed to a lot of sunlight.

Which one of these diagrams shows a pattern that might occur? Explain why you chose it.

Answer: ....

Explanation: ....

....

....

....

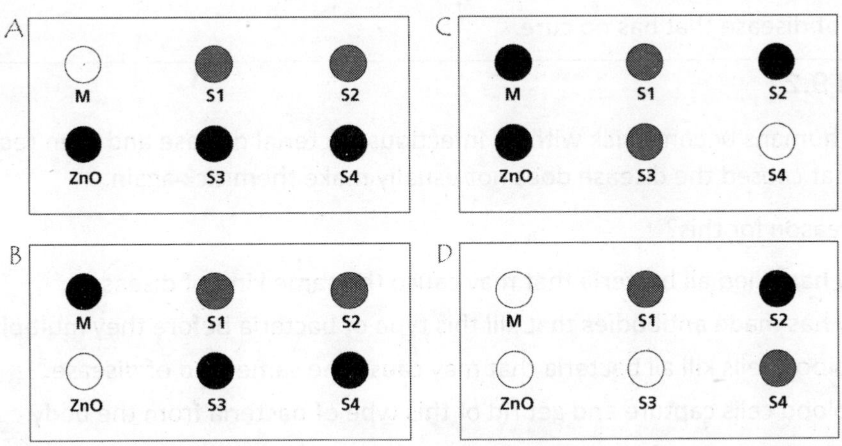

SCIENCE UNIT 9 : MARY MONTAGU

Read the following newspaper article and answer the questions that follow.

The History of Vaccination Mary Montagu was a beautiful woman. She survived an attack of smallpox in 1715 but she was left covered with scars. While living in Turkey in 1717, she observed a method called inoculation that was commonly used there. This treatment involved scratching a weak type of smallpox virus into the skin of healthy young people who then became sick, but in most cases only with a mild form of the disease. Mary Montagu was so convinced of the safety of these inoculations that she allowed her son and daughter to be inoculated.

In 1796, Edward Jenner used inoculations of a related disease, cowpox, to produce antibodies against smallpox. Compared with the inoculation of smallpox, this treatment had less side effects and the treated person could not infect others. The treatment became known as vaccination.

QUESTION 9.1

What kinds of diseases can people be vaccinated against?

A. Inherited diseases like haemophilia.

B. Diseases that are caused by viruses, like polio.

C. Diseases from the malfunctioning of the body, like diabetes.

D. Any sort of disease that has no cure.

QUESTION 9.2

If animals or humans become sick with an infectious bacterial disease and then recover, the type of bacteria that caused the disease does not usually make them sick again.

What is the reason for this?

A. The body has killed all bacteria that may cause the same kind of disease.

B. The body has made antibodies that kill this type of bacteria before they multiply.

C. The red blood cells kill all bacteria that may cause the same kind of disease.

D. The red blood cells capture and get rid of this type of bacteria from the body.

QUESTION 9.3

Give one reason why it is recommended that young children and old people, in particular, should be vaccinated against influenza (flu).

....

....

....

QUESTION 9.4 (ATTITUDE)

How much do you agree with the following statements?

Tick only one box in each row.

	Strongly Agree	Agree	Disagree	Strongly Disagree
I am in favour of research to develop vaccines for new strains of influenza.	☐ 1	☐ 2	☐ 3	☐ 4
The cause of a disease can only be identified by scientific research.	☐ 1	☐ 2	☐ 3	☐ 4
The effectiveness of unconventional treatments for diseases should be subject to scientific investigation.	☐ 1	☐ 2	☐ 3	☐ 4

SCIENCE UNIT 10 : ACID RAIN

Below is a photo of statues called Caryatids that were built on the Acropolis in Athens more than 2500 years ago. The statues are made of a type of rock called marble. Marble is composed of calcium carbonate.

In 1980, the original statues were transferred inside the museum of the Acropolis and were replaced by replicas. The original statues were being eaten away by acid rain.

QUESTION 10.1

Normal rain is slightly acidic because it has absorbed some carbon dioxide from the air. Acid rain is more acidic than normal rain because it has absorbed gases like sulfur oxides and nitrogen oxides as well.

Where do these sulfur oxides and nitrogen oxides in the air come from?

....

....

The effect of acid rain on marble can be modelled by placing chips of marble in vinegar overnight. Vinegar and acid rain have about the same acidity level. When a marble chip is placed in vinegar, bubbles of gas form. The mass of the dry marble chip can be found before and after the experiment.

QUESTION 10.2

A marble chip has a mass of 2.0 grams before being immersed in vinegar overnight. The chip is removed and dried the next day. What will the mass of the dried marble chip be?

A. Less than 2.0 grams

B. Exactly 2.0 grams

C. Between 2.0 and 2.4 grams

D. More than 2.4 grams

QUESTION 10.3

Students who did this experiment also placed marble chips in pure (distilled) water overnight.

Explain why the students included this step in their experiment.

....

....

QUESTION 10.4 (ATTITUDE)

How much do you agree with the following statements?

Tick only one box in each row.

	Strongly Agree	Agree	Disagree	Strongly Disagree
Knowing which human activities contribute most to acid rain	☐ 1	☐ 2	☐ 3	☐ 4
Learning about technologies that minimise the emission of gases that cause acid rain	☐ 1	☐ 2	☐ 3	☐ 4
Understanding the methods used to repair buildings damaged by acid rain	☐ 1	☐ 2	☐ 3	☐ 4

QUESTION 10.5 (ATTITUDE)

How much do you agree with the following statements?

Tick only one box in each row.

	Strongly Agree	Agree	Disagree	Strongly Disagree
Preservation of ancient ruins should be based on scientific evidence concerning the causes of damage.	☐ 1	☐ 2	☐ 3	☐ 4
Statements about the causes of acid rain should be based on scientific research.	☐ 1	☐ 2	☐ 3	☐ 4

SCIENCE UNIT 11 : PHYSICAL EXERCISE

Regular but moderate physical exercise is good for our health.

QUESTION 11.1

What are the advantages of regular physical exercise? Circle "Yes" or "No" for each statement.

Is this an advantage of regular physical exercise?	Yes or No?
Physical exercise helps prevent heart and circulation illnesses.	Yes / No
Physical exercise leads to a healthy diet.	Yes / No
Physical exercise helps to avoid becoming overweight.	Yes / No

QUESTION 11.2

What happens when muscles are exercised? Circle "Yes" or "No" for each statement.

Does this happen when muscles are exercised?	Yes or No?
Muscles get an increased flow of blood.	Yes / No
Fats are formed in the muscles.	Yes / No

QUESTION 11.3

Why do you have to breathe more heavily when you're doing physical exercise than when your body is resting?

....

....

....

SCIENCE UNIT 12 : GENETICALLY MODIFIED CROPS

> **GM Corn Should Be Banned**
>
> Wildlife conservation groups are demanding that a new genetically modified (GM) corn be banned. This GM corn is designed to be unaffected by a powerful new herbicide that kills conventional corn plants. This new herbicide will kill most of the weeds that grow in cornfields. The conservationists say that because these weeds are feed for small animals, especially insects, the use of the new herbicide with the GM corn will be bad for the environment. Supporters of the use of the GM corn say that a scientific study has shown that this will not happen.

Here are details of the scientific study mentioned in the above article:

- Corn was planted in 200 fields across the country.
- Each field was divided into two. The genetically modified (GM) corn treated with the powerful new herbicide was grown in one half, and the conventional corn treated with a conventional herbicide was grown in the other half.
- The number of insects found in the GM corn, treated with the new herbicide, was about the same as the number of insects in the conventional corn, treated with the conventional herbicide.

QUESTION 12.1

What factors were deliberately varied in the scientific study mentioned in the article? Circle "Yes" or "No" for each of the following factors.

Was this factor deliberately varied in the study?	Yes or No?
The number of insects in the environment	Yes / No
The types of herbicide used	Yes / No

QUESTION 12.2

Corn was planted in 200 fields across the country. Why did the scientists use more than one site?

A. So that many farmers could try the new GM corn.

B. To see how much GM corn they could grow.

C. To cover as much land as possible with the GM crop.

D. To include various growth conditions for corn.

QUESTION 12.3 (ATTITUDE)

How much do you agree with the following statements?

Tick only one box in each row.

	Strongly Agree	Agree	Disagree	Strongly Disagree
Learning about the process by which plants are genetically modified	☐ 1	☐ 2	☐ 3	☐ 4
Learning why some plants are not affected by herbicides	☐ 1	☐ 2	☐ 3	☐ 4
Understanding better the difference between crossbreeding and genetic modification of plants	☐ 1	☐ 2	☐ 3	☐ 4

SCIENCE UNIT 13: BIODIVERSITY

Read the following newspaper article and answer the questions which follow.

BIODIVERSITY IS THE KEY TO MANAGING ENVIRONMENT

An ecosystem that retains a high biodiversity (that is, a wide variety of living things) is much more likely to adapt to human-caused environment change than is one that has little.

Consider the two food webs shown in the diagram. The arrows point from the organism that gets eaten to the one that eats it. These food webs are highly simplified compared with food webs in real ecosystems, but they still illustrate a key difference between more diverse and less diverse ecosystems. Food web B represents a situation with very low biodiversity, where at some levels the food path involves only a single type of organism.

Food web A represents a more diverse ecosystem with, as a result, many more alternative feeding pathways.

Generally, loss of biodiversity should be regarded seriously, not only because the organisms that have become extinct represent a big loss for both ethical and utilitarian (useful benefit) reasons, but also because the organisms that remain have become more vulnerable (exposed) to extinction in the future.

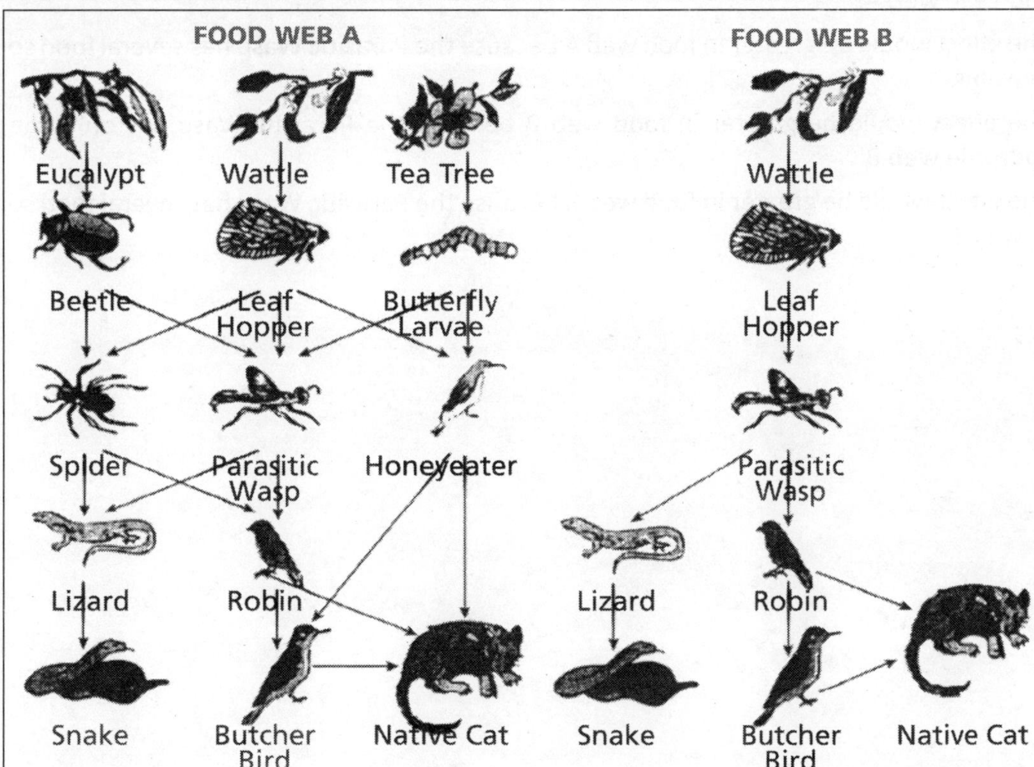

Source: Adapted from Steve Malcolm: 'Biodiversity is the key to managing environment', The Age, 16 August 1994.

QUESTION 13.1

In lines 9 and 10 it is stated that "Food web A represents a more diverse ecosystem with, as a result, many more alternative feeding pathways."

Look at FOOD WEB A. Only two animals in this food web have three direct (immediate) food sources. Which two animals are they?

A. Native Cat A. t and Parasitic Wasp
B. Native Cat and Butcher Bird
C. Parasitic Wasp and Leaf Hopper
D. Parasitic Wasp and Spider
E. Native Cat and Honeyeater

QUESTION 13.2

Food webs A and B are in different locations. Imagine if Leaf Hoppers died out in both locations. Which one of these is the best prediction and explanation for the effect this would have on the food webs?

A. The effect would be greater in food web A because the Parasitic Wasp has only one food source in web A.
B. The effect would be greater in food web A because the Parasitic Wasp has several food sources in web A.
C. The effect would be greater in food web B because the Parasitic Wasp has only one food source in web B.
D. The effect would be greater in food web B because the Parasitic Wasp has several food sources in web B.

SCIENCE UNIT 14 : BUSES

QUESTION 14.1

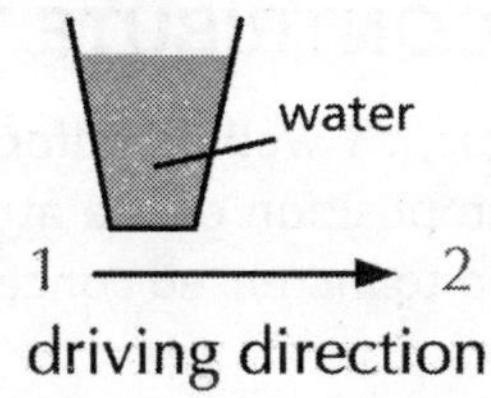

A bus is driving along a straight stretch of road. The bus driver, named Ray, has a cup of water resting on the dashboard:

Suddenly Ray has to slam on the brakes.

What is most likely to happen to the water in the cup?

A. The water will stay horizontal.

B. The water will spill over side 1.

C. The water will spill over side 2.

D. The water will spill but you cannot tell if it will spill at side 1 or side 2.

QUESTION 14.2

Ray's bus is, like most buses, powered by a petrol engine. These buses contribute to environmental pollution.

Some cities have trolley buses: they are powered by an electric engine. The voltage needed for such an electric engine is provided by overhead lines (like electric trains).

The electricity is supplied by a power station using fossil fuels. Supporters for the use of trolley buses in a city say that these buses don't contribute to environmental pollution.

Are these supporters right? Explain your answer ....

....

....

....

....

SCIENCE UNIT 15 : CLIMATE CHANGE

Read the following information and answer the questions which follow.

WHAT HUMAN ACTIVITIES CONTRIBUTE TO CLIMATE CHANGE?

The burning of coal, oil and natural gas, as well as deforestation and various agricultural and industrial practices, are altering the composition of the atmosphere and contributing to climate change. These human activities have led to increased concentrations of particles and greenhouse gases in the atmosphere.

The relative importance of the main contributors to temperature change is shown in Figure 1.

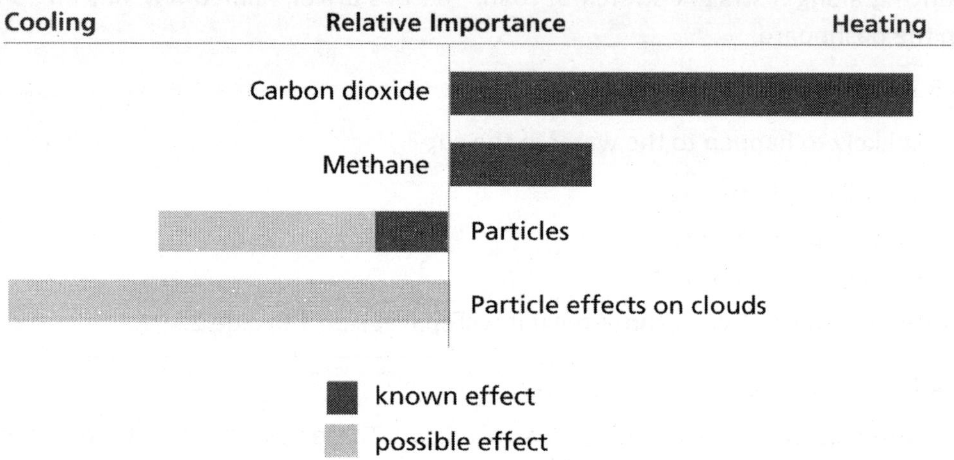

Figure 1: Relative importance of the main contributors to changes in the temperature of the atmosphere.

Figure 1 shows that increased concentrations of carbon dioxide and methane have a heating effect. Increased concentrations of particles have a cooling effect in two ways, labelled 'Particles' and 'Particle effects on clouds'.

Bars extending to the right of the centre line indicate a heating effect. Bars extending to the left of the centre line indicate a cooling effect. The relative effect of 'Particles' and 'Particle effects on clouds' are quite uncertain: in each case the possible effect is somewhere in the range shown by the light grey bar.

Source: US Global Change Research Information Office. Adapted from http://www.gcrio.org/ipcc/qa/04.html

---

QUESTION 15.1

Use the information in Figure 1 to develop an argument in support of reducing the emission of carbon dioxide from the human activities mentioned.

....

....

....

....

SCIENCE UNIT 16 : FLIES

Read the following information and answer the questions which follow.

FLIES

A farmer was working with dairy cattle at an agricultural experiment station. The population of flies in the barn where the cattle lived was so large that the animals' health was affected. So the farmer sprayed the barn and the cattle with a solution of insecticide A. The insecticide killed nearly all the flies. Some time later, however, the number of flies was again large. The farmer again sprayed with the insecticide. The result was similar to that of the first spraying. Most, but not all, of the flies were killed. Again, within a short time the population of flies increased, and they were again sprayed with the insecticide. This sequence of events was repeated five times: then it became apparent that insecticide A was becoming less and less effective in killing the flies. The farmer noted that one large batch of the insecticide solution had been made and used in all the sprayings. Therefore he suggested the possibility that the insecticide solution decomposed with age.

Source: Teaching About Evolution and the Nature of Science, National Academy Press, Washington, DC, 1998, p. 75.

QUESTION 16.1

The farmer's suggestion is that the insecticide decomposed with age. Briefly explain how this suggestion could be tested.

....

....

....

QUESTION 16.2

The farmer's suggestion is that the insecticide decomposed with age. Give two alternative explanations as to why "insecticide A was becoming less and less effective ..."

Explanation 1: ....

....

Explanation 2: ....

....

SCIENCE UNIT 17 : CALF CLONES

Read the following article about the birth of five calves.

> In February 1993 a research team of the National Institute for Agricultural Research in Bresson-Villiers (France) succeeded in producing five clones of calves. The production of the clones (animals with the same genetic material, even though born to five different cows), was a complicated process.
>
> First the researchers removed about thirty egg cells from a cow (let us say the cow's name was Blanche 1). The researchers removed the nucleus from each of the egg cells taken from Blanche 1. Then the researchers took an embryo from another cow (let us say Blanche 2). This embryo contained about thirty cells. The researchers separated the ball of cells from Blanche 2 into individual cells.
>
> 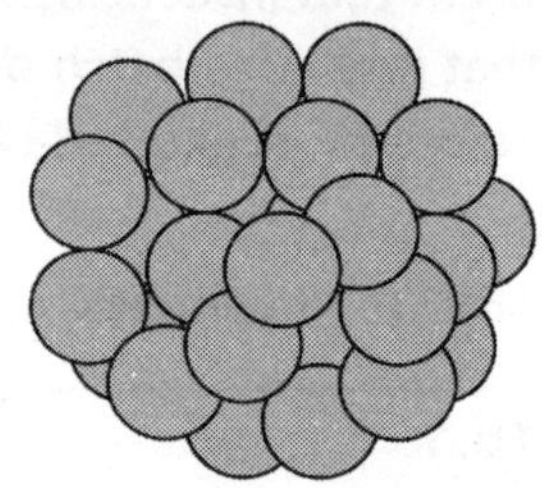
>
> Then they removed the nucleus from each of these individual cells. Each nucleus was injected separately into one of the thirty cells that came from Blanche 1 (cells from which the nuclei had been removed).
>
> Finally the thirty injected egg cells were implanted into thirty surrogate cows. Nine months later, five of the surrogate cows each gave birth to a calf clone. One of the researchers said that a large scale application of this cloning technique could be financially beneficial for cattle breeders.
>
> *Source:* Corinne Bensimon, LIBÉRATION, March 1993

QUESTION 17.1

The main idea tested in the French experiments on cows was confirmed by the results. Which main idea could have been tested in the French experiment?

....

....

QUESTION 17.2

Which of the following statements is/are true? Circle Yes or No for each.

Statement:	Yes or No
All five calves have the same type of genes.	Yes / No
All five calves have the same sex.	Yes / No
The hair of all five calves has the same colour.	Yes / No

SCIENCE UNIT 18 : CORN

Consider the following newspaper report.

DUTCHMAN USES CORN AS FUEL

Auke Ferwerda's stove contains a few logs burning quietly with low flames. From a paper bag next to the stove he takes a handful of corn and puts it onto the flames. Immediately the fire flares up brightly. "Look here," Ferwerda says, "The window of the stove stays clean and transparent. Combustion is complete." Ferwerda talks about the fact that corn can be used as fuel as well as cattle food. As far as he is concerned, this is the future.

Ferwerda points out that corn, in the form of cattle food, is in fact a type of fuel too. Cows eat corn to get energy out of it. But, Ferwerda explains, the sale of corn for fuel instead of for cattle food might be much more profitable for farmers.

Ferwerda has become convinced that, in the long run, corn will be widely used as fuel. He imagines what it will be like harvesting, storing, drying and packing the grains in bags for sale.

Ferwerda is currently investigating whether the whole corn plant could be used as fuel, but this research has not been completed yet.

What Ferwerda also needs to consider is the amount of attention being focused on carbon dioxide. Carbon dioxide is regarded as the main cause of the increase of the Greenhouse effect. The increase of the Greenhouse effect is said to be the cause of the increasing average temperature of the Earth's atmosphere.

In Ferwerda's view, however, there is nothing wrong with carbon dioxide. On the contrary, he argues, plants absorb it and convert it into oxygen for human beings.

However, Ferwerda's plans may clash with those of the government, which is actually trying to reduce the emission of carbon dioxide. Ferwerda says, "There are many scientists who say that carbon dioxide is not the main cause of the Greenhouse effect."

QUESTION 18.1

Ferwerda compares corn used as fuel to corn used as food.

The first column of the table below contains a list of things that happen when corn burns.

Do these things also happen when corn works as a fuel in an animal body?

Circle Yes or No for each.

When corn burns:	Does this also happen when corn works as a fuel in an animal body?
Oxygen is consumed	Yes / No
Carbon dioxide is produced.	Yes / No
Energy is produced.	Yes / No

QUESTION 18.2

In the article a conversion of carbon dioxide is described: "...plants absorb it and convert it into oxygen ...".

There are more substances involved in this conversion than carbon dioxide and oxygen only. The conversion can be represented in the following way:

carbon dioxide + water → oxygen + [ ]

Write in the box the name of the missing substance.

QUESTION 18.3

At the end of the article Ferwerda refers to scientists who say that carbon dioxide is not the main cause of the Greenhouse effect.

Karin finds the following table showing the relative Greenhouse effect caused by four gases:

Relative Greenhouse effect per molecule of gas			
Carbon dioxide	Methane	Nitrous oxide	Chlorofluorocarbons
1	30	160	17000

From this table Karin cannot conclude which gas is the main cause of the increase of the Greenhouse effect. The data in the table need to be combined with other data for Karin to conclude which gas is the main cause of the increase of the Greenhouse effect.

Which other data does Karin need to collect?

Data about the origin of the four gases.

A. Data about the absorption of the four gases by plants.

B. Data about the size of each of the four types of molecules.

C. Data about the amounts of each of the four gases in the atmosphere.

SCIENCE UNIT 19 : FIT FOR DRINKING

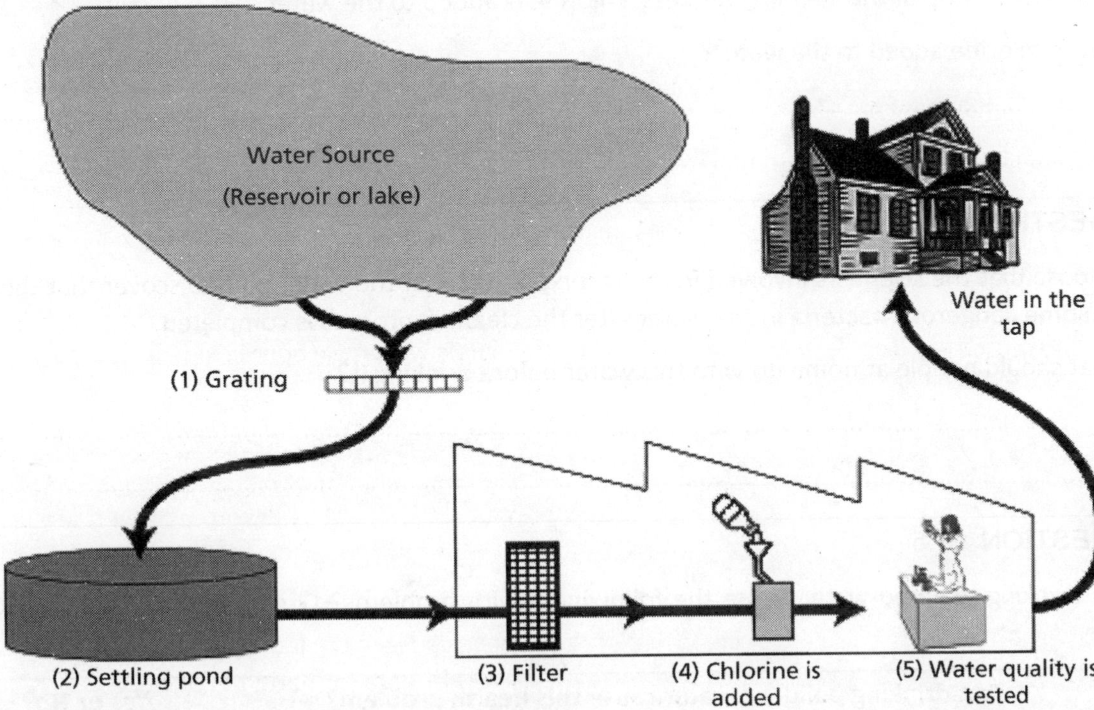

The figure above shows how water supplied to houses in cities is made fit for drinking.

QUESTION 19.1

It is important to have a source of good drinking water. Water found underground is referred to as *ground water*.

Give one reason why there is less bacteria and particle pollution in ground water than in water from surface sources such as lakes and rivers.

....

QUESTION 19.2

The cleaning of water often happens in several steps, involving different techniques. The cleaning process shown in the figure involves four steps (numbered 1–4). In the second step, the water is collected in a settling pond.

In what way does this step make the water cleaner?

A. The bacteria in the water die.

B. Oxygen is added to the water.

C. Gravel and sand sink to the bottom.

D. Toxic substances are broken down.

QUESTION 19.3

In the fourth step of the cleaning process, chlorine is added to the water.

Why is chlorine added to the water?

....

....

QUESTION 19.4

Suppose that the scientists involved in the testing of water at the water plant discover that there are some dangerous bacteria in the water after the cleaning process is completed.

What should people at home do with this water before drinking it?

....

....

QUESTION 19.5

Can drinking polluted water cause the following health problems? Circle "Yes" or "No" in each case.

Can drinking polluted water cause this health problem?	Yes or No?
Diabetes	Yes / No
Diarrhoea	Yes / No
HIV / AIDS	Yes / No

QUESTION 19.6 (ATTITUDE)

How much do you agree with the following statements?

Tick only one box in each row.

	Strongly Agree	Agree	Disagree	Strongly Disagree
Knowing how water is tested for bacterial contamination	☐ 1	☐ 2	☐ 3	☐ 4
Learning more about the chemical treatment of water supplies	☐ 1	☐ 2	☐ 3	☐ 4
Learning which diseases are transmitted in drinking water	☐ 1	☐ 2	☐ 3	☐ 4

SCIENCE UNIT 20 : TOOTH DECAY

Bacteria that live in our mouths cause dental caries (tooth decay). Caries have been a problem since the 1700s when sugar became available from the expanding sugar cane industry.

Today, we know a lot about caries. For example:

- Bacteria that cause caries feed on sugar.
- The sugar is transformed to acid.
- Acid damages the surface of teeth.
- Brushing teeth helps to prevent caries.

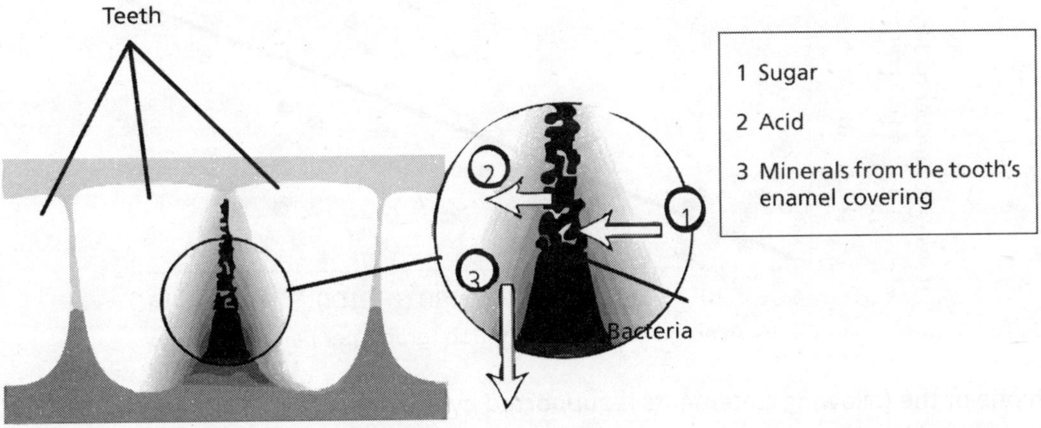

QUESTION 20.1

What is the role of bacteria in dental caries?

E. Bacteria produce enamel.
F. Bacteria produce sugar.
G. Bacteria produce minerals.
H. Bacteria produce acid.

QUESTION 20.2

The following graph shows the consumption of sugar and the amount of caries in different countries.

Each country is represented by a dot in the graph.

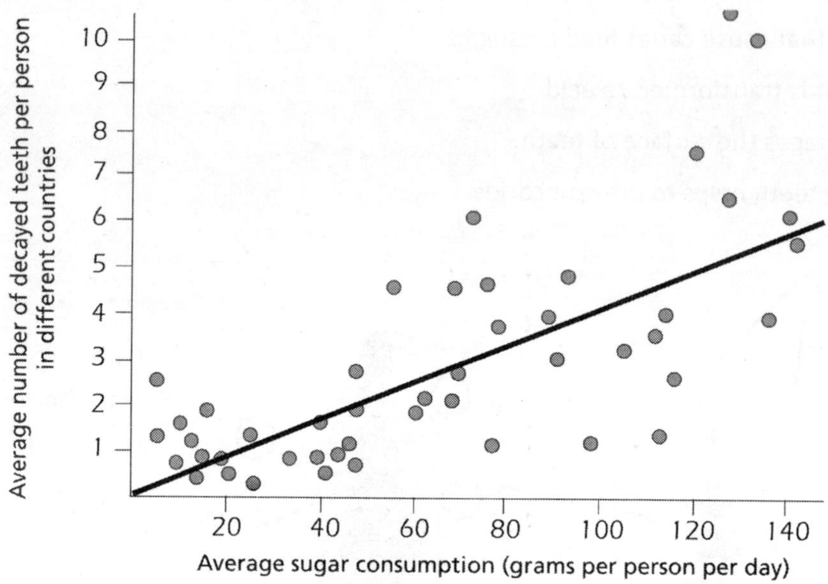

Which one of the following statements is supported by the data given in the graph?

A. In some countries, people brush their teeth more frequently than in other countries.

B. The more sugar people eat, the more likely they are to get caries.

C. In recent years, the rate of caries has increased in many countries.

D. In recent years, the consumption of sugar has increased in many countries.

QUESTION 20.3

A country has a high number of decayed teeth per person.

Can the following questions about tooth decay in that country be answered by scientific experiments?

Circle "Yes" or "No" for each question.

Can this question about tooth decay be answered by scientific experiments?	Yes or No?
What would be the effect on tooth decay of putting fluoride in the water supply?	Yes / No
How much should a visit to the dentist cost?	Yes / No

QUESTION 20.4 (ATTITUDE)

How much do you agree with the following statements?

Tick only one box in each row.

	Strongly Agree	Agree	Disagree	Strongly Disagree
Knowing what tooth decay bacteria look like under a microscope	☐ 1	☐ 2	☐ 3	☐ 4
Learning about the development of a vaccine to prevent tooth decay	☐ 1	☐ 2	☐ 3	☐ 4
Understanding how sugar-free foods can cause tooth decay	☐ 1	☐ 2	☐ 3	☐ 4

SCIENCE UNIT 21 : HOT WORK

QUESTION 21.1

Peter is working on repairs to an old house. He has left a bottle of water, some metal nails, and a piece of timber inside the boot of his car. After the car has been out in the sun for three hours, the temperature inside the car reaches about 40°C.

What happens to the objects in the car? Circle "Yes" or "No" for each statement.

Does this happen to the object(s)?	Yes or No?
They all have the same temperature.	Yes / No
After some time the water begins to boil.	Yes / No
After some time the metal nails begin to glow red.	Yes / No

QUESTION 21.2

For drinks during the day, Peter has a cup of hot coffee, at a temperature of about 90°C, and a cup of cold mineral water, with a temperature of about 5°C. The cups are of identical type and size and the volume of each drink is the same. Peter leaves the cups sitting in a room where the temperature is about 20°C.

What are the temperatures of the coffee and the mineral water likely to be after 10 minutes?

A. 70°C and 10°C

B. 90°C and 5°C

C. 70°C and 25°C

D. 20°C and 20°C

QUESTION 21.3 (ATTITUDE)

How much do you agree with the following statements?

Tick only one box in each row.

	Strongly Agree	Agree	Disagree	Strongly Disagree
Understanding how the shape of the cup influences the rate at which coffee cools	☐ 1	☐ 2	☐ 3	☐ 4
Learning about the different arrangements of atoms in wood, water and steel	☐ 1	☐ 2	☐ 3	☐ 4
Knowing why different solids conduct heat at different rates	☐ 1	☐ 2	☐ 3	☐ 4

SCIENCE UNIT 22 : MOUSEPOX

There are many types of pox viruses that cause pox diseases in animals. Each type of virus usually infects only one animal species. A magazine has reported that a scientist has used genetic engineering to modify the DNA of mousepox. The altered virus kills all the mice it infects.

The scientist says research on modifying viruses is necessary in order to control pests that damage human food. Critics of the research say viruses could escape from laboratories and infect other animals. They are also worried that a modified pox virus for one species could infect other species, especially humans.

Humans are infected with a pox virus called smallpox. Smallpox kills most people it infects. While it is thought that this disease has been eliminated from the general population, smallpox virus samples are kept in laboratories around the world.

QUESTION 22.1

Critics have expressed concern that the mousepox virus could infect species other than mice. Which one of the following reasons is the best explanation for this concern?

A. The genes of smallpox virus and the genes of modified mousepox virus are identical.

B. A mutation in mousepox DNA might allow the virus to infect other animals.

C. A mutation could make the mousepox DNA identical to smallpox DNA.

D. The number of genes in mousepox virus is the same as in other pox viruses.

QUESTION 22.2

A person who criticised the research was worried that the modified mousepox virus might escape from a laboratory. This virus could cause the extinction of some species of mice.

Are the following outcomes likely if some species of mice become extinct? Circle "Yes" or "No" in each case.

Is this outcome likely if some species of mice become extinct?	Yes or No?
Some food chains could be affected.	Yes / No
Domestic cats could die for lack of food.	Yes / No
Plants whose seeds are eaten by mice could temporarily increase in number.	Yes / No

QUESTION 22.3

One company is trying to develop a virus that will make mice sterile (i.e., unable to have babies). Such a virus could help control the number of mice.

Suppose the company is successful. Should the following questions be answered by research before releasing the virus? Circle "Yes" or "No" in each case.

Should this question be answered before releasing the virus?	Yes or No?
What is the best method for spreading the virus?	Yes / No
How soon will mice develop immunity to the virus?	Yes / No
Will the virus affect other animal species?	Yes / No

QUESTION 22.4 (ATTITUDE)

How much do you agree with the following statements?

Tick only one box in each row.

	Strongly Agree	Agree	Disagree	Strongly Disagree
Learning about the structure of viruses	☐ 1	☐ 2	☐ 3	☐ 4
Knowing how viruses mutate (change)	☐ 1	☐ 2	☐ 3	☐ 4
Understanding better how the body defends itself against viruses	☐ 1	☐ 2	☐ 3	☐ 4

SCIENCE UNIT 23: STICKLEBACK BEHAVIOUR

The stickleback is a fish that is easy to keep in an aquarium.

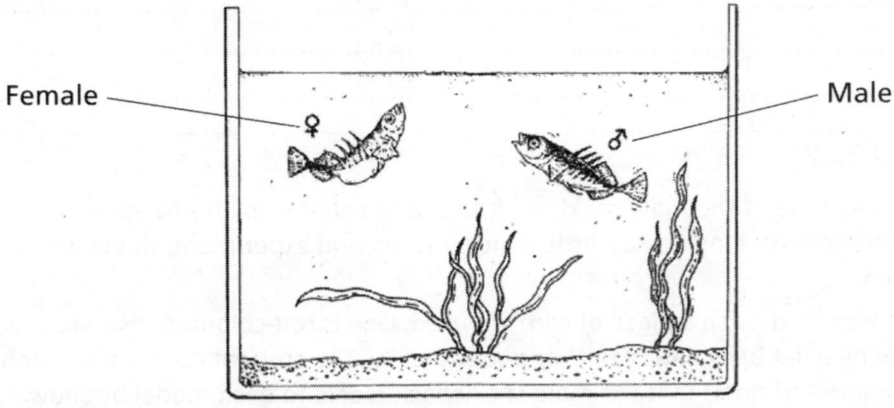

During the breeding season the male stickleback's belly turns from silver-coloured to red.

The male stickleback will attack any competing male that comes into his territory, and try to chase it away.

If a silver-coloured female approaches, he will try to guide her to his nest so she will lay her eggs there.

In an experiment a student wants to investigate what will make the male stickleback show aggressive behaviour.

A male stickleback is alone in the student's aquarium. The student has made three wax models attached to pieces of wire. He hangs them separately in the aquarium for the same amount of time. Then the student counts the number of times the male stickleback reacts aggressively by pushing against the wax figure.

The results of this experiment are shown below.

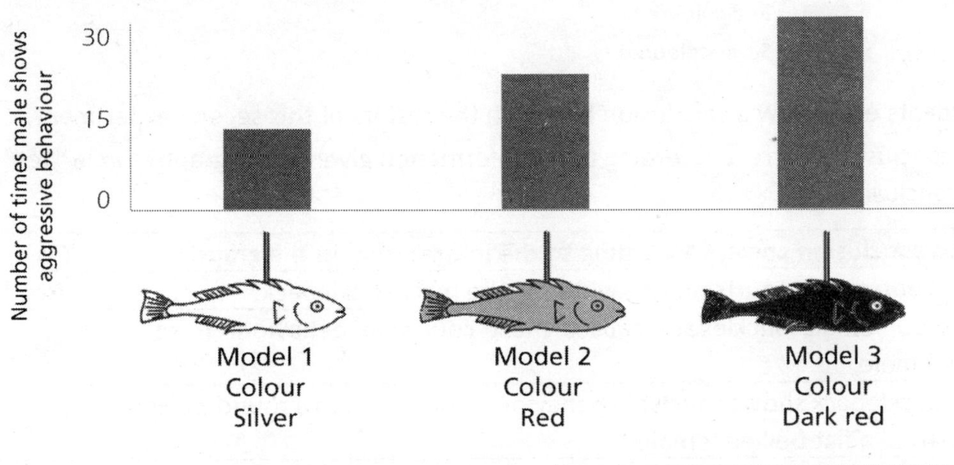

QUESTION 23.1

What is the question that this experiment is attempting to answer?

....

....

....

QUESTION 23.2

During breeding time, if the male stickleback sees a female he will try to attract the female with courtship behaviour that looks like a little dance. In a second experiment, this courtship behaviour is investigated.

Again, three wax models on a piece of wire are used. One is red-coloured; two are silver-coloured with one having a flat belly and the other a round belly. The student counts the number of times (in a given amount of time) that the male stickleback reacts to each model by showing courtship behaviour.

The results of this experiment are shown below.

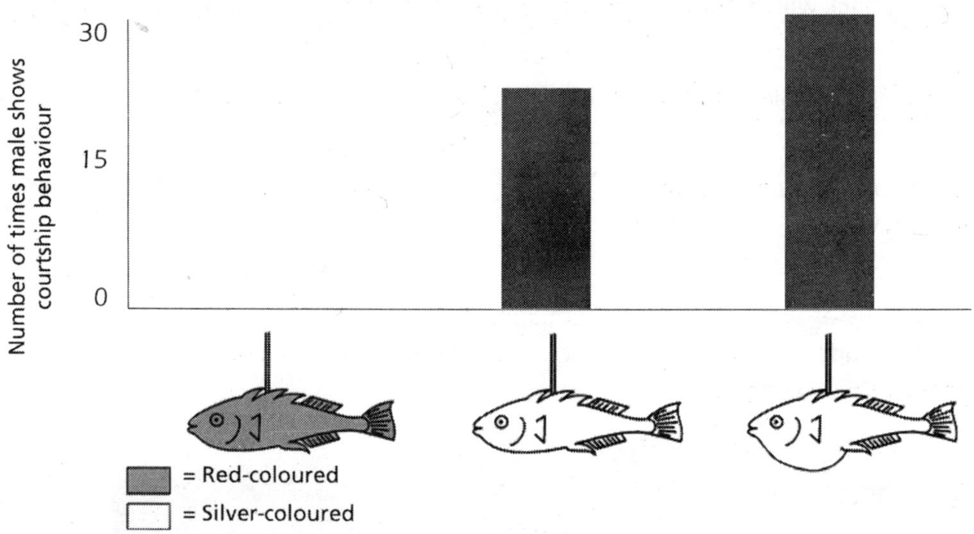

Three students each draw a conclusion based on the results of this second experiment.

Are their conclusions correct according to the information given in the graph? Circle "Yes" or "No" for each conclusion.

Is this conclusion correct according to the information in the graph?	Yes or No?
The red colour causes courtship behaviour by the male stickleback.	Yes / No
A flat-bellied female stickleback causes most courtship behaviour from a stickleback male.	Yes / No
The male stickleback shows courtship behaviour more often to a round-bellied female than to a flat-bellied female.	Yes / No

QUESTION 23.3

Experiments have shown that male sticklebacks react with aggressive behaviour to models with a red belly, and with courtship behaviour to models with a silver belly.

In a third experiment, the following four models were used in turn:

The three diagrams below show possible reactions of a male stickleback to each of the above models.

Which one of these reactions would you predict for each of the four models?

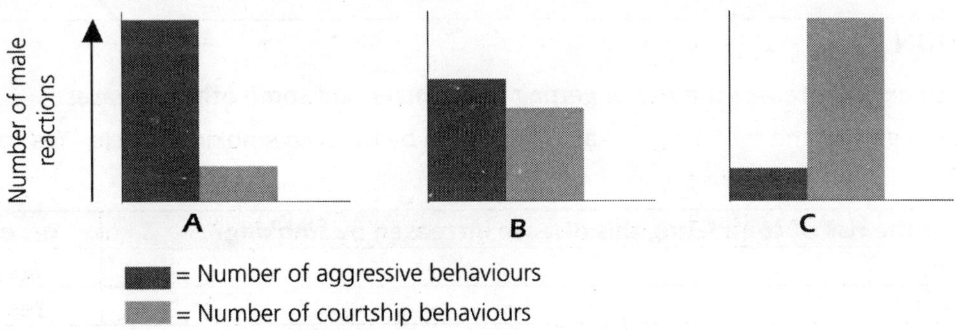

Fill in either A, B or C as the result for each model.

	Reaction
Model 1	
Model 2	
Model 3	
Model 4	

SCIENCE UNIT 24 : TOBACCO SMOKING

Tobacco is smoked in cigarettes, cigars and pipes. Research shows that tobacco-related diseases kill nearly 13 500 people worldwide every day. It is predicted that, by 2020, tobacco-related diseases will cause 12% of all deaths globally.

Tobacco smoke contains many harmful substances. The most damaging substances are tar, nicotine and carbon monoxide.

QUESTION 24.1

Tobacco smoke is inhaled into the lungs. Tar from the smoke is deposited in the lungs and this prevents the lungs from working properly.

Which one of the following is a function of the lungs?

A. To pump oxygenated blood to all parts of your body

B. To transfer some of the oxygen that you breathe to your blood

C. To purify your blood by reducing the carbon dioxide content to zero

D. To convert carbon dioxide molecules into oxygen molecules

QUESTION 24.2

Tobacco smoking increases the risk of getting lung cancer and some other diseases.

Is the risk of getting the following diseases increased by tobacco smoking? Circle "Yes" or "No" in each case.

Is the risk of contracting this disease increased by smoking?	Yes or No?
Bronchitis	Yes / No
HIV/AIDS	Yes / No
Chicken pox	Yes / No

QUESTION 24.3

Some people use nicotine patches to help them to give up smoking. The patches are put on skin and release nicotine into the blood. This helps to relieve cravings and withdrawal symptoms when people have stopped smoking.

To study the effectiveness of nicotine patches, a group of 100 smokers who want to give up smoking is chosen randomly. The group is to be studied for six months. The effectiveness of the nicotine patches is to be measured by finding out how many people in the group have not resumed smoking by the end of the study.

Which one of the following is the best experimental design?

A. All the people in the group wear the patches.

B. All wear patches except one person who tries to give up smoking without them.

C. People choose whether or not they will use patches to help give up smoking.

D. Half are randomly chosen to use patches and the other half do not use them.

QUESTION 24.4

Various methods are used to influence people to stop smoking.

Are the following ways of dealing with the problem based on technology? Circle "Yes" or "No" in each case.

Is this method of reducing smoking based on technology?	Yes or No?
Increase the cost of cigarettes.	Yes / No
Produce nicotine patches to help make people give up cigarettes.	Yes / No
Ban smoking in public areas.	Yes / No

QUESTION 24.5 (ATTITUDE)

How much do you agree with the following statements?

Tick only one box in each row.

	Strongly Agree	Agree	Disagree	Strongly Disagree
Knowing how tar in tobacco reduces lung efficiency	☐ 1	☐ 2	☐ 3	☐ 4
Understanding why nicotine is addictive	☐ 1	☐ 2	☐ 3	☐ 4
Learning how the body recovers after stopping smoking	☐ 1	☐ 2	☐ 3	☐ 4

SCIENCE UNIT 25 : STARLIGHT

Toshio likes to look at stars. However, he cannot observe stars very well at night because he lives in a large city.

Last year Toshio visited the countryside where he observed a large number of stars that he cannot see when he is in the city.

QUESTION 25.1

Why can many more stars be observed in the countryside than in large cities?

A. The moon is brighter in cities and blocks out the light from many stars.

B. There is more dust to reflect light in country air than in city air.

C. The brightness of city lights makes many stars hard to see.

D. The air is warmer in cities due to heat emitted by cars, machinery and houses.

QUESTION 25.2

Toshio uses a telescope with a large diameter lens in order to observe stars of low brightness.

Why does using a telescope with a large diameter lens make it possible to observe stars of low brightness?

A. The larger the lens the more light is collected.

B. The larger the lens the more it magnifies.

C. Larger lenses allow more of the sky to be seen.

D. Larger lenses can detect the dark colours in stars.

SCIENCE UNIT 26 : ULTRASOUND

In many countries, images can be taken of a foetus (developing baby) by ultrasound imaging (echography). Ultrasounds are considered safe for both the mother and the foetus.

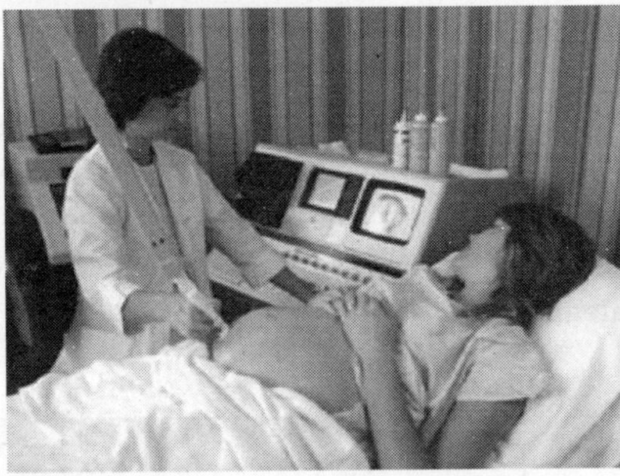

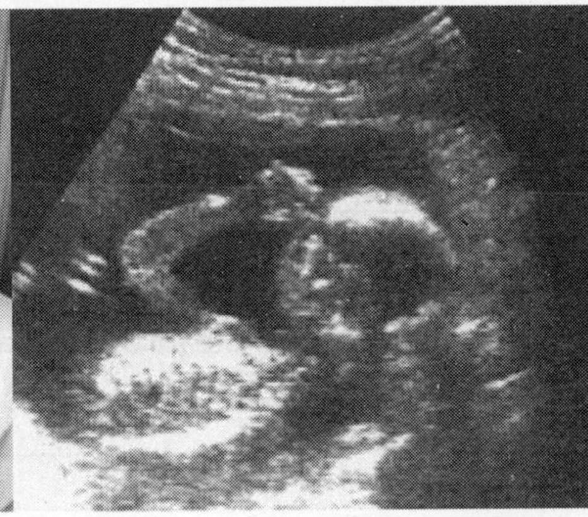

The doctor holds a probe and moves it across the mother's abdomen. Ultrasound waves are transmitted into the abdomen. Inside the abdomen they are reflected from the surface of the foetus. These reflected waves are picked up again by the probe and relayed to a machine that can produce an image.

QUESTION 26.1

To form an image the ultrasound machine needs to calculate the distance between the foetus and the probe.

The ultrasound waves move through the abdomen at a speed of 1540 m/s. What measurement must the machine make so that it can calculate the distance?

....

....

....

QUESTION 26.2

An image of a foetus can also be obtained using X-rays. However, women are advised to avoid having X-rays of their abdomens during pregnancy.

Why should a woman avoid having her abdomen X-rayed during pregnancy in particular?

....

....

....

QUESTION 26.3

Can ultrasound examinations of expectant mothers provide answers to the following questions? Circle "Yes" or "No" for each question.

Can an ultrasound examination answer this question?	Yes or No?
Is there more than one baby?	Yes / No
What colour are the baby's eyes?	Yes / No
Is the baby about the right size?	Yes / No

QUESTION 26.4 (ATTITUDE)

How much do you agree with the following statements?

Tick only one box in each row.

	Strongly Agree	Agree	Disagree	Strongly Disagree
Understanding how ultrasound can penetrate your body without harming it	☐ 1	☐ 2	☐ 3	☐ 4
Learning more about the differences between X-rays and ultrasound	☐ 1	☐ 2	☐ 3	☐ 4
Knowing about other medical uses of ultrasound	☐ 1	☐ 2	☐ 3	☐ 4

SCIENCE UNIT 27 : LIP GLOSS

The table below contains two different recipes for cosmetics you can make yourself.

The lipstick is harder than the lip gloss, which is soft and creamy.

Lip gloss	Lipstick
Ingredients:	**Ingredients:**
5 g castor oil 0.2 g beeswax 0.2 g palm wax 1 teaspoon of colouring substance 1 drop of food flavouring	5 g castor oil 1 g beeswax 1 g palm wax 1 teaspoon of colouring substance 1 drop of food flavouring
Instructions:	**Instructions:**
Heat the oil and the waxes in a container placed in hot water until you have an even mixture. Then add the colouring substance and the flavouring, and mix them in.	Heat the oil and the waxes in a container placed in hot water until you have an even mixture. Then add the colouring substance and the flavouring, and mix them in.

QUESTION 27.1

In making the lip gloss and lipstick, oil and waxes are mixed together. The colouring substance and flavouring are then added.

The lipstick made from this recipe is hard and not easy to use. How would you change the proportion of ingredients to make a softer lipstick?

....

....

....

QUESTION 27.2

Oils and waxes are substances that will mix well together. Oils cannot be mixed with water, and waxes are not soluble in water.

Which one of the following is most likely to happen if a lot of water is splashed into the lipstick mixture while it is being heated?

A. A creamier and softer mixture is produced.

B. The mixture becomes firmer.

C. The mixture is hardly changed at all.

D. Fatty lumps of the mixture float on the water.

QUESTION 27.3

When substances called emulsifiers are added, they allow oils and waxes to mix well with water.

Why does soap and water remove lipstick?

A. Water contains an emulsifier that allows the soap and lipstick to mix.

B. The soap acts as an emulsifier and allows the water and lipstick to mix.

C. Emulsifiers in the lipstick allow the soap and water to mix.

D. The soap and lipstick combine to form an emulsifier that mixes with the water.

SCIENCE UNIT 28 : EVOLUTION

Most horses today are streamlined and can run fast.

Scientists have found the fossil skeletons of animals that are similar to horses. They consider them to be the ancestors of the present-day horse. The scientists have also been able to determine the period during which the fossil species were living.

The table below provides information on three of these fossils and on the present-day horse.

ANIMAL NAME:	HYRACOTHERIUM	MESOHIPPUS	MERYCHIPPUS	EQUUS (present-day horse)
Period of existence:	55 to 50 million years ago	39 to 31 million years ago	19 to 11 million years ago	2 million years ago to the present day
Skeleton of the leg (same scale):	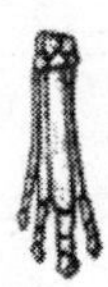	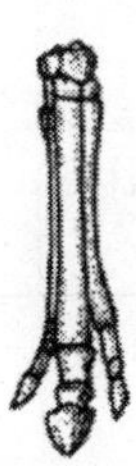		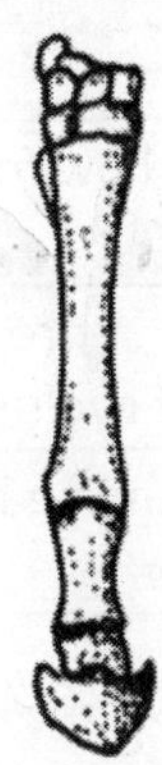

QUESTION 28.1

What information in the table is strong evidence that present-day horses may have evolved over time from the other three animals?

....

....

....

QUESTION 28.2

What further research can scientists undertake to find out how horses have evolved over time?

Circle "Yes" or "No" for each of these statements.

Would this research help find out how horses have evolved over time?	Yes or No?
Compare the number of horses living at different periods.	Yes / No
Search for skeletons belonging to ancestors of the horse that lived 50 to 40 million years ago.	Yes / No

QUESTION 28.3

Which one of the following statements best applies to the scientific theory of evolution?

A. The theory cannot be believed because it is not possible to see species changing.

B. The theory of evolution is possible for animals but cannot be applied to humans.

C. Evolution is a scientific theory that is currently based on extensive evidence.

D. Evolution is a theory that has been proven to be true by scientific experiments.

QUESTION 28.4 (ATTITUDE)

How much interest do you have in the following information?

Tick only one box in each row.

	High Interest	Medium Interest	Low Interest	No Interest
Knowing how fossils can be identified	☐ 1	☐ 2	☐ 3	☐ 4
Learning more about the development of the theory of evolution	☐ 1	☐ 2	☐ 3	☐ 4
Understanding better the evolution of the present-day horse	☐ 1	☐ 2	☐ 3	☐ 4

SCIENCE UNIT 29 : BREAD DOUGH

To make bread dough, a cook mixes flour, water, salt and yeast. After mixing, the dough is placed in a container for several hours to allow the process of fermentation to take place. During fermentation, a chemical change occurs in the dough: the yeast (a single-celled fungus) helps to transform the starch and sugars in the flour into carbon dioxide and alcohol.

QUESTION 29.1

Fermentation causes the dough to rise. Why does the dough rise?

A. The dough rises because alcohol is produced and turns into a gas.

B. The dough rises because of single-celled fungi reproducing in it.

C. The dough rises because a gas, carbon dioxide, is produced.

D. The dough rises because fermentation turns water into a vapour.

QUESTION 29.2

A few hours after mixing the dough, the cook weighs the dough and observes that its weight has decreased.

The weight of the dough is the same at the start of each of the four experiments shown below. Which two experiments should the cook compare to test if the yeast is the cause of the loss of weight?

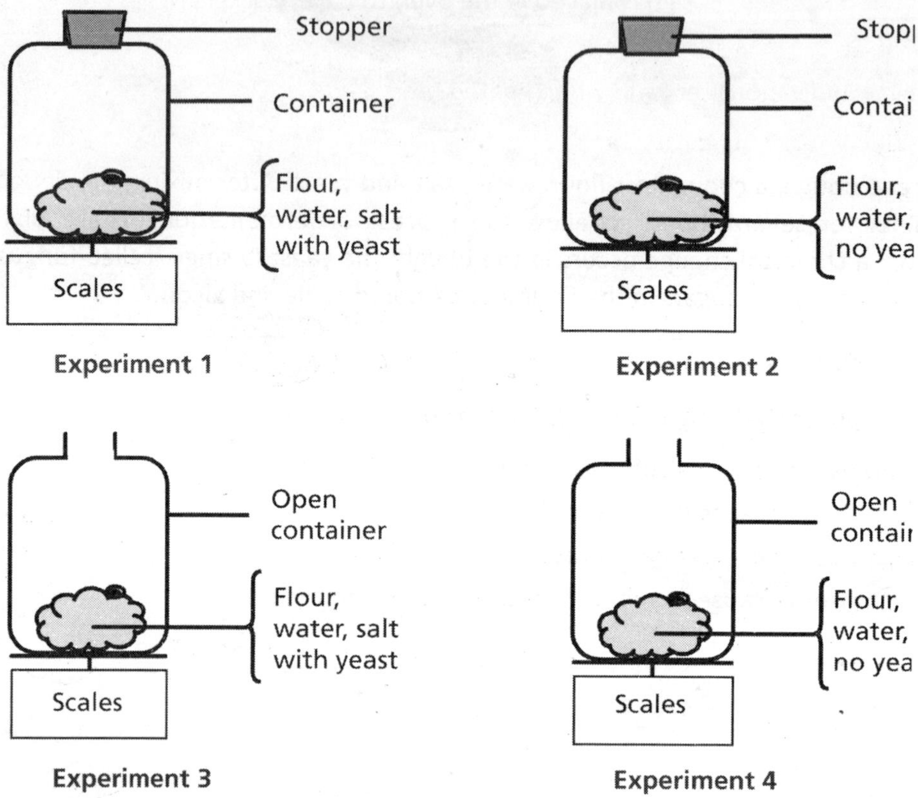

A. The cook should compare experiments 1 and 2.

B. The cook should compare experiments 1 and 3.

C. The cook should compare experiments 2 and 4.

D. The cook should compare experiments 3 and 4.

QUESTION 29.3

In the dough, yeast helps to transform starch and sugars in the flour. A chemical reaction occurs during which carbon dioxide and alcohol form.

Where do the carbon atoms that are present in carbon dioxide and alcohol come from? Circle “Yes” or “No” for each of the following possible explanations.

Is this a correct explanation of where the carbon atoms come from?	Yes or No?
Some carbon atoms come from the sugars.	Yes / No
Some carbon atoms are part of the salt molecules.	Yes / No
Some carbon atoms come from the water.	Yes / No

QUESTION 29.4

When the risen (leavened) dough is placed in the oven to bake, pockets of gas and vapours in the dough expand.

Why do the gas and vapours expand when heated?

A. Their molecules get bigger.

B. Their molecules move faster.

C. Their molecules increase in number.

D. Their molecules collide less frequently.

SCIENCE UNIT 30 : TRANSIT OF VENUS

On 8 June 2004, the planet Venus could be seen passing in front of the Sun when viewed from many places on Earth. This is called a "transit" of Venus and happens when its orbit takes Venus between the Sun and Earth. The previous transit of Venus occurred in 1882 and another is predicted to occur in 2012.

Below is a picture of the transit of Venus in 2004. A telescope was pointed at the Sun and the image projected onto a white card.

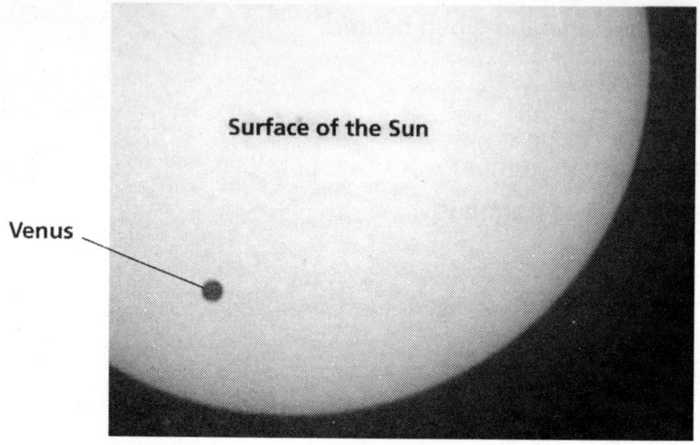

QUESTION 30.1

Why was the transit observed by projecting the image onto a white card, rather than by looking directly through the telescope?

A. The Sun's light was too bright for Venus to show up.

B. The Sun is big enough to see without magnification.

C. Viewing the Sun through a telescope may damage your eyes.

D. The image needed to be made smaller by projecting it onto a card.

QUESTION 30.2

When viewed from Earth, which one of the following planets can be seen in transit across the face of the Sun at certain times?

A. Mercury

B. Mars

C. Jupiter

D. Saturn

QUESTION 30.3

Several words have been underlined in the following statement.

<u>Astronomers predict</u> that, as seen from <u>Neptune</u>, there will be a <u>transit</u> of <u>Saturn</u> across the <u>Sun's</u> face later this <u>century</u>.

Which *three* of the underlined words would be most useful in an internet or library search to find out when this transit might occur?

....

....

....

SCIENCE UNIT 31 : HEALTH RISK?

Imagine that you live near a large chemical factory that produces fertilisers for use in agriculture. In recent years there have been several cases of people in the area suffering from long-term breathing problems. Many local people believe that these symptoms are caused by the emission of toxic fumes from the nearby chemical fertiliser factory.

A public meeting was held to discuss the potential dangers of the chemical factory to the health of local residents. Scientists made the following statements at the meeting.

Statement by scientists working for the chemical company
"We have made a study of the toxicity of soil in the local area. We have found no evidence of toxic chemicals in the samples we have taken."
Statement by scientists working for concerned citizens in the local community
"We have looked at the number of cases of long-term breathing problems in the local area and compared this with the number of cases in an area far away from the chemical factory. There are more incidents in the area close to the chemical factory."

QUESTION 31.1

The owner of the chemical factory used the statement of the scientists working for the company to argue that "the emission fumes from the factory are not a health risk to local residents".

Give one reason, other than the statement by scientists working for the concerned citizens, for doubting that the statement by scientists working for the company supports the owner's argument.

....

....

QUESTION 31.2

The scientists working for the concerned citizens compared the number of people with long-term breathing problems close to the chemical factory with those in an area far away from the factory.

Describe one possible difference in the two areas that would make you think that the comparison was not a valid one.

....

....

QUESTION 31.3 (ATTITUDE)

How much do you agree with the following statements?

Tick only one box in each row.

	Strongly Agree	Agree	Disagree	Strongly Disagree
Knowing more about the chemical composition of agricultural fertilisers	☐ 1	☐ 2	☐ 3	☐ 4
Understanding what happens to toxic fumes emitted into the atmosphere	☐ 1	☐ 2	☐ 3	☐ 4
Learning about respiratory diseases that can be caused by chemical emissions	☐ 1	☐ 2	☐ 3	☐ 4

SCIENCE UNIT 32 : CATALYTIC CONVERTER

Most modern cars are fitted with a catalytic converter that makes the exhaust fumes of the car less harmful to people and to the environment.

About 90% of harmful gases are converted into less harmful ones. Here are some of the gases that go into the converter and how they come out of it.

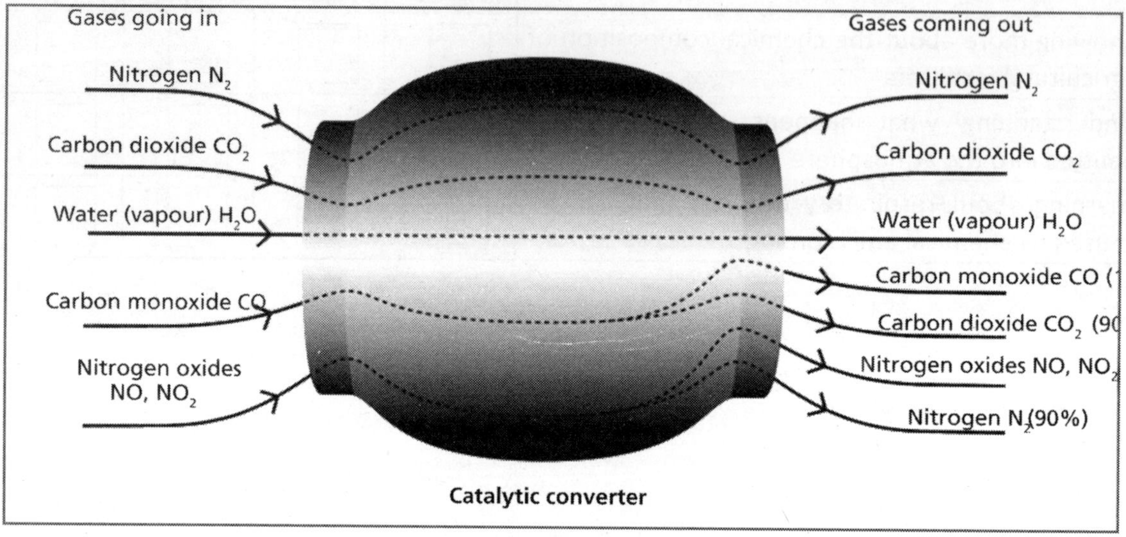

Catalytic converter

QUESTION 32.1

Use the information in the diagram above to give an example of how the catalytic converter makes exhaust fumes less harmful.

....

....

QUESTION 32.2

Changes take place to gases inside the catalytic converter. Explain what is happening in terms of atoms AND molecules.

....

....

....

QUESTION 32.3

Examine the gases emitted by the catalytic converter. What is one problem that engineers and scientists working on the catalytic converter should try to solve to produce less harmful exhaust fumes?

....

QUESTION 32.4 (ATTITUDE)

How much do you agree with the following statements?

Tick only one box in each row.

	Strongly Agree	Agree	Disagree	Strongly Disagree
Knowing how car fuels differ in the amounts of toxic fumes they produce	☐ 1	☐ 2	☐ 3	☐ 4
Understanding more about what happens inside a catalytic converter	☐ 1	☐ 2	☐ 3	☐ 4
Learning about vehicles that do not emit toxic exhaust fumes	☐ 1	☐ 2	☐ 3	☐ 4

SCIENCE UNIT 33: MAJOR SURGERY

Major surgery, performed in specially equipped operating theatres, is necessary to treat many diseases.

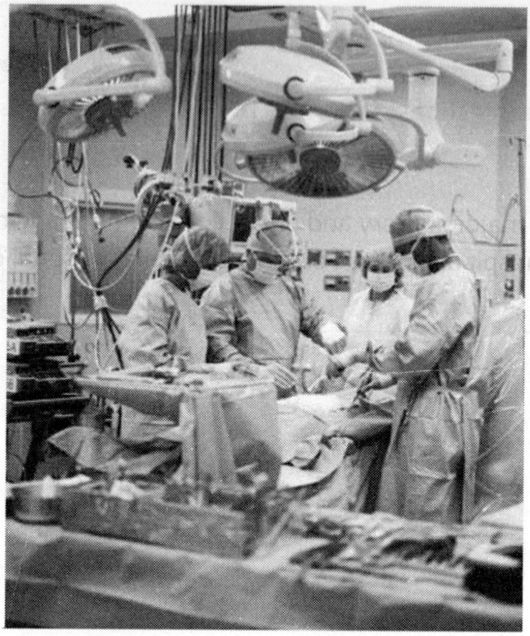

QUESTION 33.1

While undergoing major surgery, patients are anaesthetised so they don't feel any pain. The anaesthetic is often administered as a gas through a face mask that covers the nose and mouth.

Are the following human systems involved in the action of anaesthetic gases? Circle "Yes" or "No" for each system.

Is this system involved in the action of anaesthetic gases?	Yes or No?
Digestive system	Yes / No
Nervous system	Yes / No
Respiratory system	Yes / No

QUESTION 33.2

Explain why surgical instruments used in operating theatres are sterilised.

....

....

....

QUESTION 33.3

Patients may be unable to eat and drink after surgery and so they are put on a drip (infusion) that contains water, sugars and mineral salts. Sometimes antibiotics and tranquillisers are also added to the drip.

Why are the sugars that are added to the drip important for the post-operative patient?

A. To avoid dehydration

B. To control post-operative pain

C. To cure post-operative infections

D. To provide necessary nutrition

QUESTION 33.4

Organ transplants involve major surgery and are becoming more and more common. In the graph below, the numbers of transplants carried out in a particular hospital during 2003 are given.

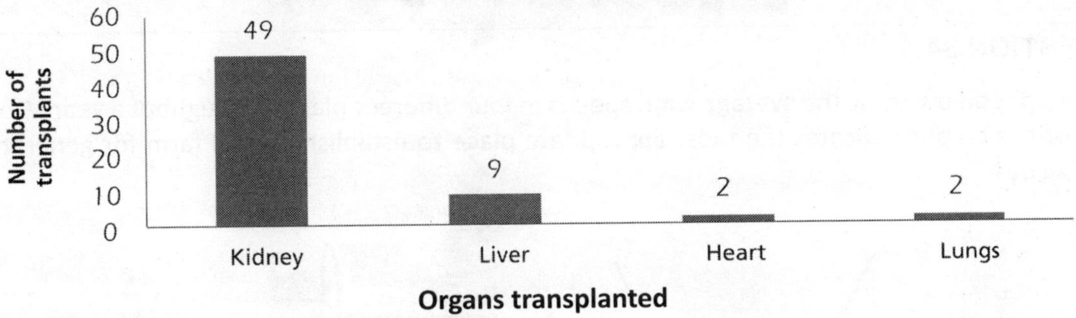

Can the following conclusions be drawn from the graph above? Circle "Yes" or "No" for each conclusion.

Can this conclusion be drawn from the graph?	Yes or No?
If the lungs are transplanted, the heart must be transplanted too.	Yes / No
Kidneys are the most important organs in the human body.	Yes / No
Most of the patients that have a transplant have suffered from a kidney disease.	Yes / No

QUESTION 33.5 (ATTITUDE)

How much do you agree with the following statements?

Tick only one box in each row.

	Strongly Agree	Agree	Disagree	Strongly Disagree
Learning how surgical instruments are sterilised	☐ 1	☐ 2	☐ 3	☐ 4
Knowing about the different types of anaesthetics that are used	☐ 1	☐ 2	☐ 3	☐ 4
Understanding how a patient's level of consciousness is monitored during surgery	☐ 1	☐ 2	☐ 3	☐ 4

SCIENCE UNIT 34 : WIND FARMS

Many people believe that wind should replace oil and coal as a source of energy for producing electricity. The structures in the picture are windmills with blades that are rotated by the wind. These rotations cause electricity to be produced by generators that are turned by the windmills.

A wind farm

QUESTION 34.1

The graphs below show the average wind speeds in four different places throughout a year. Which one of the graphs indicates the most appropriate place to establish a wind farm for generating electricity?

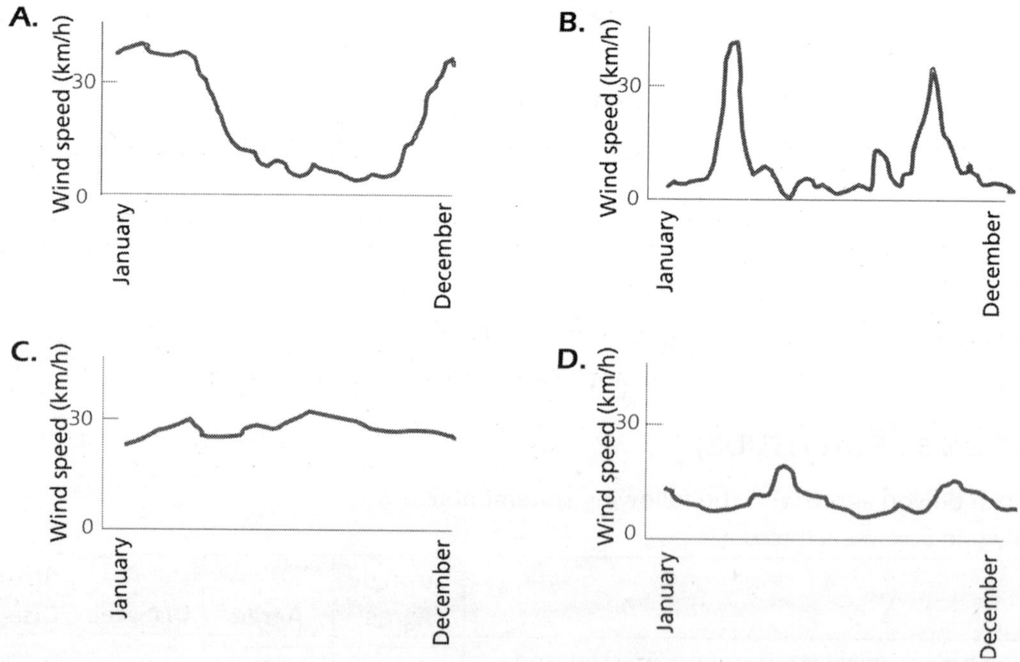

QUESTION 34.2

The stronger the wind, the faster the windmill blades rotate and the greater the electric power output.

However, there is not a direct relationship between wind speed and electric power in a real setting.

Below are four working conditions of electricity generation in a real wind farm.

The windmill blades start rotating when the wind speed reaches V_1.

The electric power output reaches a maximum (W) when the wind speed is V_2.

For safety reasons, the blades are prevented from rotating faster than they do when the wind speed is V_2.

The blades stop rotating when the wind speed reaches V_3.

Which one of the following graphs best represents the relationship between wind speed and electric power output under these working conditions?

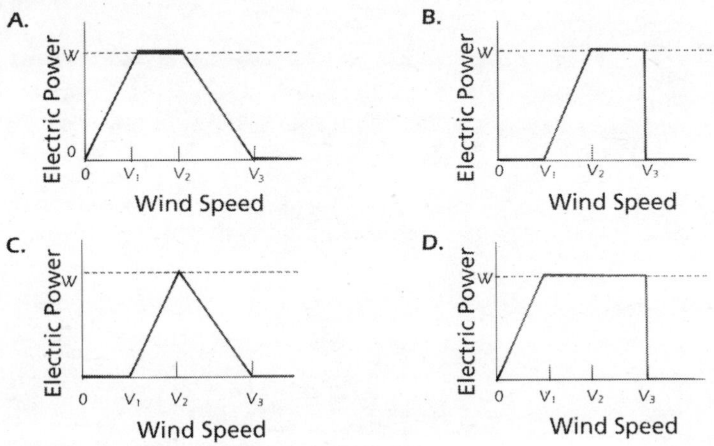

QUESTION 34.3

The higher the altitude the more slowly windmills rotate at the same wind speed.

Which one of the following is the best reason why the blades of windmills rotate more slowly in higher places at the same wind speed?

A. The air is less dense as altitude increases.

B. The temperature is lower as altitude increases.

C. Gravity becomes less as altitude increases.

D. It rains more often as altitude increases.

QUESTION 34.4

Describe one specific advantage, and one specific disadvantage, of using wind to generate electricity compared with using fossil fuels like coal and oil.

An advantage ....

....

A disadvantage ....

....

ANSWERS

CHAPTER 2
Reading sample tasks

LAKE CHAD SCORING 1.1

Full credit: A. About two metres.

Answering this question correctly corresponds to a difficulty of 478 score points on the PISA reading scale. Across OECD countries, 65% of students answered correctly. To do so, they correctly retrieved information.

LAKE CHAD SCORING 1.2

Full credit: 11,000 BC (or approximation between 10,500 and 12,000; or other indication that the student has extrapolated from the scale)

- 11,000
- 11,000 BC
- 10,500 BC
- Just before 10,000 BC
- About 12,000
- About 11,000 BC

Answering this question correctly corresponds to a difficulty of 540 score points on the PISA reading scale. Across OECD countries, 50% of students answered correctly. To do so, they correctly retrieved information.

LAKE CHAD SCORING 1.3

Full credit: Refers to <u>reappearance of lake</u>. Note: answer may receive full credit even if previous answer is incorrect.

- Lake Chad reappeared in 11,000 BC after disappearing completely around 20,000
- BC.
- The lake disappeared during the Ice Age and then came back at about this time.
- It reappeared then.
- About 11,000 BC it came back.

- Then the lake reappeared after being gone for 9000 years.

Answering this question correctly corresponds to a difficulty of 600 score points on the PISA reading scale. Across OECD countries, 37% of students answered correctly. To do so, they reflected on and evaluated the text.

LAKE CHAD SCORING 1.4

Full credit: A. the animals in the rock art were present in the area at the time they were drawn.

Answering this question correctly corresponds to a difficulty of 397 score points on the PISA reading scale. Across OECD countries, 77% of students answered correctly. To do so, they interpreted the text correctly.

LAKE CHAD SCORING 1.5

Full credit: C. after the level of Lake Chad had been falling for over a thousand years.

Answering this question correctly corresponds to a difficulty of 508 score points on the PISA reading scale. Across OECD countries, 57% of students answered correctly. To do so, they interpreted the text correctly.

FLU SCORING 2.1

Full credit: B. Immunisations will be given during working hours.

Answering this question correctly corresponds to a difficulty of 443 score points on the PISA reading scale. Across OECD countries, 70% of students answered correctly. To do so, they correctly retrieved information.

FLU SCORING 2.2

Full credit:

- Refers accurately to the text and relates style to purpose, consistent with "friendly and encouraging". The answer must do AT LEAST ONE of the following:

  (1) refer to one of the features in detail (layout, style of writing, pictures or other graphics; or other similar) – that is, to a specific part or quality of a feature; AND/OR

  (2) use evaluative terms other than "friendly" and "encouraging". (Note that such terms as "interesting", "easy to read" and "clear" are not considered to be adequately specific.)

  Opinion about whether Fiona succeeded may be stated or implied.

- No, it was a bad idea to put a picture of a syringe near the beginning. That looks scary. *[Refers to one specific part of the design: a particular picture (1). Uses own evaluative term: "scary" (2).]*
- Yes, the pictures break up the writing and make it easy to read. *[Describes a specific aspect of layout (1).]*
- The cartoon-like picture of the virus is friendly. *[Refers to a specific aspect ("cartoon-like") of one illustration (1).]*
- No, the pictures are childish and irrelevant. *[Uses own terms ("childish", "irrelevant") to evaluate one of the features mentioned in the stem (2).]*
- Yes, the written style is relaxed and informal. *[Uses own terms ("relaxed", "informal") to evaluate one of the features mentioned in the stem (2).]*
- Yes, the style was warm and inviting. *[Uses own terms to evaluate style (2).]*
- There is too much writing. People wouldn't bother reading it. *[Refers to a relevant feature of the presentation: amount of text (1). Uses own evaluative terms (2).]*
- She doesn't put pressure on people to get the injection, and that would encourage people. *[Implicit reference to manner or register: an aspect of style (2).]*
- No, the writing style is very formal. *[Debatable but plausible application of own evaluative term: "formal" (2).]*

Partial credit:

- <u>Refers accurately to the text</u> and <u>relates purpose to information and content</u> (rather than style), consistent with "friendly and encouraging". Opinion about whether Fiona succeeded may be stated or implied.
  - No, there is no way that a message about having an injection could be friendly and encouraging.
  - Yes she succeeded. She's giving many opportunities and arranging times for a flu immunisation. She also gave suggestions about health.

Answering this question correctly corresponds to a difficulty of 583 score points on the PISA reading scale. Giving a partially correct answer to this question corresponds to a difficulty of 542 score points on the PISA reading scale. Across OECD countries, 44% of students answered correctly. To do so, they reflected on and evaluated the text.

FLU SCORING 2.3

Full credit: B. a good idea, but not a substitute for exercise and a healthy diet.

Answering this question correctly corresponds to a difficulty of 521 score points on the PISA reading scale. Across OECD countries, 53% of students answered correctly. To do so, they interpreted the text correctly.

FLU SCORING 2.4

Full credit:

- Evaluates the section of text in relation to the term "misleading" by indicating that there is a potential contradiction. ("Who should be immunised? Anyone..." vs "Who should not be immunised?"). May or may not explain what the contradiction is. Agreement or disagreement may be stated or implied.
    - Yes, because it would be dangerous for some people to have the immunisation (*e.g.* pregnant women). *[Describes contradiction.]*
    - No, because you only have to read another couple of lines to realise that some people shouldn't have the injection, and on the whole she wants people to have it.
    - Yes, because she says "anyone" can and later she states the people who should not be immunised. *[Contradiction identified.]*
    - This line suggests that all people should get the vaccine, which is untrue. *[Contradiction briefly indicated.]*
    - Yes, to some extent! Maybe: "Anyone interested in being protected against the virus, but who doesn't suffer from any of the following symptoms or diseases." *[Suggested rewording implies recognition of the contradiction.]*
- Evaluates the section of text in relation to the term "misleading" by indicating that the statement may be an exaggeration. (*i.e.* Not everyone needs the immunisation, or the immunisation does not offer complete protection.) May or may not explain what the exaggeration is. Agreement or disagreement may be stated or implied.
    - Leave out because having the immunisation is not a guarantee that you won't get the flu.
    - I don't agree, even though it makes it sound as if you will definitely get the flu if you don't have the injection.
    - Having the injection is not a complete protection.
    - Leave out because not everyone gets the flu, especially if you are fit and well.
    - Yes I agree because it makes the shot sound better than it is. *[Implies an exaggeration, though unspecified.]*

Answering this question correctly corresponds to a difficulty of 637 score points on the PISA reading scale. Across OECD countries, 37% of students answered correctly. To do so, they reflected on and evaluated the text.

FLU SCORING 2.5

Full credit: D. Michael from accounts who would like to be immunised but will be on leave in the week of May 17.

Answering this question correctly corresponds to a difficulty of 562 score points on the PISA reading scale. Across OECD countries, 45% of students answered correctly. To do so, they interpreted the text correctly.

GRAFFITI SCORING 3.1

Full credit: B. present an opinion about graffiti.

Answering this question correctly corresponds to a difficulty of 421 score points on the PISA reading scale. Across OECD countries, 76% of students answered correctly. To do so, they interpreted the text correctly.

GRAFFITI SCORING 3.2

Full credit:

- Recognises that a <u>comparison</u> is being drawn between graffiti and advertising. Answer is consistent with the idea that advertising is a legal form of graffiti.

    - To show us that advertising can be as invasive as graffiti.
    - Because some people think advertising is just as ugly as spray-painting.
    - She's saying that advertising is just a legal form of graffiti.
    - She thinks advertising is like graffiti.
    - Because they don't ask your permission to put up billboards. *[The comparison between advertising and graffiti is implicit.]*
    - Because advertisements are placed in society without our permission, as is graffiti.
    - Because the billboards are like graffiti. *[A minimal answer. Recognises a similarity without elaborating on what the similarity is.]*
    - Because it is another form of display.
    - Because advertisers stick posters on the wall and she thinks it is graffiti as well.
    - Because it is on the walls too.
    - Because they are equally nice or ugly to look at.
    - She refers to advertising because it is acceptable unlike graffiti. *[Similarity of graffiti and advertising is implied by contrasting attitudes to the two.]*

- Recognises that referring to advertising is a strategy to defend graffiti.
  - So that we will see that graffiti is legitimate after all.

Answering this question correctly corresponds to a difficulty of 542 score points on the PISA reading scale. Across OECD countries, 53% of students answered correctly. To do so, they interpreted the text correctly.

GRAFFITI SCORING 3.3

Full credit: Explains point of view by <u>referring to the content of one or both letters</u>. May refer to the writer's general position (*i.e.* for or against) or to a detail of her argument. Interpretation of writer's argument must be <u>plausible</u>. Explanation may take the form of paraphrase of part of the text, but must not be wholly or largely copied without alteration or addition.

- I agree with Helga. Graffiti is illegal and that makes it vandalism.
- Helga because I am against graffiti. *[Minimum answer]*
- Sophia. I think it's hypocritical to fine graffiti artists and then make millions by copying their designs.
- I sort of agree with both of them. It should be illegal to paint over walls in public places but these people should be given the opportunity to do their work somewhere else.
- Sophia's because she cares about art.
- I agree with both. Graffiti is bad but advertising is just as bad so I won't be hypocritical.
- Helga because I don't really like graffiti either but I understand Sophia's point of view and how she didn't want to condemn people for doing something they believe in.
- Helga's because it really is a pity to spoil the reputation of young people for nothing. *[Borderline case: some direct quotation, but embedded in other text.]*
- Sophia. It is true that patterns and colours stolen from graffiti appear in stores and are accepted by people who consider graffiti dreadful. *[The explanation is a combination of phrases from the text, but the amount of manipulation indicates that it has been well understood.]*

Answering this question correctly corresponds to a difficulty of 471 score points on the PISA reading scale. Across OECD countries, 67% of students answered correctly. To do so, they reflected on and evaluated the text.

GRAFFITI SCORING 3.4

Full credit: Explains opinion with <u>reference to the style or form</u> of one or both letters. Refers to criteria such as style of writing, structure of argument, cogency of argument, tone, register used, strategies for persuading audience. Terms like "better arguments" must be substantiated.

- Helga's. She gave you lots of different points to consider and she mentioned the environmental damage that graffiti artists do which I think is very important.
- Helga's letter was effective because of the way she addressed the graffiti artists directly.
- I think Helga's letter was the better one of the two. I thought Sophia's was a bit biased.
- I thought Sophia put forward a very strong argument but Helga's was structured better.
- Sophia, because she didn't really aim it at anyone. *[Explains his/her choice in terms of quality of content. Explanation is intelligible when interpreted as "Doesn't attack anyone".]*
- I like Helga's letter. She was quite dominant getting her opinion out.

Answering this question correctly corresponds to a difficulty of 581 score points on the PISA reading scale. Across OECD countries, 45% of students answered correctly. To do so, they reflected on and evaluated the text.

LABOUR SCORING 4.1

Full credit: D. In the labour force and not in the labour force.

Answering this question correctly corresponds to a difficulty of 477 score points on the PISA reading scale. Across OECD countries, 63% of students answered correctly. To do so, they interpreted the text correctly.

LABOUR SCORING 4.2

Full credit: Indicates that the number in the tree diagram AND the "000s" in the title/footnote have been integrated: 949,900. Allow approximations 949,000 and 950,000 in figures or words. Also accept 900,000 or one million (in words or figures) with qualifier.

- 949,900
- just under nine hundred and fifty thousand
- 950,000
- 949.9 thousand
- almost a million
- about 900 thousand
- 949.9 X 1000
- 949(000)

Partial credit: Indicates that number in tree diagram has been located, but that the "000s" in the title/footnote has not been correctly integrated. Answers 949.9 in words or figures. Allow approximations comparable to those for Code 2.

- 949.9
- 94,900
- almost a thousand
- just under 950
- about 900
- just under 1000

Answering this question correctly corresponds to a difficulty of 631 score points on the PISA reading scale. Giving a partially correct answer to this question corresponds to a difficulty of 485 score points on the reading scale. Across OECD countries, 46% of students answered correctly. To do so, they correctly retrieved information.

LABOUR SCORING 4.3

	"In labour force: employed"	"In labour force: unemployed"	"Not in labour force"	Not included in any category
A part-time waiter, aged 35	☒	☐	☐	☐
A business woman, aged 43, who works a sixty hour week	☒	☐	☐	☐
A full-time student, aged 21	☐	☐	☒	☐
A man, aged 28, who recently sold his shop and is looking for work	☐	☒	☐	☐
A woman, aged 55, who has never worked or wanted to work outside the home	☐	☐	☒	☐
A grandmother, aged 80, who still works a few hours a day at the family's market stall	☐	☐	☐	☒

Full credit: 5 correct.

Partial credit: 3 or 4 correct.

Answering this question correctly corresponds to a difficulty of 727 score points on the PISA reading scale. Giving a partially correct answer to this question corresponds to a difficulty of 473 score points on the reading scale. Across OECD countries, 39% of students answered correctly. To do so, they interpreted the text correctly.

LABOUR SCORING 4.4

Features of Tree Diagram	Answer
The labels in each box (e.g. "In labour force")	Change / **No change**
The percentages (e.g. "64.2%")	**change** / No change
The numbers (e.g. "2656.5")	**change** / No change
The footnotes under the tree diagram	Change / **No change**

Full credit: 3 correct.

Answering this question correctly corresponds to a difficulty of 445 score points on the PISA reading scale. Across OECD countries, 69% of students answered correctly. To do so, they reflected on and evaluated the text.

LABOUR SCORING 4.5

Full credit: C. Categories within each group.

Answering this question correctly corresponds to a difficulty of 486 score points on the PISA reading scale. Across OECD countries, 62% of students answered correctly. To do so, they reflected on and evaluated the text.

PLAN INTERNATIONAL SCORING 5.1

Note: The correct answer is B: "The level of activity was comparatively low in Ethiopia". This question is for information only and will not independently contribute to the student's score. The answer is taken into account in assessing the response to Question 5.2

PLAN INTERNATIONAL SCORING 5.2

Full credit: Student has answered Question 5.1 correctly. Explains the level of PLAN's activity by drawing on ALL the information supplied, with explicit or implicit reference to the type of activity conducted in Ethiopia by PLAN. Answer must also be consistent with (though does not need to refer to) BOTH of the following:

(1) PLAN's low level of activity in Ethiopia (information supplied in the table); AND

(2) Ethiopia's poverty (information given in the stem).

- Aid organisations often start their work in a country by training local people so I would say PLAN had just started working in Ethiopia in 1996.
- Training community workers might be the only kind of aid they can give there. There

might not be the hospitals or schools in which they could base the other kinds of aid work.

- Other foreign aid groups might be helping with medicine etc. and PLAN sees they need to know how to run the country. *[Implicitly refers to training community leaders.]*

Partial credit:

- Student has answered Question 5.1 correctly. Explains the level of PLAN's work by drawing on MOST of the information supplied. Answer must be consistent with (though does not need to refer to) BOTH of the following:

  (1) PLAN's low level of activity in Ethiopia (information supplied in the table); AND

  (2) Ethiopia's poverty (information given in the stem).

  - It might be hard to distribute aid there because things are in such a mess.
  - There may be a war on so it would be hard to give aid.
  - They don't know how to help there.
  - If other organisations are helping in Ethiopia, there is less for PLAN to do.
  - I could imagine that the other countries received help first and that Ethiopia will be helped in the near future.
  - The people of Ethiopia may have a certain culture which makes it difficult to interact with foreigners.
  - I think they are giving a bit too much help in other countries and Ethiopia is missing out. Plan International might not have enough funding and money for all the countries in need.

- Student has answered Question 5.1 correctly. Explains the level of PLAN's work by drawing on PART of the information supplied. Answer must be consistent with (though does not need to refer to) PLAN's low level of activity in Ethiopia (information supplied in the table).

  - Ethiopia does not need PLAN's help as much as the other countries. *[Draws on information in the table but does not take into account the information about Ethiopia's relative poverty supplied in the stem.]*
  - Ethiopia is not as poor as the other countries so it doesn't need PLAN's help as much. *[Draws on information in the table but is inconsistent with information about Ethiopia's relative poverty supplied in the stem.]*
  - Ethiopia might only need more help with their community leaders than other countries. *[Draws in detail on information in the table but does not take into account the information about Ethiopia's relative poverty supplied in the stem.]*

- Student has answered Question 5.1 incorrectly. Explains the level of PLAN's work by drawing on PART of the information supplied. Answer must be consistent with (though does not need to refer to) BOTH of the following:

  (1) the level of activity in Ethiopia which the student has indicated in Question 4A (the explanation itself need not be true); AND

(2) Ethiopia's poverty (information given in the stem).

- *[Answer to Question 4A: The level of activity is comparatively high in Ethiopia.]* Ethiopia is poorer than other countries in the region and therefore needs more help.
- *[Answer to Question 4A: It is about the same as in other countries in the region.]* Aid is distributed equally so there is no rivalry between countries.

Answering this question correctly corresponds to a difficulty of 822 score points on the PISA reading scale. Giving a partially correct answer to this question corresponds to a difficulty of 705 score points on the reading scale. Across OECD countries, 11% of students answered correctly. To do so, they reflected on and evaluated the text.

POLICE SCORING 6.1

Full credit: B. The order of the pearls is different.

Answering this question correctly corresponds to a difficulty of 515 score points on the PISA reading scale. Across OECD countries, 61% of students answered correctly. To do so, they correctly retrieved information.

POLICE SCORING 6.2

Full credit: C. how cells are analysed to find the pattern of DNA.

Answering this question correctly corresponds to a difficulty of 518 score points on the PISA reading scale. Across OECD countries, 58% of students answered correctly. To do so, they interpreted the text correctly.

POLICE SCORING 6.3

Full credit: C. To inform.

Answering this question correctly corresponds to a difficulty of 406 score points on the PISA reading scale. Across OECD countries, 80% of students answered correctly. To do so, they interpreted the text correctly.

POLICE SCORING 6.4

Full credit: B. carrying out genetic analyses.

Answering this question correctly corresponds to a difficulty of 402 score points on the PISA reading scale. Across OECD countries, 81% of students answered correctly. To do so, they interpreted the text correctly.

RUNNERS SCORING 7.1

Full credit: D. That it is very important for young sports players to wear good sports shoes.

Answering this question correctly corresponds to a difficulty of 356 score points on the PISA reading scale. Across OECD countries, 85% of students answered correctly. To do so, they interpreted the text correctly.

RUNNERS SCORING 7.2

Full credit: Refers to restriction of movement.

- They restrict movement.
- They prevent you from running easily.

Answering this question correctly corresponds to a difficulty of 392 score points on the PISA reading scale. Across OECD countries, 79% of students answered correctly. To do so, they correctly retrieved information.

RUNNERS SCORING 7.3

Full credit: Refers to the four criteria in italics in the text. Each reference may be a direct quotation, a paraphrase or an elaboration of the criterion. Criteria may be given in any order. The four criteria are:

(1) To provide exterior protection

(2) To support the foot

(3) To provide good stability

(4) To absorb shocks

- 1. Exterior protection
  2. Support of the foot
  3. Good stability
  4. Shock absorption
- It must provide exterior protection, support the foot, provide the player with good stability and must absorb shocks.
- Protect, support, stabilise, absorb. *[Quotes sub-heading of this section of text.]*

Answering this question correctly corresponds to a difficulty of 405 score points on the PISA reading scale. Across OECD countries, 76% of students answered correctly. To do so, they correctly retrieved information.

RUNNERS SCORING 7.4

Full credit: D. Gives the solution to the problem described in the first part.

Answering this question correctly corresponds to a difficulty of 402 score points on the PISA reading scale. Across OECD countries, 78% of students answered correctly. To do so, they reflected on and evaluated the text.

GIFT SCORING 8.1

Full credit: C. Her house has been surrounded by flood waters.

Answering this question correctly corresponds to a difficulty of 447 score points on the PISA reading scale. Across OECD countries, 73% of students answered correctly. To do so, they interpreted the text correctly.

GIFT SCORING 8.2

Full credit: C. intending to shoot the cat.

Answering this question correctly corresponds to a difficulty of 603 score points on the PISA reading scale. Across OECD countries, 40% of students answered correctly. To do so, they interpreted the text correctly.

GIFT SCORING 8.3

Full credit: Goes beyond a literal interpretation of the story while interpreting it in a way which is consistent with accurate literal comprehension. Evaluates the ending in terms of thematic completeness, by relating the last sentence to central relationships, issues or metaphors in the story. Answer may refer, for example, to the relationship between the panther and the woman; to survival; or to a gift or thanks. Opinion about appropriateness may be stated or implied.

- Yes. The story has brought the woman into contact with what is really essential in life, and the clean white bone is a symbol of that.
- Yes. I suppose that what was left of the ham by the panther was also a gift, the message being "live and let live".
- Yes. The bone is like a gift, and that is the theme of the story.
- Yes. The ham bone reminds us of what could have happened to the woman.
- It is appropriate because the animal sort of thanked her for the ham.

Partial credit:

- Goes beyond a literal interpretation of the story while interpreting it in a way which is consistent with accurate literal comprehension. Evaluates the ending in terms of style or mood, by relating the last sentence to the general style or mood of the rest of the story. Opinion about appropriateness may be stated or implied.
    - Yes, it fits the matter-of-fact telling of the story.
    - Yes, it continues the effect of something eerie.
    - No, it is too abrupt when most of the story is given in great detail.
- Responds at a literal level, in a way which is consistent with accurate literal comprehension of the story. Evaluates the ending in terms of narrative sequence, by relating the last sentence to explicit events, (*e.g.* the cat having eaten the meat; the visit of the panther to the house; the subsiding of the flood). Opinion about appropriateness may be stated or implied.
    - Yes it gives you an answer to the question of whether the cat ate the food.
    - No. The part about the meat was already finished.
    - It is finished because the meat is finished and so is the story.
    - Yes. Now that the flood has subsided and it has eaten the meat, there is no reason for the cat to stay.
    - I think it was a good ending because it proves that she had a panther on her porch. *[Understanding at a literal level that the events in the story "really happened".]*
    - No, it is not a suitable end, it was not a gift, but it was very dangerous. *[Indicates a wholly literal reading.]*
    - It is appropriate to describe that it was after the rain. *[Reference to the end of the flood.]*

Answering this question correctly corresponds to a difficulty of 652 score points on the PISA reading scale. Giving a partially correct answer to this question corresponds to a difficulty of 567 score points on the reading scale. Across OECD countries, 37% of students answered correctly. To do so, they reflected on and evaluated the text.

GIFT SCORING 8.4

Full credit: B. It began to float.

Answering this question correctly corresponds to a difficulty of 367 score points on the PISA reading scale. Across OECD countries, 85% of students answered correctly. To do so, they correctly retrieved information.

GIFT SCORING 8.5

Full credit: Recognises that the descriptions are intended to evoke pity. Reference to writer's intention or effect on the reader may be stated or implied. Reference to what happens in the rest of the story may be stated or implied. May suggest that:

(1) the descriptions quoted link the panther with the woman (or humans generally) in suffering; OR

(2) the descriptions quoted prepare for the woman's later compassionate behavior towards the panther; OR

(3) the panther is presented as an object of compassion.

- The panther sounds almost like a human, so it is like the woman, and you feel sorry for both of them. *[Explicit reference to the link between the panther and the woman/humans. (1) Explicit reference to the effect on the reader.]*
- It makes you realise straight away that the panther is also a victim of the flood. *[Implicit reference to the link between the panther and humans in "also". (1) Explicit reference to the effect on the reader.]*
- The woman seems to feel sorry for it before she knows what it is. *[Links the extracts with the the woman's later compassionate behaviour (2), without explicit reference to intention or effect.]*
- It makes you feel sorry for the panther. *[Implied accurate understanding of descriptions' nuances. (3) Explicit reference to effect on reader.]*
- It sounds sad and distressed. *[Implied understanding of descriptions' nuances (3), with implicit reference to author's intention.]*

Partial credit:

- Refers to possible intentions (or effects) of the quoted descriptions, other than that of evoking pity. Comment is consistent with comprehension of the text. Reference to writer's intention or effect on the reader may be stated or implied. References to what happens in the rest of the story may be stated or implied. May refer to:

(1) the intention/effect of creating suspense or mystery (Note that such terms as "frightening" and "scary" are considered to show lack of comprehension of the quoted descriptions; and "interesting", "easy to read" and "clear" are not considered to be adequately specific); OR

- the idea that the panther is presented from the woman's point of view.
- Because it creates suspense. You don't really know what was crying. *[1]*
- It introduces the panther slowly. *[1]*
- It's exciting. *[1]*
- You don't know what it is, just like the woman. *[Combination of (1) and (2).]*

- It describes the woman's feelings about the panther. *[2]*

- Refers to the literal information given in the quoted descriptions. Comment is consistent with comprehension of the text. Reference to writer's intention or effect on the reader may be stated or implied. References to what happens in the rest of the story may be stated or implied. May refer to:
  (1) the realistic depiction of the panther; OR
  (2) the way the descriptions fit with the literal setting and situation.

- The panther is a wild animal and wild animals cry. *[1]*
- The panther was hungry, and these animals make a noise when they are hungry. *[1]*
- She would notice the sounds it made because it was dark so she couldn't see it. *[2]*
- Hearing the panther now makes her remember when she has heard one before. *[2]*

Answering this question correctly corresponds to a difficulty of 645 score points on the PISA reading scale. Giving a partially correct answer to this question corresponds to a difficulty of 539 score points on the reading scale. Across OECD countries, 43% of students answered correctly. To do so, they interpreted the text correctly.

GIFT SCORING 8.6

Full credit:

- Recognises the implication that the woman is motivated by pity or empathy towards the panther. May also mention that the woman does not consciously understand her own motivation.

- She felt sorry for it.
- Because she knew what it felt like to be hungry.
- Because she's a compassionate person.
- To help it live.

Answering this question correctly corresponds to a difficulty of 529 score points on the PISA reading scale. Across OECD countries, 57% of students answered correctly. To do so, they interpreted the text correctly.

GIFT SCORING 8.7

GIFT SCORING 8.7A (Speaker 1 – "heartless and cruel")

Full credit: Provides evidence from the story to support the idea that the woman is heartless and cruel. May refer to her intention to shoot the panther, or to the fact that she actually shoots at the panther. May use quotation or close paraphrase.

- She tries to shoot the panther.
- She's cruel because her first thought is to kill the panther.
- She laughs when she thinks about killing the cat.
- When she was eating she laughed at the cat's whining.
- And taking up the rifle she fired it through the window. *[Quotation]*

GIFT SCORING 8.7 B (Speaker 2 – "compassionate")

Full credit: Provides evidence from the story to support the idea that the woman is compassionate. May refer to her action in feeding the panther, or to suggestions about her capacity for compassion towards the panther or more generally. May use quotation or close paraphrase.

- She's generous because she shares her food with the cat.
- She gives it ham.
- She took down what was left of the ham and shoved it through the broken pane. *[Quotation]*
- When she first hears the panther she thinks it sounds sad, not scary. *[Evidence of capacity for compassion towards the panther.]*
- It says "she wanted to cry, for herself, for all the people, for everything in the flood". *[Quoted evidence of more general compassion.]*

Answering this question correctly corresponds to a difficulty of 537 score points on the PISA reading scale. Across OECD countries, 64% of students answered correctly. To do so, they reflected on and evaluated the text.

AMANDA AND THE DUCHESS SCORING 9.1

Full credit: C. to get Amanda to make the Prince forget his grief.

Answering this question correctly corresponds to a difficulty of 423 score points on the PISA reading scale. Across OECD countries, 74% of students answered correctly. To do so, they interpreted the text correctly.

AMANDA AND THE DUCHESS SCORING 9.2

Full credit: Refers to italics. Allow non-technical descriptions. May mention parentheses as well as italics.

- (They are in) italics.
- Slanting writing.

- Like this: *[Imitates italic style.]*
- Handwriting.
- Writing in italics and also the use of brackets.
- They are in a skinny type of writing.

Answering this question correctly corresponds to a difficulty of 561 score points on the PISA reading scale. Across OECD countries, 44% of students answered correctly. To do so, they reflected on and evaluated the text.

AMANDA AND THE DUCHESS SCORING 9.3

AMANDA AND THE DUCHESS SCORING 9.3A (Props manager)

Full credit: Indicates suitcase OR bicycle. May quote a phrase from the stage directions.

- Her small suitcase
- Bicycle

AMANDA AND THE DUCHESS SCORING 9.3B (Sound technician)

Full credit: Indicates bird song OR (evening) birds OR twittering OR bicycle bell OR wind OR silence. May quote a phrase from the stage directions.

- A bicycle bell is heard in the evening air.
- Only the wind can be heard.
- Evening birds
- The evening birds have now taken over.

AMANDA AND THE DUCHESS SCORING 9.3C (Lighting technician)

Full credit: Indicates shadows OR pale blur OR [completely] dark OR evening

- The grounds are filled with shadows.
- The deeper shadows of the trees
- Evening is falling.
- In the evening air

Answering this question correctly corresponds to a difficulty of 567 score points on the PISA reading scale. Across OECD countries, 44% of students answered correctly. To do so, they interpreted the text correctly.

AMANDA AND THE DUCHESS SCORING 9.4

Full credit: Marks A by the obelisk and D behind or near the trees.

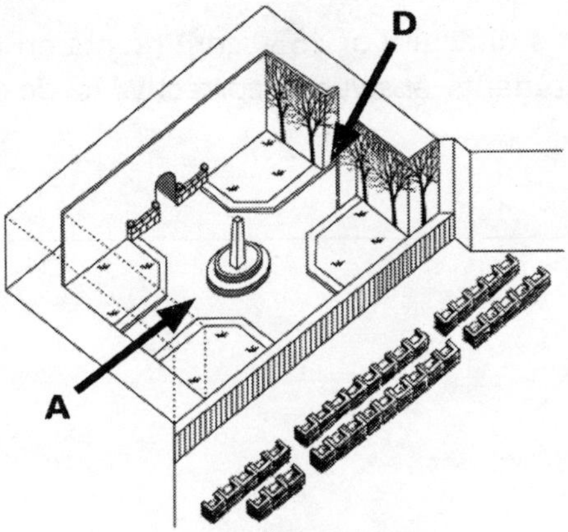

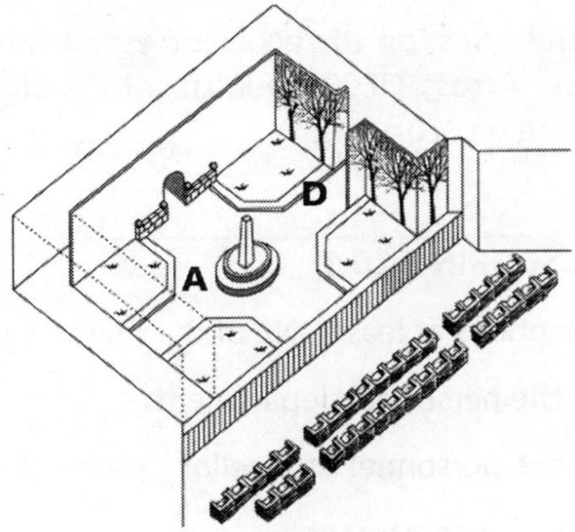

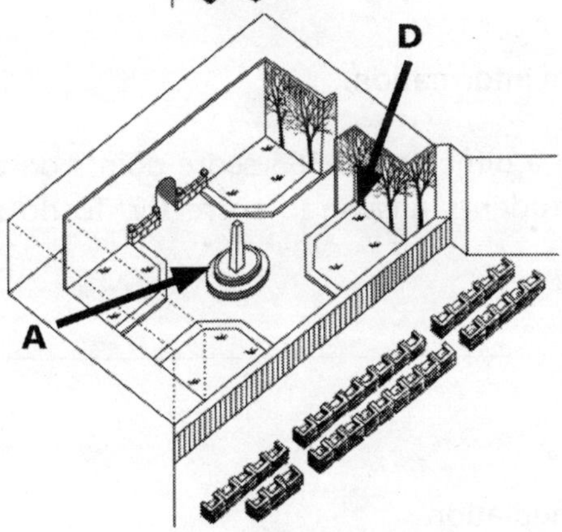

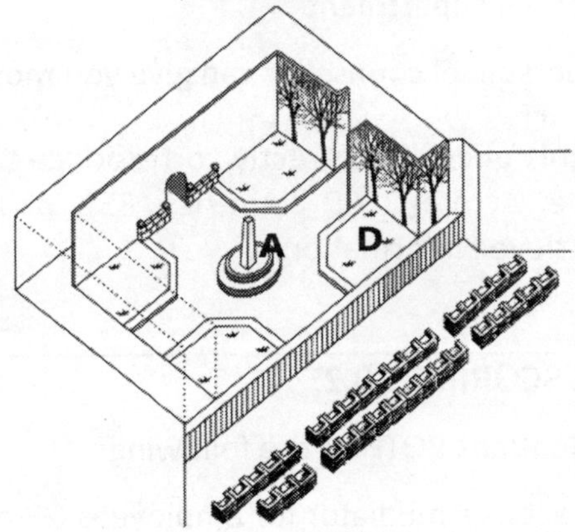

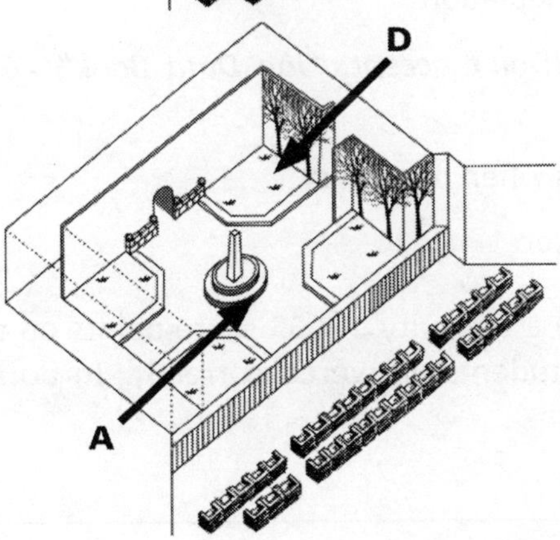

Answering this question correctly corresponds to a difficulty of 608 score points on the PISA reading scale. Across OECD countries, 37% of students answered correctly. To do so, they correctly retrieved information.

AMANDA AND THE DUCHESS SCORING 9.5

Full credit: D. That the Prince didn't notice that Amanda looked like Léocadia.

Answering this question correctly corresponds to a difficulty of 455 score points on the PISA reading scale. Across OECD countries, 67% of students answered correctly. To do so, they interpreted the text correctly.

PERSONNEL SCORING 10.1

Full credit: Mentions at least ONE of the following:

(1) From the personnel department

(2) From the personnel counsellor

- Personnel department
- The personnel counsellor can give you more information.

Answering this question correctly corresponds to a difficulty of 363 score points on the PISA reading scale. Across OECD countries, 85% of students answered correctly. To do so, they correctly retrieved information.

PERSONNEL SCORING 10.2

Full credit: Mentions BOTH of the following:

(1) They act as a mediator for employees OR mediation

(2) They assist with finding new positions. *[Don't accept: "Job Data Bank", "Guidance", "Courses", or "Career Change Projects".]*

- mediator assists with finding new positions when necessary
- acts as a mediator helps you to find a new job

Answering this question correctly corresponds to a difficulty of 655 score points on the PISA reading scale. Across OECD countries, 32% of students answered correctly. To do so, they correctly retrieved information.

NEW RULES SCORING 11.1

Full credit: Underlines OR circles the sentence OR a part of the sentence that contains at least ONE of the following:

(1) "set up a commission"

(2) "three months be allowed for public opinion to respond to the commission recommendation...."

- [Underlining] ...The Australians set up a commission to study the matter... [Student has underlined one of the relevant sentences.]
- [Underlining] ...The Australians set up a commission to study the matter... and ...they urged that three months be allowed for public opinion to respond to the commission recommendation... [Student has underlined both of the relevant sections of the text.]
- [Underlining] ...The Australians set up a commission to study the matter. ...and ...In France, a woman recently had to go to court to be allowed to bear a child from her deceased husband's frozen sperm... [One section of the text is correctly underlined; the other underlining seems to be related to answering the next question, so accept.]

Answering this question correctly corresponds to a difficulty of 558 score points on the PISA reading scale. Across OECD countries, 48% of students answered correctly. To do so, they interpreted the text correctly.

NEW RULES SCORING 11.2

Full credit: Mentions at least TWO of the following:

(1) When the Rioses died, there was a controversy over what was to be done with the embryos. [Don't accept controversies in paragraph 4 (e.g., "What was the hospital to do with the frozen embryos?" "Were the embryos entitled to the estate?") unless the respondent explicitly links these controversies to the death of the embryo donors (the Rioses).]

(2) A woman in France had to go to court to be allowed to use her deceased husband's sperm.

(3) What should the rules be for a surrogate mother who refused to give up the infant she bore?

- It showed a need for the producer to specify what should be done to the embryos if something happens to them, and for laws about what is to be done should a surrogate mother refuse to give up the child.

Partial credit: Mentions ONE of the examples given above relating to bio-technology ((1), (2) or (3)) AND (the destructive potential of) atomic power.

Answering this question correctly corresponds to a difficulty of 669 score points on the PISA reading scale. Across OECD countries, 26% of students answered correctly. To do so, they interpreted the text correctly.

MORELAND SCORING 12.1

Full credit: 5 p.m. / 5 o'clock

To answer this question correctly students had to retrieve information.

MORELAND SCORING 12.2

Full credit: C. Coburg Library

To answer this question correctly students had to retrieve information.

WARRANTY SCORING 13.1

Each piece receives a separate mark, which is combined to yield a single score.

A) MODEL

Full credit: Correctly identifies model.

- Rolly Fotonex 250 zoom.
- Rolly Fotonex.
- Fotonex.

B) SERIAL NUMBER

Full credit: *30910963*

C) DATE OF PURCHASE

Full credit: 18/10/99

Date may be given in another form, but must include date, month and year.

- 18 October 1999

May give redundant related information (time).

- 18/10/99, 12:10 pm

D) PURCHASE PRICE

Full credit: ($) 249.08

To answer this question correctly students had to retrieve information.

WARRANTY SCORING 13.2

Full credit: Indicates 10 days.

- Ten days.
- Within 10 days of purchase.

To answer this question correctly students had to retrieve information.

WARRANTY SCORING 13.3

Full credit: A tripod.

To answer this question correctly students had to retrieve information.

WARRANTY SCORING 13.4

Full credit: Refers either explicitly or implicitly to development of the business–customer relationship.

- It's good for business to be nice to you.
- To create a good relationship with the customer.
- They want you to come back.

To answer this question correctly students had to reflect on and evaluate the text.

JUST JUDGE SCORING 14.1

Full credit: D. He wanted to see the judge at work in his usual way, uninfluenced by the presence of the king.

To answer this question correctly students had to interpret the text.

JUST JUDGE SCORING 14.2

Full credit: D. By testing her skill in work that she needed to perform for her husband.

To answer this question correctly students had to retrieve information.

JUST JUDGE SCORING 14.3

Full credit: Evaluates the fairness of the punishments in relation to each other, in terms of similarity or difference of offences. Shows accurate understanding of the crimes.

- No, it is a much more serious crime to try to steal someone's wife than to steal their money or their horse.
- All three criminals tried to cheat someone and then lied about it, so it was fair that they were punished in the same way.
- It's hard to say. The peasant, the oil merchant and the beggar all wanted to steal something. On the other hand the things they wanted to steal were not equally valuable.
- No, some of the crimes were worse than others. *[Minimal correct answer: gives a criterion ("worse") for the varying punishments.]*

- Yes, they all lied.

To answer this question correctly students had to reflect on and evaluate the text.

JUST JUDGE SCORING 14.4

Full credit: B. Wise justice.

To answer this question correctly students had to interpret the text.

JUST JUDGE SCORING 14.5

Consider the first part of the response only ("similar").

Full credit: Describes one similarity. Shows accurate comprehension of the story. Comparison with a feature of the national legal system is either explicitly stated or may be readily inferred. Accurate knowledge of national legal systems is not essential, but take into account what background knowledge about the law in your country it would be reasonable to expect of a 15 year old.

- Rulings made on evidence.
- Both sides allowed to give their version of the truth.
- Equality before the law (it doesn't matter who you are).
- There is a judge presiding over the court.
- The same punishment is given for similar offences.
- The people in court are judged by different evidence which can be found.
- Each person gets to have their say.
- That they were taken to court to discuss the outcome.
- The justice system in this story has an impartial person to decide the truth, the judge.
- Court system. *[Unlike "punishment" (Code 0) not all systems of law have courts.]*
- Both people's arguments were heard.
- Judges also have to be wise and just in our system. *[Value judgment, consistent with accurate understanding of the story.]*

Consider the second part of the response only ("different").

Full credit: Describes one difference. Shows accurate comprehension of the story. Comparison with a feature of the national legal system is either explicitly stated or may be readily inferred. Accurate knowledge of national legal systems is not essential. (For example "no jury" may be accepted as a "difference", although in some modern courts there is no jury.)Take into account what background knowledge about the law in your country it would be reasonable to expect of a 15 year old.

- No lawyers.
- Judge carries out his own investigation.
- It's very quick, whereas in modern courts usually cases take weeks.
- No jury; there doesn't seem to be any way of appealing.
- The punishment is much harsher. *[A qualitative comment on the kind of punishment]*
- The same punishment is given regardless of the offence.
- A board of 12 judges – a jury – is used instead of a single judge.
- There weren't any lawyers or a jury.
- No jury or hard evidence.
- The judge's word was final.
- We do the judging inside the courtroom.
- The judges don't use little "tests" like the just judge.
- The story had a just judge. *[States or implies value judgment or opinion about national legal system. Answer is consistent with accurate understanding of the story, so credit even though it happens to be identical with the story's title.]*

To answer this question correctly students had to reflect on and evaluate the text.

JUST JUDGE SCORING 14.6

Full credit: A. A folk tale.

To answer this question correctly students had to reflect on and evaluate the text.

IN POOR TASTE SCORING 15.1

Full credit: A. Guilt.

To answer this question correctly students had to interpret the text.

IN POOR TASTE SCORING 15.2

Full credit:

- Government/individuals should spend more on (overseas) aid.
  - People donating more money to overseas aid.
  - Donate money to charities.

- People should spend less on chocolate and more on the poor.
- People spending less money on chocolate and more on the overseas sick. *[Limited sense of aid, but still gets main thrust.]*
- That people don't spend all their money on chocolate rather than overseas. *[Poorly expressed but has some sense of the interrelationship Jago refers to.]*
- An increase in the spending of people and Government towards overseas aid to help the poor. He also wants people to feel guilty and buy less chocolate or to donate money to overseas aid for the poor.
- People instead of buying and eating chocolate should give to a good cause and not be so self-indulgent.

- Government/individuals should change their priorities or awareness.

- Change our priorities.
- He would like people to raise their awareness about how we spend our resources.
- People stirred up to think more of helping others than indulging in personal pleasures. [Focuses on attitude ("think more") rather than action.]
- People's awareness that the poor need our help, for people to do something about it. [Emphasis on awareness.]

To answer this question correctly students had to reflect on and evaluate the text.

BULLYING SCORING 16.1

Full credit: Relates the bullying-suicide incident to public concern and / or the survey OR refers to the idea that the death was associated with extreme bullying. Connection may be explicitly stated or readily inferred.

- To explain why the survey was conducted.
- To give the background to why people are so concerned about bullying in Japan.
- He was a boy who committed suicide because of bullying.
- To show how far bullying can go.
- It was an extreme case.
- He hanged himself and he left a note saying that he was bullied in many hurtul ways. e.g. bulllies took his money and they also dunked him in a nearby stream many times. *[A description of the extremity of the case.]*
- This is mentioned because they feel it is important to try and stop bullying and for parents and teachers to keep a close eye on the children because they might do the same thing if it goes on for too long without help. *[A very long winded way of saying that the incident showed how much public awareness needed to be raised.]*

To answer this question correctly students had to interpret the text.

BULLYING SCORING 16.2

Full credit: Circles A (letter A or graph).

To answer this question correctly students had to retrieve information.

BEES SCORING 17.1

Full credit: B. To indicate where the foragers have found food.

To answer this question correctly students had to interpret the text.

BEES SCORING 17.2

Base scoring on the following responses:

a: fruit trees

b: clover

c: flowering trees

d: trees

e: flowers

Full credit: abc, abe, bde (in any order)

To answer this question correctly students had to retrieve information.

BEES SCORING 17.3

Full credit: A. The proportion of water in the substance.

To answer this question correctly students had to interpret the text.

BEES SCORING 17.4

Full credit: Indicates that information is given BOTH by shaking of abdomen AND by the length of time the abdomen is shaken.

- How long the bee shakes her abdomen for.
- It shakes its abdomen for a certain length of time.

Partial credit:

- Mentions <u>shaking of abdomen only</u>. (Answer may be partly inaccurate.)
    - She shakes her abdomen.
    - She shows how far it is by how fast she shakes her abdomen.
- Mentions length of time without mentioning shaking of abdomen..
    - How long she dances for.

To answer this question correctly students had to interpret the text.

CHAPTER 3
MATHEMATICS SAMPLE TASKS

FARMS SCORING 1.1

Full credit: 144 (unit already given)

Answering this question correctly corresponds to a difficulty of 492 score points on the PISA mathematics scale. Across OECD countries, 61% of students answered correctly. To answer the question correctly students have to draw on skills from the reproduction competency cluster.

FARMS SCORING 1.2

Full credit: 6 (unit already given)

Answering this question correctly corresponds to a difficulty of 524 score points on the PISA mathematics scale. Across OECD countries, 55% of students answered correctly. To answer the question correctly students have to draw on skills from the connections competency cluster.

WALKING SCORING 2.1

Full credit:

	$70/p = 140$	
0.5 m or 50 cm,1/2 (unit not required)	$70 = 140p$	70/140
	$p = 0.5$	

Answering this question correctly corresponds to a difficulty of 611 score points on the PISA mathematics scale. Across OECD countries, 34% of students answered correctly. To answer the question correctly students have to draw on skills from the reproduction competency cluster.

WALKING SCORING 2.2

Full credit: Correct answers (unit not required) for both metres/minute and km/hour:

- n = 140 x .80 = 112.
- Per minute he walks 112 x .80 metres = 89.6 metres.
- His speed is 89.6 metres per minute.
- So his speed is 5.38 or 5.4 km/hr.

- As long as both correct answers are given (89.6 and 5.4), whether working out is shown or not. Note that errors due to rounding are acceptable. For example, 90 metres per minute and 5.3 km/hr (89 X 60) are acceptable.
    - 89.6, 5.4.
    - 90, 5.376 km/h.
    - 89.8, 5376 m/hour.

Partial credit (2-point):

- Fails to multiply by 0.80 to convert from steps per minute to metres per minute. For example, his speed is 112 metres per minute and 6.72 km/hr.
    - 112, 6.72 km/h.
- The speed in metres per minute correct (89.6 metres per minute) but conversion to kilometers per hour incorrect or missing.
    - 89.6 metres/minute, 8960 km/hr.
    - 89.6, 5376.
    - 89.6, 53.76.
    - 89.6, 0.087 km/h.
    - 89.6, 1.49 km/h.
- Correct method (explicitly shown) with minor calculation error(s). No answers correct.
    - n = 140 x .8 = 1120; 1120 x 0.8 = 896. He walks 896 m/min, 53.76km/h.
    - n = 140 x .8 = 116; 116 x 0.8 =92.8. 92.8 m/min -> 5.57km/h.
- Only 5.4 km/hr is given, but not 89.6 metres/minute (intermediate calculations not shown).
    - 5.4.
    - 5.376 km/h.
    - 5376 m/h.

Partial credit (1-point):

- *n* = 140 x .80 = 112. No further working out is shown or incorrect working out from this point.
    - 112.
    - n = 112, 0.112 km/h.
    - n = 112, 1120 km/h.
    - 112 m/min, 504 km/h.

Answering this question correctly corresponds to a difficulty of 708 score points on the PISA mathematics scale. The difficulty of the higher partial credit response corresponds to a difficulty of 659 score points on the mathematics scale. The difficulty of the lower partial credit response corresponds to a difficulty of 600 score points on the mathematics scale. Across OECD countries, 19% of students answered correctly. To answer the question correctly students have to draw on skills from the connections competency cluster.

APPLES SCORING 3.1

Complete the table:

n	Number of apple trees	Number of conifer trees
1	1	8
2	4	16
3	9	24
4	16	32
5	25	40

Full credit: All 7 entries correct.

Answering this question correctly corresponds to a difficulty of 548 score points on the PISA mathematics scale. Across OECD countries, 49% of students answered correctly. To answer the question correctly students have to draw on skills from the connections competency cluster.

APPLES SCORING 3.2

Full credit: Responses with the correct answer, n=8, such as:

- $n^2 = 8n$, $n^2 - 8n = 0$, $n(n - 8)=0$, $n = 0$ & $n = 8$, so $n = 8$.
- $n^2 = 8^2 = 64$, $8n = 8 . 8 = 64$.
- $n^2 = 8n$. This gives n=8.
- 8 x 8 = 64, n=8
- n = 8.
- $8 \times 8 = 8^2$.

- Responses including both the answers n = 8 AND n = 0.

Answering this question correctly corresponds to a difficulty of 655 score points on the PISA mathematics scale. Across OECD countries, 25% of students answered correctly. To answer the question correctly students have to draw on skills from the connections competency cluster.

APPLES SCORING 3.3

Full credit: Correct response (apple trees) accompanied by a valid explanation. For example:

- Apple trees = n × n and conifer trees = 8 × n both formulas have a factor n, but apple trees have another n which will get larger where the factor 8 stays the same. The number of apple trees increases more quickly.
- The number of apple trees increases faster because that number is being squared instead of multiplied by 8.
- Number of apple trees is quadratic. Number of conifer trees is linear. So apple trees will increase faster.
- Response uses graph to demonstrate that n_2 exceeds 8n after n = 8.

Partial credit: Correct response (apple trees) based on specific examples or based on extending the table.

- The number of apple trees will increase more quickly because, if we use the table (previous page), we find that the no. of apple trees increases faster than the no. of conifer trees. This happens especially after the no. of apple trees and the number of conifer trees are equivalent.
- The table shows that the number of apple trees increases faster.

OR

Correct response (apple trees) with SOME evidence that the relationship between n^2 and 8n is understood, but not very clearly expressed.

- Apple trees after n > 8.
- After 8 rows, the number of apple trees will increase more quickly than conifer trees.
- Conifer trees until you get to 8 rows, then there will be more apple trees.

Answering this question correctly corresponds to a difficulty of 723 score points on the PISA mathematics scale. Giving a partially correct answer corresponds to a difficulty of 672 score points on the mathematics scale. Across OECD countries, 13% of students answered correctly. To answer the question correctly students have to draw on skills from the reflection competency cluster.

CUBES SCORING 4.1

Full credit: Top row (1 5 4) Bottom Row (2 6 5). Equivalent answer shown as dice faces is also acceptable.

1	**5**	**4**
2	**6**	**5**

Answering this question correctly corresponds to a difficulty of 516 score points on the PISA mathematics scale. Across OECD countries, 58% of students answered correctly. To answer the question correctly students have to draw on skills from the reproduction competency cluster.

CONTINENT AREA SCORING 5.1

Full credit: Responses using the correct method AND getting the correct answer.

- Estimated by drawing a square or rectangle - between 12 000 000 sq kms and 18 000 000 sq kms (units not required).
- Estimated by drawing a circle - between 12 000 000 sq kms and 18 000 000 sq kms.
- Estimated by adding areas of several regular geometric figures - between 12 000 000 and 18 000 000 sq kms.
- Estimated by other correct method – between 12 000 000 sq kms and 18 000 000 sq kms.
- Correct answer (between 12 000 000 sq kms and 18 000 000 sq kms) but no working out is shown.

Partial credit: Responses using the correct method BUT getting incorrect or incomplete answer.

- Estimated by drawing a square or rectangle – correct method but incorrect answer or incomplete answer.
    - Draws a rectangle and multiplies width by length, but the answer is an over estimation or an under estimation (e.g., 18 200 000).
    - Draws a rectangle and multiplies width by length, but the number of zeros are incorrect (e.g., 4000 X 3500 = 140 000).
    - Draws a rectangle and multiplies width by length, but forgets to use the scale to convert to square kilometres (e.g., 12cm X 15cm = 180).
    - Draws a rectangle and states the area is 4000km x 3500km. No further working out.
- Estimated by drawing a circle – correct method but incorrect answer or incomplete answer.
- Estimated by adding areas of several regular geometric figures – correct method but incorrect answer or incomplete answer.
- Estimated by other correct method – but incorrect answer or incomplete answer.

Answering this question correctly corresponds to a difficulty of 712 score points on the PISA mathematics scale. Giving a partially correct answer corresponds to a difficulty of 629 score points on the mathematics scale. Across OECD countries, 19% of students answered correctly. To answer the question correctly students have to draw on skills from the connections competency cluster.

GROWING UP SCORING 6.1

Full credit: 168.3 cm (unit already given).

Answering this question correctly corresponds to a difficulty of 506 score points on the PISA mathematics scale. Across OECD countries, 61% of students answered correctly. To answer the question correctly students have to draw on skills from the reproduction competency cluster.

GROWING UP SCORING 6.2

Full credit: The key here is that the response should refer to the "change" of the gradient of the graph for female. This can be done explicitly or implicitly.

- Refers to the reduced steepness of the curve from 12 years onwards, using daily-life language, not mathematical language.
    - It does no longer go straight up, it straightens out.
    - The curve levels off.
    - It is more flat after 12.
    - The line of the girls starts to even out and the boys line just gets bigger.
    - It straightens out and the boys graph keeps rising.
- Refers to the reduced steepness of the curve from 12 years onwards, using mathematical language.
    - You can see the gradient is less.
    - The rate of change of the graph decreases from 12 years on.
    - *[The student computed the angles of the curve with respect to the x-axis before and after 12 years.]*

  In general, if words like "gradient", "slope", or "rate of change" are used, regard it as using mathematical language.
- Comparing actual growth (comparison can be implicit).
    - From 10 to 12 the growth is about 15 cm, but from 12 to 20 the growth is only about 17 cm.
    - The average growth rate from 10 to 12 is about 7.5 cm per year, but about 2 cm per year from 12 to 20 years.

Answering this question correctly corresponds to a difficulty of 559 score points on the PISA mathematics scale. Across OECD countries, 46% of students answered correctly. To answer the question correctly students have to draw on skills from the connections competency cluster.

GROWING UP SCORING 6.3

Full credit:

- Gives the correct interval, from 11-13 years.
  - Between age 11 and 13.
  - From 11 years old to 13 years old, girls are taller than boys on average.
  - 11-13.
- States that girls are taller than boys when they are 11 and 12 years old. (This answer is correct in daily-life language, because it means the interval from 11 to 13).
  - Girls are taller than boys when they are 11 and 12 years old.
  - 11 and 12 years old.

Partial credit: Other subsets of (11, 12, 13), not included in the full credit section.

- 12 to 13.
- 12.
- 13.
- 11.
- 11.2 to 12 .8.

Answering this question correctly corresponds to a difficulty of 529 score points on the PISA mathematics scale. Giving a partially correct answer corresponds to a difficulty of 415 score points on the mathematics scale. Across OECD countries, 69% of students answered correctly. To answer the question correctly students have to draw on skills from the reproduction competency cluster.

SPEED OF RACING CAR SCORING 7.1

Full credit: B. 1.5 km

Answering this question correctly corresponds to a difficulty of 492 score points on the PISA mathematics scale. Across OECD countries, 67% of students answered correctly. To answer the question correctly students have to draw on skills from the connections competency cluster.

SPEED OF RACING CAR SCORING 7.2

Full credit: C. at about 1.3 km.

Answering this question correctly corresponds to a difficulty of 403 score points on the PISA mathematics scale. Across OECD countries, 83% of students answered correctly. To answer the question correctly students have to draw on skills from the reproduction competency cluster.

SPEED OF RACING CAR SCORING 7.3

Full credit: B. The speed of the car is increasing.

Answering this question correctly corresponds to a difficulty of 413 score points on the PISA mathematics scale. Across OECD countries, 83% of students answered correctly. To answer the question correctly students have to draw on skills from the reproduction competency cluster.

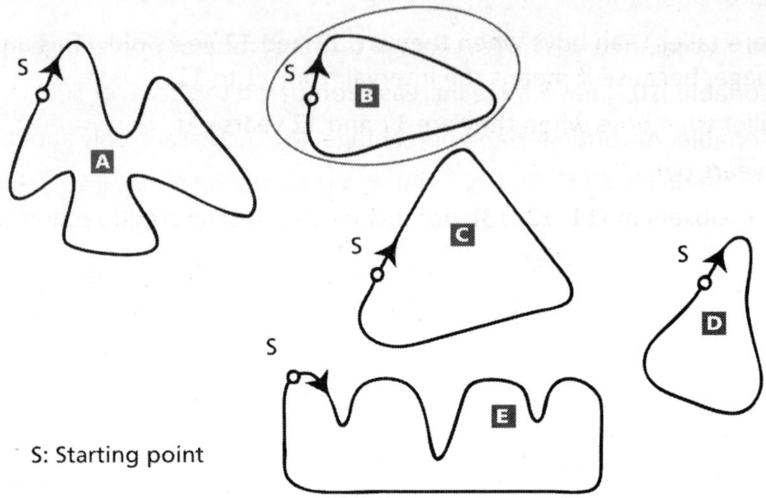

SPEED OF RACING CAR SCORING 7.4

Full credit: B

Answering this question correctly corresponds to a difficulty of 655 score points on the PISA mathematics scale. Across OECD countries, 28% of students answered correctly. To answer the question correctly students have to draw on skills from the connections competency cluster.

TRIANGLES SCORING 8.1

Full credit: Answer D.

Answering this question correctly corresponds to a difficulty of 537 score points on the PISA mathematics scale. Across OECD countries, 58% of students answered correctly. To answer the question correctly students have to draw on skills from the reproduction competency cluster.

ROBBERIES SCORING 9.1

Full credit:

- No, not reasonable. Focuses on the fact that only a **small part** of the graph is shown.

- Not reasonable. The entire graph should be displayed.
- I don't think it is a reasonable interpretation of the graph because if they were to show the whole graph you would see that there is only a slight increase in robberies.
- No, because he has used the top bit of the graph and if you looked at the whole graph from 0 – 520, it wouldn't have risen so much.
- No, because the graph makes it look like there's been a big increase but you look at the numbers and there's not much of an increase.

\- No, not reasonable. Contains correct arguments in terms of ratio or percentage increase.

- No, not reasonable. 10 is not a huge increase compared to a total of 500.
- No, not reasonable. According to the percentage, the increase is only about 2%.
- No. 8 more robberies is 1.5% increase. Not much in my opinion!
- No, only 8 or 9 more for this year. Compared to 507, it is not a large number.

\- Trend data is required before a judgement can be made.

- We can't tell whether the increase is huge or not. If in 1997, the number of robberies is the same as in 1998, then we could say there is a huge increase in 1999.
- There is no way of knowing what "huge" is because you need at least two changes to think one huge and one small.

Partial credit:

Note: As the scale on the graph is not that clear, accept between 5 and 15 for the increase of the exact number of robberies.

\- No, not reasonable, but explanation lacks detail.

- Focuses ONLY on an increase given by the exact number of robberies, but does not compare with the total.
- Not reasonable. It increased by about 10 robberies. The word "huge" does not explain the reality of the increased number of robberies. The increase was only about 10 and I wouldn't call that "huge".
- From 508 to 515 is not a large increase.
- No, because 8 or 9 is not a large amount.
- Sort of. From 507 to 515 is an increase, but not huge.

\- No, not reasonable, with correct method but with minor computational errors.

- Correct method and conclusion but the percentage calculated is 0.03%.

Answering this question correctly corresponds to a difficulty of 710 score points on the PISA mathematics scale. Giving a partially correctly answer corresponds to a difficulty of 609 score points on the mathematics scale. Across OECD countries, 26% of students answered correctly. To answer the question correctly students have to draw on skills from the connections competency cluster.

CARPENTER SCORING 10.1

Full credit: All four correct: Yes, No, Yes, Yes in that order.

Answering this question correctly corresponds to a difficulty of 700 score points on the PISA mathematics scale. Across OECD countries, 20% of students answered correctly. To answer the question correctly students have to draw on skills from the connections competency cluster.A

INTERNET RELAY CHAT SCORING 11.1

Full credit: 10 AM or 10:00.

Answering this question correctly corresponds to a difficulty of 533 score points on the PISA mathematics scale. Across OECD countries, 54% of students answered correctly. To answer the question correctly students have to draw on skills from the connections competency cluster.

INTERNET RELAY CHAT SCORING 11.2

Full credit: Any time or interval of time satisfying the 9 hours time difference and taken from one of these intervals:

Sydney: 4:30 PM – 6:00 PM; Berlin: 7:30 AM – 9:00 AM

OR

Sydney: 7:00 AM – 8:00 AM; Berlin: 10:00 PM – 11:00 PM

- Sydney 17:00, Berlin 8:00.

Note: If an interval is given, the entire interval must satisfy the constraints. Also, if morning (AM) or evening (PM) is not specified, but the times could otherwise be regarded as correct, the response should be given the benefit of the doubt, and counted as correct.

Answering this question correctly corresponds to a difficulty of 636 score points on the PISA mathematics scale. Across OECD countries, 29% of students answered correctly. To answer the question correctly students have to draw on skills from the reflection competency cluster.

EXCHANGE RATE SCORING 12.1

Full credit: 12 600 ZAR (unit not required).

Answering this question correctly corresponds to a difficulty of 406 score points on the PISA mathematics scale. Across OECD countries, 80% of students answered correctly. To answer the question correctly students have to draw on skills from the reproduction competency cluster.

EXCHANGE RATE SCORING 12.2

Full credit: 975 SGD (unit not required).

Answering this question correctly corresponds to a difficulty of 439 score points on the PISA mathematics scale. Across OECD countries, 74% of students answered correctly. To answer the question correctly students have to draw on skills from the reproduction competency cluster.

EXCHANGE RATE SCORING 12.3

Full credit: 'Yes', with adequate explanation.

- Yes, by the lower exchange rate (for 1 SGD) Mei-Ling will get more Singapore dollars for her South African rand.
- Yes, 4.2 ZAR for one dollar would have resulted in 929 ZAR. *[Note: student wrote ZAR instead of SGD, but clearly the correct calculation and comparison have been carried out and this error can be ignored]*
- Yes, because she received 4.2 ZAR for 1 SGD, and now she has to pay only 4.0 ZAR to get 1 SGD.
- Yes, because it is 0.2 ZAR cheaper for every SGD.
- Yes, because when you divide by 4.2 the outcome is smaller than when you divide by 4.
- Yes, it was in her favour because if it didn't go down she would have got about $50 less.

Answering this question correctly corresponds to a difficulty of 586 score points on the PISA mathematics scale. Across OECD countries, 40% of students answered correctly. To answer the question correctly students have to draw on skills from the reflection competency cluster.

EXPORTS SCORING 13.1

Full credit: 27.1 million zeds or 27 100 000 zeds or 27.1 (unit not required).

Answering this question correctly corresponds to a difficulty of 427 score points on the PISA mathematics scale. Across OECD countries, 79% of students answered correctly. To answer the question correctly students have to draw on skills from the reproduction competency cluster.

EXPORTS SCORING 13.2

Full credit: E. 3.8 million zeds.

Answering this question correctly corresponds to a difficulty of 565 score points on the PISA mathematics scale. Across OECD countries, 48% of students answered correctly. To answer the question correctly students have to draw on skills from the connections competency cluster.

COLOURED CANDIES SCORING 14.1

Full credit: B. 20%.

Answering this question correctly corresponds to a difficulty of 549 score points on the PISA mathematics scale. Across OECD countries, 50% of students answered correctly. To answer the question correctly students have to draw on skills from the reproduction competency cluster.

SCIENCE TESTS SCORING 15.1

Full credit: 64.

Answering this question correctly corresponds to a difficulty of 556 score points on the PISA mathematics scale. Across OECD countries, 47% of students answered correctly. To answer the question correctly students have to draw on skills from the reproduction competency cluster.

BOOKSHELVES SCORING 16.1

Full credit: 5.

Answering this question correctly corresponds to a difficulty of 499 score points on the PISA mathematics scale. Across OECD countries, 61% of students answered correctly. To answer the question correctly students have to draw on skills from the connections competency cluster.

LITTER SCORING 17.1

Full credit: Reason focuses on big variance in data.

- The difference in the lengths of the bars of the bar graph would be too big.
- If you make a bar with length 10 centimetres for polystyrene, the one for cardboard boxes would be 0.05 centimetres.

OR

Reason focuses on the variability of the data for some categories.

- The length of the bar for "polystyrene cups" is undetermined.
- You cannot make one bar for 1–3 years or one bar for 20–25 years.

Answering this question correctly corresponds to a difficulty of 551 score points on the PISA mathematics scale. Across OECD countries, 52% of students answered correctly. To answer the question correctly students have to draw on skills from the reflection competency cluster.

EARTHQUAKE SCORING 18.1

Full credit: C. The likelihood that there will be an earthquake in Zed City at some time during the next 20 years is higher than the likelihood of no earthquake.

Answering this question correctly corresponds to a difficulty of 557 score points on the PISA mathematics scale. Across OECD countries, 46% of students answered correctly. To answer the question correctly students have to draw on skills from the reflection competency cluster.

CHOICES SCORING 19.1

Full credit: 6.

Answering this question correctly corresponds to a difficulty of 559 score points on the PISA mathematics scale. Across OECD countries, 49% of students answered correctly. To answer the question correctly students have to draw on skills from the connections competency cluster.

TEST SCORES SCORING 20.1

Full credit: One valid argument is given. Valid arguments could relate to the number of students passing, the disproportionate influence of the outlier, or the number of students with scores in the highest level.

- More students in Group A than in Group B passed the test.
- If you ignore the weakest Group A student, the students in Group A do better than those in Group B.
- More Group A students than Group B students scored 80 or over.

Answering this question correctly corresponds to a difficulty of 620 score points on the PISA mathematics scale. Across OECD countries, 32% of students answered correctly. To answer the question correctly students have to draw on skills from the connections competency cluster.

SKATEBOARD SCORING 21.1

Full credit: Both the minimum (80) and the maximum (137) correct.

Partial credit: Only the minimum (80) correct or only the maximum (137) correct.

Answering this question correctly corresponds to a difficulty of 496 score points on the PISA mathematics scale. Giving a partially correct answer corresponds to a difficulty of 464 score points on the mathematics scale. Across OECD countries, 72% of students answered correctly. To answer the question correctly students have to draw on skills from the reproduction competency cluster.

SKATEBOARD SCORING 21.2

Full credit: D. 12.

Answering this question correctly corresponds to a difficulty of 570 score points on the PISA mathematics scale. Across OECD countries, 46% of students answered correctly. To answer the question correctly students have to draw on skills from the reproduction competency cluster.

SKATEBOARD SCORING 21.3

Full credit: 65 zeds on a deck, 14 on wheels, 16 on trucks and 20 on hardware.

Answering this question correctly corresponds to a difficulty of 554 score points on the PISA mathematics scale. Across OECD countries, 50% of students answered correctly. To answer the question correctly students have to draw on skills from the connections competency cluster.

STAIRCASE SCORING 22.1

Full credit: 18.

Answering this question correctly corresponds to a difficulty of 421 score points on the PISA mathematics scale. Across OECD countries, 78% of students answered correctly. To answer the question correctly students have to draw on skills from the reproduction competency cluster.

NUMBER CUBES SCORING 23.1

Full credit: No, Yes, Yes, No, in that order.

Answering this question correctly corresponds to a difficulty of 503 score points on the PISA mathematics scale. Across OECD countries, 63% of students answered correctly. To answer the question correctly students have to draw on skills from the connections competency cluster.

SUPPORT FOR THE PRESIDENT SCORING 24.1

Full credit: Newspaper 3. The poll is more recent, with larger sample size, a random selection of the sample, and only voters were asked. (Give at least two reasons). Additional information (including irrelevant or incorrect information) should be ignored.

- Newspaper 3, because they have selected more citizens randomly with voting rights.
- Newspaper 3 because it has asked 1000 people, randomly selected, and the date is closer to the election date so the voters have less time to change their mind.
- Newspaper 3 because they were randomly selected and they had voting rights.

- Newspaper 3 because it surveyed more people closer to the date.
- Newspaper 3 because the 1000 people were randomly selected.

Answering this question correctly corresponds to a difficulty of 615 score points on the PISA mathematics scale. Across OECD countries, 36% of students answered correctly. To answer the question correctly students have to draw on skills from the connections competency cluster.

THE BEST CAR SCORING 25.1

Full credit: 15 points.

Answering this question correctly corresponds to a difficulty of 447 score points on the PISA mathematics scale. Across OECD countries, 73% of students answered correctly. To answer the question correctly students have to draw on skills from the reproduction competency cluster.

THE BEST CAR SCORING 25.2

Full credit: Correct rule that will make "Ca" the winner.

Answering this question correctly corresponds to a difficulty of 657 score points on the PISA mathematics scale. Across OECD countries, 25% of students answered correctly. To answer the question correctly students have to draw on skills from the reflection competency cluster.

STEP PATTERN SCORING 26.1

Full credit: 10.

Answering this question correctly corresponds to a difficulty of 484 score points on the PISA mathematics scale. Across OECD countries, 66% of students answered correctly. To answer the question correctly students have to draw on skills from the reproduction competency cluster.

LICHEN SCORING 27.1

Full credit: 14mm (units not required). Full credit should be given as long as the correct answer is 14 whether working out is shown or not.

$d = 7.0 \times \sqrt{16-12}$

$d = 14$

14mm

14

$d = 7.0 \times \sqrt{16-12}$

$d = 7.0 \times \sqrt{4}$

$d = 14$ *years*

(Note that here the calculations are all correct, but the unit is wrong. We will assume for now that it is the slip of the pen)

Partial credit: Partial responses including:

- Correct substitution of value in the formula but incorrect answer Or missing answer.
- Incomplete answers (eg, $7\sqrt{4}$).

$d = 7.0 \times \sqrt{16 - 12}$ (wrong answer but correct substitution)

$d = 16$

$d = 7.0 \times \sqrt{16 - 12}$ (incomplete answer)

$d = 7\sqrt{4}$

To answer the question correctly students have to draw on skills from the reproduction competency cluster.

LICHEN SCORING 27.2

Full credit: 37 years (unit not required) whether working out is shown or not.

$35 = 7\times \sqrt{t - 12}$

$5 = \sqrt{t - 12}$

$25 = t - 12$

$t = 37$

$35 \div 7 = 5$

$7 \times 5 = 7 \times \sqrt{25}$

$= 7 \times \sqrt{25 + 12}$

$= 7 \times 37$

$\therefore$ 37 *years*

35/7 = 5

$5^2 = 25$

25 + 12 = 37

(Strictly incorrect algebraic representation, but we know what the student is trying to do)

t = 15 d = 12.1

t = 25 d = 25.2

t = 40 d = 37.0

t = 35 d = 33.6

t = 37 d = 35

So 37 years after the ice disappeared

(Note that here the answer 37 is embedded in an equation that is correct)

$756 = 35 = 7 \times \sqrt{(37 - 12)} = 7 \times \sqrt{25} = 7 \times 5 = 35$

Partial credit: Correct substitution of values in the formula but incorrect answer or missing answer.

OR

36 years or 38 years. (Students may arrive at these answers using the trial and error method)

$35 = 7 \times \sqrt{t-12}$	$35 = 7\times \sqrt{t-12}$	$35 = 7\times \sqrt{t-12}$
$35^2 = 7^2 \times t - 12$	$5 = \sqrt{t-12}$	$5 = \sqrt{t-12}$
$49t = 1237$	$25 = t - 12$	$5 = \sqrt{t} - \sqrt{12}$
$t = 25$	$t = 13$	*Too hard!*

To answer the question correctly students have to draw on skills from the connections competency cluster

COINS SCORING 28.1

Full credit: 15 – 20 – 26 – 34 – 45. It is possible that the response could be presented as actual drawings of the coins of the correct diameters. This should be coded as 1 as well.

Partial credit: Gives a set of coins that satisfy the three criteria, but not the set that contains as many coins as possible, eg., 15 – 21 – 29 – 39, or 15 – 30 – 45

OR

The first three diameters correct, the last two incorrect (15 – 20 – 26 -)

OR

The first four diameters correct, the last one incorrect (15 – 20 – 26 – 34 -)

To answer the question correctly students have to draw on skills from the connections competency cluster.

PIZZAS SCORING 29.1

Full credit: Gives general reasoning that the surface area of pizza increases more rapidly than the price of pizza to conclude that the larger pizza is better value.

- The diameter of the pizzas is the same number as their price, but the amount of pizza you get is found using diameter$_2$, so you will get more pizza per zeds from the larger one

Partial credit: Calculates the area and amount per zed for each pizza to conclude that the larger pizza is better value.

- Area of smaller pizza is $0.25 \times \pi \times 30 \times 30 = 225\pi$; amount per zed is 23.6 cm^2 area of larger pizza is $0.25 \times \pi \times 40 \times 40 = 400\pi$; amount per zed is 31.4 cm^2 so larger pizza is better value

To answer the question correctly students have to draw on skills from the connections competency cluster.

SHAPES SCORING 30.1

Full credit: Shape B, supported with plausible reasoning.

- It's the largest area because the others will fit inside it.
- B. It doesn't have indents in it which decreases the area. A and C have gaps.
- B, because it's a full circle, and the others are like circles with bits taken out.
- B, because it has no open areas: 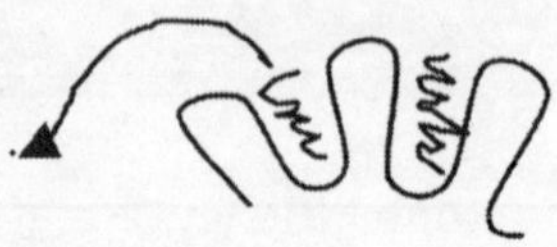

To answer the question correctly students have to draw on skills from the reproduction competency cluster.

SHAPES SCORING 30.2

Full credit: Reasonable method:

- Draw a grid of squares over the shape and count the squares that are more than half filled by the shape.
- Cut the arms off the shape and rearrange the pieces so that they fill a square then measure the side of the square.
- Build a 3D model based on the shape and fill it with water. Measure the amount of water used and the depth of the water in the model. Derive the area from the information.
- You could fill the shape with lots of circles, squares and other basic shapes so there is not a gap. Work out the area of all of the shapes and add together.
- Redraw the shape onto graph paper and count all of the squares it takes up.
- Drawing and counting equal size boxes. Smaller boxes = better accuracy *(Here the student's description is brief, but we will be lenient about student's writing skills and regard the method offered by the student as correct)*
- Make it into a 3D model and filling it with exactly 1cm of water and then measure the volume of water required to fill it up.

Partial credit:

- The student suggests to find the area of the circle and subtract the area of the cut out pieces. However, the student does not mention about how to find out the area of the cut out pieces.
- Add up the area of each individual arm of the shape

- Find the area of B then find the areas of the cut out pieces and subtract them from the main area.
- Minus the shape from the circle
- Add up the area of each individual piece e.g.,

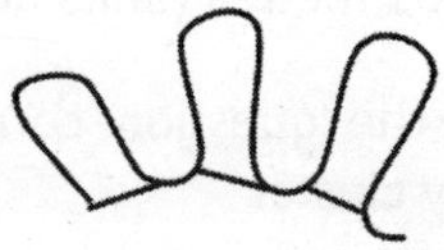

- Use a shape like that and pour a liquid into it.
- Use graph
- Half of the area of shape B
- Figure out how many are in one little leg things and times it by 8.

To answer the question correctly students have to draw on skills from the connections competency cluster.

SHAPES SCORING 30.3

Full credit: Reasonable method:

- Lay a piece of string over the outline of the shape then measure the length of string used.
- Cut the shape up into short, nearly straight pieces and join them together in a line, then measure the length of the line.
- Measure the length of some of the arms to find an average arm length then multiply by 8 (number of arms) X 2.
- Wool or string!!!

  (Here although the answer is brief, the student did offer a METHOD for measuring the perimeter)
- Cut the side of the shape into sections. Measure each then add them together. (Here the student did not explicitly say that each section needs to be approximately straight, but we will give the benefit of the doubt, that is, by offering the METHOD of cutting the shape into pieces, each piece is assumed to be easily measurable)

To answer the question correctly students have to draw on skills from the connections competency cluster.

BRAKING SCORING 31.1

Full credit: 22.9 metres (units not required)

To answer the question correctly students have to draw on skills from the connections competency cluster.

BRAKING SCORING 31.2

Full credit: 101 metres (units not required)

To answer the question correctly students have to draw on skills from the connections competency cluster

BRAKING SCORING 31.3

Full credit: 5.84 seconds (units not required)

To answer the question correctly students have to draw on skills from the connections competency cluster.

BRAKING SCORING 31.4

Full credit: 78.1 metres (units not required)

To answer the question correctly students have to draw on skills from the connections competency cluster.

BRAKING SCORING 31.5

Full credit: 90 kmph (units not necessary)

To answer the question correctly students have to draw on skills from the connections competency cluster.

PATIO SCORING 32.1

Full credit: 1275, 1276 or 1275.75 (unit not required).

- 5.25 X 3 = 15.75 X 81 = 1276

Partial credit:

15.75 (units not required)

OR

1215 bricks for 5m X 3m

(This score is used for students who are able to calculate the number of bricks for an integer number of square metres, but not for fractions of square metres. See example response.)

OR

Error in calculating the area, but multiplied by 81 correctly

OR

Rounded off the area and then multiplied by 81 correctly

- 5.25 X 3 = 15.75
- 15.75 X 81 = 9000
- 81 X 15 = 1215; 1215 + 21 = 1236
- 5.25 X 3.0 = 15.75 m^2; so 15.75 X 1275.75 = 1376 bricks.

  (Here the student got the first part right, but the second part wrong. Give credit for the first part and ignore the second part. So score as 1)

To answer the question correctly students have to draw on skills from the connections competency cluster.

DRUG CONCENTRATIONS SCORING 33.1

Full credit: All three table entries correct.

Time	0800	0900	1000	1100
Penicillin (mg)	300	180	108	64.8 or 65

Partial credit: One or two table entries correct.

To answer the question correctly students have to draw on skills from the connections competency cluster.

DRUG CONCENTRATIONS SCORING 33.2

Full credit: D. 32mg.

To answer the question correctly students have to draw on skills from the reproduction competency cluster.

DRUG CONCENTRATIONS SCORING 33.3

Full credit: C. 40%.

To answer the question correctly students have to draw on skills from the connections competency cluster.

BUILDING BLOCKS SCORING 34.1

Full credit: 12 cubes.

To answer the question correctly students have to draw on skills from the reproduction competency cluster.

BUILDING BLOCKS SCORING 34.2

Full credit: 27 cubes.

To answer the question correctly students have to draw on skills from the reproduction competency cluster.

BUILDING BLOCKS SCORING 34.3

Full credit: 26 cubes.

To answer the question correctly students have to draw on skills from the connections competency cluster.

BUILDING BLOCKS SCORING 34.4

Full credit: 96 cubes.

To answer the question correctly students have to draw on skills from the reflection competency cluster.

REACTION TIME SCORING 35.1

Full credit:

Medal	Lane	Reaction time (secs)	Final time (secs)
GOLD	3	0.197	9.87
SILVER	2	0.136	9.99
BRONZE	6	0.216	10.8

To answer the question correctly students have to draw on skills from the reproduction competency cluster.

REACTION TIME SCORING 35.2

Full credit: Yes, with adequate explanation.

- Yes. If he had a reaction time of 0.05 sec faster, he would have equalled second place.

- Yes, he would have a chance to win the Silver medal if his reaction time was less than or equal to 0.166 sec.
- Yes, with the fastest possible reaction time he would have done a 9.93 which is good enough for silver medal.

To answer the question correctly students have to draw on skills from the connections competency cluster.

WATER TANK SCORING 36.1

Full credit: B.

To answer the question correctly students have to draw on skills from the connections competency cluster.

SPRING FAIR SCORING 37.1

Full credit: B. Not very likely.

To answer the question correctly students have to draw on skills from the connections competency cluster.

SWING SCORING 38.1

Full credit: A.

To answer the question correctly students have to draw on skills from the connections competency cluster.

STUDENT HEIGHTS SCORING 39.1

Full credit: 'No' for all conclusions.

To answer the question correctly students have to draw on skills from the reflection competency cluster.

PAYMENTS BY AREA SCORING 40.1

Full credit: Incorrect, Correct, Incorrect, Correct, in that order.

To answer the question correctly students have to draw on skills from the connections competency cluster.

PAYMENTS BY AREA SCORING 40.2

Full credit: 102,000 zeds, with or without the calculation shown, and unit not required.

- Apartment 2: 102 000 zeds.

  $Apt-2: \frac{85}{250} \times 300000 = 102000\ zeds$

  $= \frac{300000}{250}$ 1200 *zeds* for each square metre, so Apartment 2 is 102 000.

Partial credit: Correct method, but minor computational error/s.

- Apt – 2: $\frac{85}{250} \times 300000 = 10200$ zeds

To answer the question correctly students have to draw on skills from the connections competency cluster.

SHOES FOR KIDS SCORING 41.1

Full credit: 26.

To answer the question correctly students have to draw on skills from the reproduction competency cluster.

TABLE TENNIS TOURN SCORING 42.1

Full credit: Four remaining matches correctly described and distributed over rounds 2 and 3.

- E.g.

	Practice Table 1	Practice Table 2
Round 1	Teun - Riek	Bep - Dirk
Round 2	Teun - Bep	Riek – Dirk
Round 3	Teun - Dirk	Riek - Bep

To answer the question correctly students have to draw on skills from the reproduction competency cluster.

LIGHTHOUSE SCORING 43.1

Full credit: C. 5 seconds.

To answer the question correctly students have to draw on skills from the connections competency cluster.

LIGHTHOUSE SCORING 43.2

Full credit: D. 24.

To answer the question correctly students have to draw on skills from the connections competency cluster.

LIGHTHOUSE SCORING 43.3

Full credit: The graph shows a pattern of light and dark with flashes for 3 seconds in every 6 seconds, and with a period of 6 seconds. This can be done in the following ways:

- 1 one-second flash and a two-second flash (and this can be shown in several ways),

OR

- 1 three-second flash (which can be shown in four different ways).
- If two periods are shown, the pattern must be identical for each period.

Partial credit: The graph shows a pattern of light and dark with flashes for 3 seconds in every 6 seconds, but the period is not 6 seconds. If two periods are shown, the pattern must be identical for each period.

- Three one-second flashes, alternating with 3 one-second dark periods.

To answer the question correctly students have to draw on skills from the reflection competency cluster.

DECREASING CO_2 LEVELS SCORING 44.1

Full credit: Correct subtraction, and correct calculation of percentage.

- $6727 - 6049 = 678, \frac{678}{6049} \times 100\% = 11\%$

Partial credit: Subtraction error and percentage calculation correct, or subtraction correct but dividing by 6727.

$\frac{6049}{6727} \times 100 = 89.9\%$, and $100 - 89.9 = 10.1\%$.

To answer the question correctly students have to draw on skills from the connections competency cluster.

DECREASING CO_2 LEVELS SCORING 44.2

Full credit: No, with correct argumentation.

- No, other countries from the EU can have increases e.g. the Netherlands so the total decrease in the EU can be smaller than the decrease in Germany.

To answer the question correctly students have to draw on skills from the connections competency cluster.

DECREASING CO_2 LEVELS SCORING 44.3

Full credit: Response identifies both mathematical approaches (the largest absolute increase and the largest relative increase), and names the USA and Australia.

- USA has the largest increase in millions of tons, and Australia has the largest increase in percentage.

Partial credit: Response identifies or refers to both the largest absolute increase and the largest relative increase, but the countries are not identified, or the wrong countries are named.

- Russia had the biggest increase in the amount of CO_2 (1078 tons), but Australia had the biggest percentage increase (15%).

To answer the question correctly students have to draw on skills from the reflection competency cluster.

TWISTED BUILDING SCORING 45.1

Full credit: Accept answers from 50 to 90 metres if a correct explanation is given.

- One floor of the building has a height of about 2.5 meters. There is some extra room between floors. Therefore an estimate is 21 x 3 = 63 metres.
- Allow 4 m for each story, so 20 of these gives 80 m, plus 10 m for the ground floor, so a total of 90 m.

Partial credit: Correct calculation method and explanation, but using 20 stories instead of 21.

- Each apartment could be 3.5 metres high, 20 stories of 3.5 metres gives a total height of 70 m.

To answer the question correctly students have to draw on skills from the connections competency cluster.

TWISTED BUILDING SCORING 45.2

Full credit: C. From the East.

To answer the question correctly students have to draw on skills from the connections competency cluster.

TWISTED BUILDING SCORING 45.3

Full credit: D. From the South East.

To answer the question correctly students have to draw on skills from the connections competency cluster.

TWISTED BUILDING SCORING 45.4

Full credit: A correct drawing, meaning correct rotation point and anti-clockwise rotation. Accept angles from 40° to 50°.

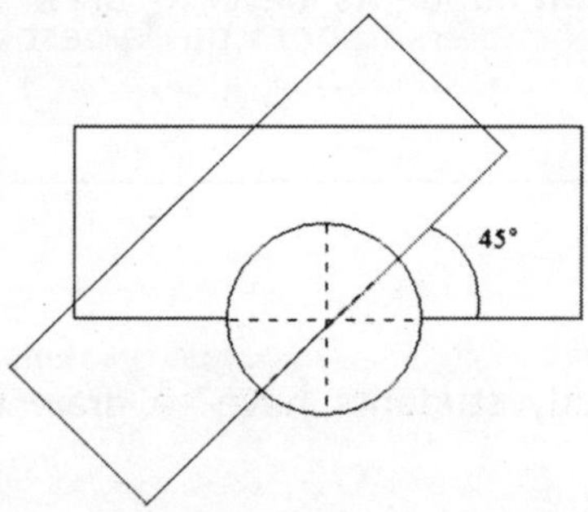

Partial credit: One of the rotation angle, the rotation point, or the rotation direction incorrect.

To answer the question correctly students have to draw on skills from the connections competency cluster.

HEARTBEAT SCORING 46.1

Full credit: Accept 41, or 40.

- 220 – *age* = 208 – 0.7 × *age* results in *age* = 40, so people above 40 will have a higher recommended maximum heart rate under the new formula.

To answer the question correctly students have to draw on skills from the connections competency cluster.

HEARTBEAT SCORING 46.2

Full credit: Any formula that is the equivalent of multiplying the formula for recommended maximum heart rate by 80%.

- heart rate = 166 – 0.56 x age.
- heart rate = 166 – 0.6 x age.
- h = 166 – 0.56 x a.

- h = 166 – 0.6 x a.
- heart rate = (208 – 0.7age) x 0.8.

To answer the question correctly students have to draw on skills from the connections competency cluster.

SPACE FLIGHT SCORING 47.1

Full credit: C. 11 000.

To answer the question correctly students have to draw on skills from the connections competency cluster.

ROCK CONCERT SCORING 48.1

Full credit: C. 20 000.

To answer the question correctly students have to draw on skills from the connections competency cluster.

MOVING WALKWAYS SCORING 49.1

Full credit: Accept a line below the two lines, but it must be closer to the line of "A person walking on the ground" than to the baseline.

To answer the question correctly students have to draw on skills from the reflection competency cluster.

POSTAL CHARGES SCORING 50.1

Full credit: C.

To answer the question correctly students have to draw on skills from the connections competency cluster.

POSTAL CHARGES SCORING 50.2

Full credit: It will be cheaper to send the items as two separate parcels. The cost will be 1.71 zeds for two separate parcels, and 1.75 zeds for one single parcel containing both items.

To answer the question correctly students have to draw on skills from the connections competency cluster.

CHAPTER 4

SCIENCE SAMPLE TASKS

SEMMELWEIS' DIARY SCORING 1.1

Full credit: Responses that refer to the difference between the numbers of deaths (per 100 deliveries) in both wards, such as:

- Due to the fact that the first ward had a high rate of women dying compared to women in the second ward, obviously shows that it had nothing to do with earthquakes.
- Not as many people died in ward 2 so an earthquake couldn't have occurred without causing the same number of deaths in each ward.
- Because the second ward isn't as high, maybe it had something to do with ward 1.
- It is unlikely that earthquakes cause the fever since death rates are so different for the two wards.

Partial credit:

- Responses that refer to the fact that earthquakes don't occur frequently, for example:
- It would be unlikely to be caused by earthquakes because earthquakes wouldn't happen all the time.
- Responses that refer to the fact that earthquakes also influence people outside the wards, for example:
- If there were an earthquake, women from outside the hospital would have got puerperal fever as well.
- If an earthquake were the reason, the whole world would get puerperal fever each time an earthquake occurs (not only the wards 1 and 2).
- Responses that refer to the thought that when earthquakes occur, men don't get puerperal fever for example:
- If a man were in the hospital and an earthquake came, he didn't get puerperal fever, so earthquakes cannot be the cause.
- Because girls get it and not men.

Answering this question correctly corresponds to a difficulty of 666 score points on the PISA 2000 science scale. 22% of students across OECD countries answered it correctly and 28% of students across OECD countries gave a partially correct answer. The question was part of the PISA 2000 scientific process drawing or evaluating conclusions.

SEMMELWEIS' DIARY SCORING 1.2

Full credit: A. Having students clean themselves after dissections should lead to a decrease of puerperal fever.

The difficulty of this question corresponds to 493 score points on the PISA 2000 science scale. On average across OECD countries, 64% of students gave the correct answer. This question falls into the PISA 2000 scientific process recognising questions.

SEMMELWEIS' DIARY SCORING 1.3

Full credit:

- Responses that refer to *killing* of *bacteria*.
  - Because with the heat many bacteria will die.
  - Bacteria will not stand the high temperature.
  - Bacteria will be burnt by the high temperature.
  - Bacteria will be cooked.
- Responses that refer to *killing* of microorganisms, germs or viruses.
  - Because high heat kills small organisms which cause disease.
  - It's too hot for germs to live.
- Responses that refer to the *removal* (not killing) of bacteria.
  - The bacteria will be gone.
  - The number of bacteria will decrease.
  - You wash the bacteria away at high temperatures.
  - Because you won't have the germ on your body.
- Responses that refer to the *removal* (not killing) of microorganisms, germs or viruses or to the sterilisation of the sheets.

The difficulty of this question corresponds to 467 score points on the PISA 2000 science scale. 68% of students across OECD countries gave the correct answer. The question falls into the scientific process demonstrating knowledge and understanding.

SEMMELWEIS' DIARY SCORING 1.4

Full credit: B. Bacteria become resistant to antibiotics.

The difficulty of this question corresponds to 508 score points on the PISA 2000 science scale. 60% of students across OECD countries gave the correct answer. The question is part of the process category demonstrating knowledge and understanding.

OZONE SCORING 2.1

Full credit: Answers which mention the following three aspects:

First aspect: an oxygen molecule or some oxygen molecules (each consisting of two oxygen atoms) are split into oxygen atoms (picture 1).

- The splitting should be described using the correct words (see lines 5 and 6) for O (atom or atoms) and O_2 (molecule or molecules).
- If O and/or O_2 have been described only as "particles" or "small parts" no credit should be given for this aspect.

Second aspect: the splitting (of oxygen molecules) takes place under the influence of sunlight (picture 1).

- The sun's influence should be related to the splitting of O_2 (an oxygen molecule or oxygen molecules).
- If the sun's influence is related to the forming of an ozone molecule from an oxygen atom and an oxygen molecule (pictures 2 and 3) no credit should be given for this second aspect.

Note: Aspects 1 and 2 may typically be given in the one sentence.

Third aspect: the oxygen atoms combine with other oxygen molecules to form ozone molecules (pictures 2 and 3).

- Credit (one point) should be given for this aspect if the answer contains any description of an O combining with an O_2. If the formation of O_3 is described as the combining of (three, separate) O atoms, credit should not be given for this third aspect.
- If O_3 is not described as a molecule or molecules but for example as "a group of atoms" this can be tolerated for the third aspect.

Examples of such answers:

- When the sun shines on the O_2 molecule the two atoms separate. The two O atoms look for other O_2 molecules to join with. When the O_1 and O_2 join they form O_3, which is ozone.
- The strip illustrates the formation of ozone. If an oxygen molecule is affected by the sun, it breaks into two separate atoms. These separate atoms, O, float around looking for a molecule to link up to; they link up to existing O_2 molecules and form an O_3 molecule, as three atoms are now joined together; O_3 forms ozone.

- The little guys are O, or oxygen atoms. When two are joined they make O_2 or oxygen molecules. The sun causes these to decompose into oxygen again. The O_2 atoms then bond with O_2 molecules creating O_3, which is ozone . *[Note: this answer can be regarded as correct. There is only one slip of the pen ("O_2 atoms" after having mentioned "oxygen atoms" previously).]*

Partial credit:

- Answers which correctly mention only the first and second aspects. For example:
  - The sun decomposes the oxygen molecules into single atoms. The atoms fuse into groups. The atoms form groups of 3 atoms together.
- Answers which correctly mention only the first and third aspects. For example:
  - Each of the little fellows stand for one atom of oxygen. O is one oxygen atom, O_2 is an oxygen molecule and O_3 is a group of atoms all joined together. The processes shown are one pair of oxygen atoms (O_2) getting split and then each joining with 2 other pairs forming two groups of 3 (O_3).
  - The little fellows are oxygen atoms. O_2 means one oxygen molecule (like a pair of little fellows holding hands) and O_3 means three oxygen atoms. The two oxygen atoms of one pair break apart and one joins each of the other pairs and out of the three pairs, two sets of three oxygen olecules (O_3) are formed.
- Answers which correctly mention only the second and third aspects. For example:
  - The oxygen is broken up by the sun's radiation. It splits in half. The two sides go and join other oxygen "particles" forming ozone.
  - Most of the time in pure oxygen (O_2) environments oxygen comes in pairs of 2 so there are 3 pairs of 2. 1 pair is getting too hot and they fly apart going into another pair making O_3 instead of O_2. *[Note: Although "one pair is getting too hot" is not a very good description for the sun's influence, credit should be given for the second aspect; the third aspect can also be regarded as correct.]*
- Answers which correctly mention the first aspect only. For example:
  - Oxygen molecules are breaking down. They form O atoms. And sometimes there are ozone molecules. The ozone layer remains the same because new molecules are formed and others die.
- Answers which correctly mention only the second aspect. For example:
  - O represents an oxygen molecule, O_2 = oxygen, O_3 = ozone. Sometimes both oxygen molecules, joining each other, are separated by the sun. The single molecules join another pair and form ozone (O_3).
- Answers which correctly mention only the third aspect. For example:
  - <u>The 'O' (oxygen) molecules are forced to bond with O_2 (2 x oxygen molecules) to form O_3 (3 x oxygen molecules)</u>, by the heat of the sun. *[Note: the underlined part of the answer shows the third aspect. No credit can be given for the second aspect, because the sun is*

not involved in the formation of ozone from $O + O_2$ but only in breaking down bonds in O_2.]

Answering this question correctly corresponds to a difficulty of 682 score points on the PISA 2000 science scale. Giving a partially correct answer corresponds to a difficulty of 628 score points on the PISA 2000 science scale. Across OECD countries, 28% of students answered correctly. The question assesses student's ability to communicate valid conclusions from evidence/data.

OZONE SCORING 2.2

Full credit: B. Bad. It is formed in the troposphere.

Answering this question correctly corresponds to a difficulty of 642 score points on the PISA 2000 science scale. Across OECD countries, 35% of students answered correctly. To answer this question, students need to critically evaluate scientific evidence/data.

OZONE SCORING 2.3

Full credit: Answers which refer to skin cancer. For example:

- Skin cancer.
- Melonoma. *[Note: this answer can be regarded as correct, despite the fact that it has a spelling mistake.]*

Answering this question correctly corresponds to a difficulty of 547 score points on the PISA 2000 science scale. Across OECD countries, 54% of students answered correctly. To answer this question, students have to apply scientific knowledge to the presented situation.

DAYLIGHT SCORING 3.1

Full credit: A. The Earth rotates on its axis.

Answering this question correctly corresponds to a difficulty of 592 score points on the PISA 2003 science scale. Across OECD countries, 43% of students answered correctly. This question assesses the process describing, explaining and predicting scientific phenomena.

DAYLIGHT SCORING 3.2

The important features when marking this question are:

- The Earth's axis is drawn tilted towards the Sun within the range 10° and 45° from vertical for credit: Outside of 10° and 45° to vertical range: no credit.
- The presence or absence of clearly labelled Northern and Southern Hemispheres, or one Hemisphere only labelled, the other implied.

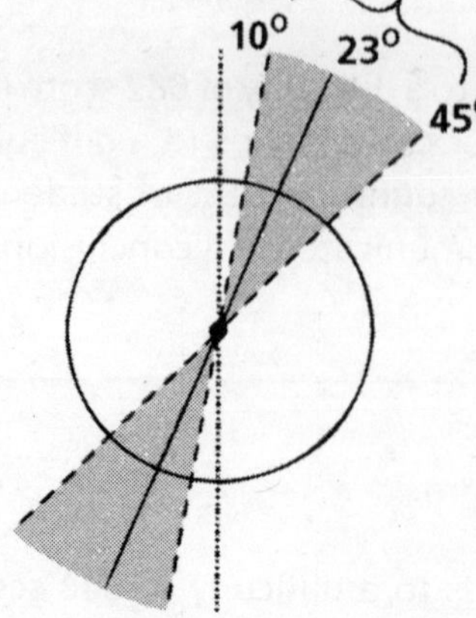

- The equator is drawn at a tilt towards the Sun within the range 10° and 45° above horizontal for credit: refer to the following diagram: The equator may be drawn as an elliptical line or straight line.

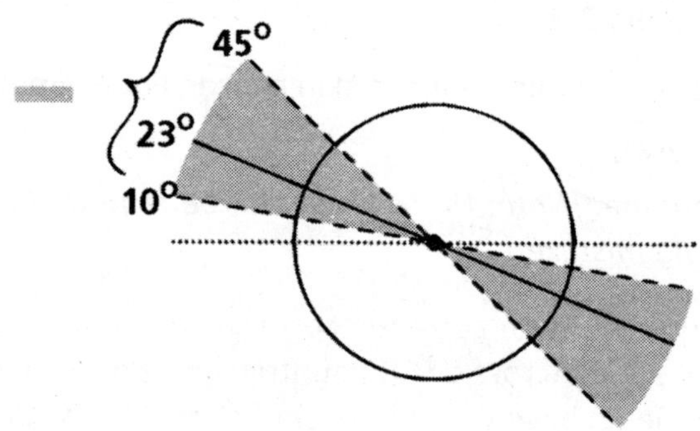

- Outside of 10° and 45° to horizontal range: no credit.

Full credit:

Diagram with Equator tilted towards the Sun at an angle between 10° and 45° and Earth's axis tilted towards the Sun within the range 10° and 45° from vertical, and the Northern and or Southern emispheres correctly labelled (or one only labelled, the other implied).

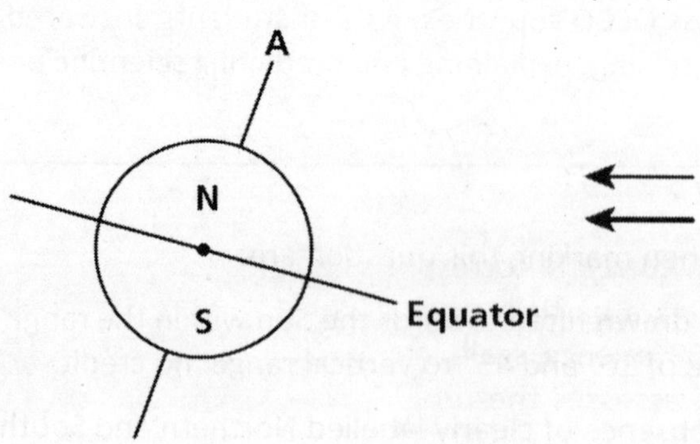

Partial credit:

Angle of tilt of axis between 10° and 45°, Northern and / or Southern Hemispheres correctly labelled (or one only labelled, the other implied), but angle of tilt of Equator not between 10° and 45°; or Equator missing.

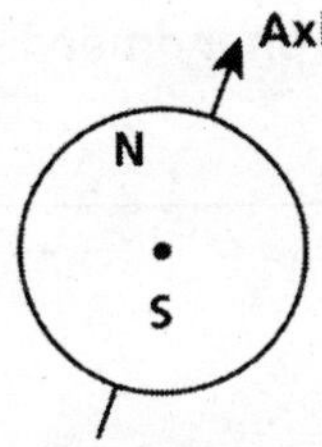

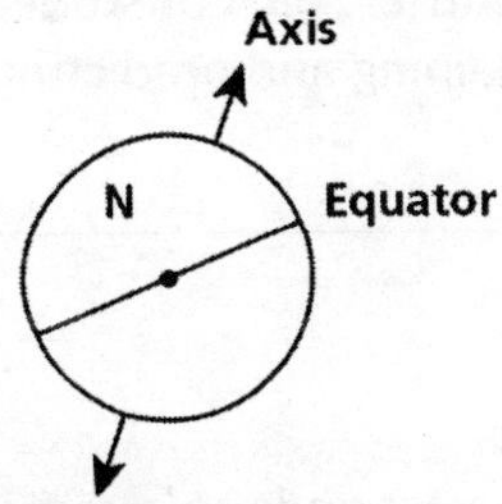

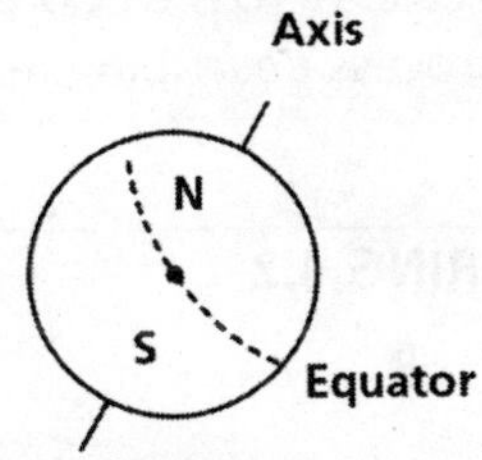

Angle of tilt of Equator between 10° and 45°, Northern and / or Southern Hemispheres correctly labelled (or one only labelled, the other implied), but angle of tilt of axis not between 10° and 45°; or axis missing.

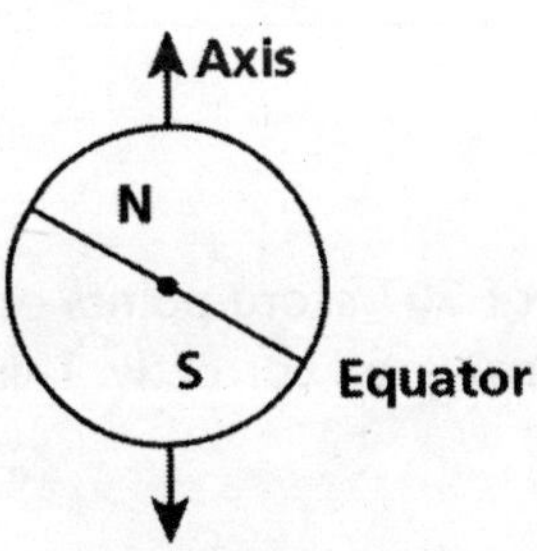

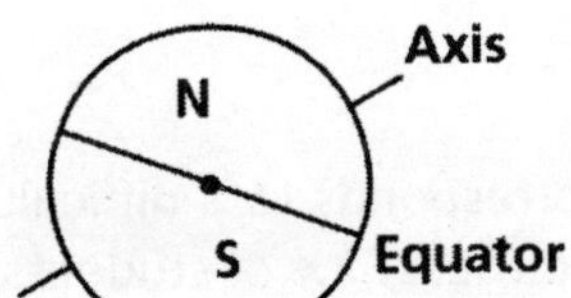

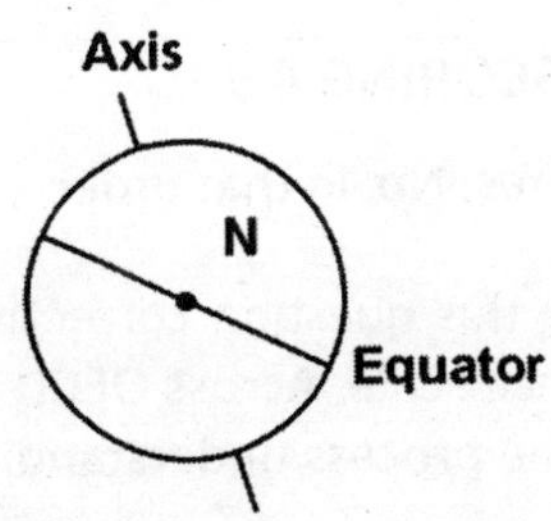

Angle of tilt of Equator between 10° and 45°, and angle of tilt of axis between 10° and 45°, but Northern and Southern Hemispheres not correctly labelled (or one only labelled, the other implied, or both missing).

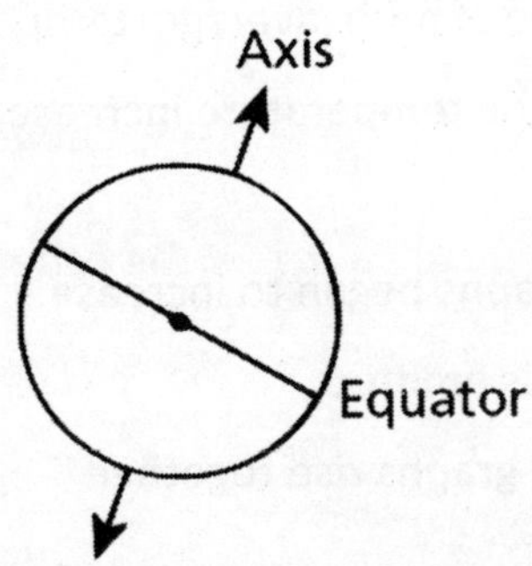

Answering this question correctly corresponds to a difficulty of 720 score points on the PISA 2003 science scale. Giving a partially correct answer corresponds to a difficulty of 667 score points on the PISA 2003 science scale. Across OECD countries, 19% of students answered correctly. This question assesses the process describing, explaining and predicting scientific phenomena.

CLONING SCORING 4.1

Full credit: A. Sheep 1.

Answering this question correctly corresponds to a difficulty of 494 score points on the PISA 2003 science scale. Across OECD countries, 65% of students answered correctly. This question assesses the process describing, explaining and predicting scientific phenomena.

CLONING SCORING 4.2

Full credit: A. a cell.

Answering this question correctly corresponds to a difficulty of 572 score points on the PISA 2003 science scale. Across OECD countries, 47% of students answered correctly. This question assesses the process describing, explaining and predicting scientific phenomena.

CLONING SCORING 4.3

Full credit: Yes, No, in that order.

Answering this question correctly corresponds to a difficulty of 507 score points on the PISA 2003 science scale. Across OECD countries, 62% of students answered correctly. This question assesses the process understanding scientific investigation.

GREENHOUSE SCORING 5.1

Full credit:

- Responses that refer to the increase of both (average) temperature and carbon dioxide emission.
    - As the emissions increased the temperature increased.
    - Both graphs are increasing.
    - Because in 1910 both the graphs began to increase.
    - Temperature is rising as CO_2 is emitted.
    - The information lines on the graphs rise together.
    - Everything is increasing.
    - The more CO_2 emission, the higher the temperature.
- Responses that refer (in general terms) to a positive relationship between temperature and carbon dioxide emission.
    - The amount of CO_2 and average temperature of the Earth is directly proportional.

- They have a similar shape indicating a relationship.

Answering this question correctly corresponds to a difficulty of 529 score points on the PISA 2006 science scale. Across OECD countries, 54% of students answered correctly. This question assesses students' competencies in using scientific evidence.

GREENHOUSE SCORING 5.2

Full credit: Responses that refer to one particular part of the graphs in which the curves are not both descending or both climbing and gives the corresponding explanation, such as:

- In 1900–1910 (about) CO_2 was increasing, whilst the temperature was going down.
- In 1980–1983 carbon dioxide went down and the temperature rose.
- The temperature in the 1800's is much the same but the first graph keeps climbing.
- Between 1950 and 1980 the temperature didn't increase but the CO_2 did.
- From 1940 until 1975 the temperature stays about the same but the carbon dioxide emission shows a sharp rise.
- In 1940 the temperature is a lot higher than in 1920 and they have similar carbon dioxide emissions.

Partial credit:

- Responses that mention a correct period, without any explanation.
- Responses that mention only one particular year (not a period of time), with an acceptable explanation.
    - In 1980 the emissions were down but the temperature still rose.
- Responses that give an example that doesn't support André's conclusion but makes a mistake in mentioning the period. *[Note: There should be evidence of this mistake – e.g. an area clearly illustrating a correct answer is marked on the graph and then a mistake made in transferring this information to the text.]*
    - Between 1950 and 1960 the temperature decreased and the carbon dioxide emission increased.
- Responses that refer to differences between the two curves, without mentioning a specific period.
    - At some places the temperature rises even if the emission decreases.
    - Earlier there was little emission but nevertheless high temperature.
    - When there is a steady increase in graph 1, there isn't an increase in graph 2, it stays constant. *[Note: It stays constant "overall".]*

- Because at the start the temperature is still high where the carbon dioxide was very low.

- Responses that refer to an irregularity in one of the graphs.
  - It is about 1910 when the temperature had dropped and went on for a certain period of time.
  - In the second graph there is a decrease in temperature of the Earth's atmosphere just before 1910.
- Responses that indicate difference in the graphs, but explanation is poor.
- In the 1940's the heat was very high but the carbon dioxide very low.

Answering this question correctly corresponds to a difficulty of 659 score points on the PISA 2006 science scale. Giving a partially correct answer corresponds to a difficulty of 568 score points on the PISA 2000 science scale. Across OECD countries, 35% of students answered correctly. The question assesses students' competencies in using scientific evidence.

GREENHOUSE SCORING 5.3

Full credit:

- Responses that give a factor referring to the energy/radiation coming from the Sun.
  - The sun heating and maybe the earth changing position.
  - Energy reflected back from Earth. *[Assuming that by "Earth" the student means "the ground".]*
- Responses that give a factor referring to a natural component or a potential pollutant.
  - Water vapour in the air.
  - Clouds.
  - The things such as volcanic eruptions.
  - Atmospheric pollution (gas, fuel).
  - The amount of exhaust gas.
  - CFC's.
  - The number of cars.
  - Ozone (as a component of air).

Answering this question correctly corresponds to a difficulty of 709 score points on the PISA 2006 science scale. Across OECD countries, 19% of students answered correctly. The question assesses students' competencies in explaining phenomena scientifically.

CLOTHES SCORING 6.1

Full credit: Yes, Yes, Yes, No, in that order.

Answering this question correctly corresponds to a difficulty of 567 score points on the PISA 2006 science scale. Across OECD countries, 48% of students answered correctly. The question assesses students' competencies in identifying scientific issues.

CLOTHES SCORING 6.2

Full credit: A. Voltmeter.

Answering this question correctly corresponds to a difficulty of 399 score points on the PISA 2006 science scale. Across OECD countries, 79% of students answered correctly.

This question assesses students' competencies in explaining phenomena scientifically.

THE GRAND CANYON SCORING 7.1

Full credit: D. Freezing water expands in the rock cracks.

Answering this question correctly corresponds to a difficulty of 451 score points on the PISA 2006 science scale. Across OECD countries, 68% of students answered correctly. The question assesses students' competencies in explaining phenomena scientifically.

THE GRAND CANYON SCORING 7.2

Full credit: C. An ocean covered this area at that time and then receded later.

Answering this question correctly corresponds to a difficulty of 411 score points on the PISA 2006 science scale. Across OECD countries, 76% of students answered correctly. This question assesses students' competencies in explaining phenomena scientifically.

THE GRAND CANYON SCORING 7.3

Full credit: Yes, No in that order.

Answering this question correctly corresponds to a difficulty of 485 score points on the PISA 2006 science scale. Across OECD countries, 61% of students answered correctly. The question assesses students' competencies in identifying scientific issues.

SUNSCREENS SCORING 8.1

Full credit: D. Mineral oil and zinc oxide are both reference substances.

Answering this question correctly corresponds to a difficulty of 588 score points on the PISA 2006 science scale. Across OECD countries, 41% of students answered correctly. This question assesses students' competencies in identifying scientific issues.

SUNSCREENS SCORING 8.2

Full credit: A. How does the protection for each sunscreen compare with the others?

Answering this question correctly corresponds to a difficulty of 499 score points on the PISA 2006 science scale. Across OECD countries, 58% of students answered correctly. The question assesses students' competencies in identifying scientific issues.

SUNSCREENS SCORING 8.3

Full credit: D. To make the drops the same thickness.

Answering this question correctly corresponds to a difficulty of 574 score points on the PISA 2006 science scale. Across OECD countries, 43% of students answered correctly. The question assesses students' competencies in identifying scientific issues.

SUNSCREENS SCORING 8.4

Full credit: A. with explanation that the ZnO spot has stayed dark grey (because it blocks sunlight) and the M spot has gone white (because mineral oil absorbs very little sunlight), such as:

- A. ZnO has blocked the sunlight as it should and M has let it through.
- I chose A because the mineral oil needs to be the lightest shade while the zinc oxide is the darkest.

Partial credit: A. and gives a correct explanation for either the ZnO spot or the M spot, but not both, such as:

- A. Mineral oil provides the lowest resistance against UVL. So with other substances the paper would not be white.
- A. Zinc oxide absorbs practically all rays and the diagram shows this.
- A because ZnO blocks the light and M absorbs it.

Answering this question correctly corresponds to a difficulty of 629 score points on the PISA 2006 science scale. Giving a partially correct answer corresponds to a difficulty of 616 score points on the PISA 2000 science scale. Across OECD countries, 27% of students answered correctly. The question assesses students' competencies in using scientific evidence.

MARY MONTAGU SCORING 9.1

Full credit: B. Diseases that are caused by viruses, like polio.

Answering this question correctly corresponds to a difficulty of 436 score points on the PISA 2006 science scale. Across OECD countries, 75% of students answered correctly. The question assesses students' competencies in explaining phenomena scientifically.

MARY MONTAGU SCORING 9.2

Full credit: B. The body has made antibodies that kill this type of bacteria before they multiply.

Answering this question correctly corresponds to a difficulty of 431 score points on the PISA 2006 science scale. Across OECD countries, 75% of students answered correctly. The question assesses students' competencies in explaining phenomena scientifically.

MARY MONTAGU SCORING 9.3

Full credit: Responses referring to young and/or old people having weaker immune systems than other people, or similar, such as:

- These people have less resistance to getting sick.
- The young and old can't fight off disease as easily as others.
- They are more likely to catch the flu.
- If they get the flu the effects are worse in these people.
- Because organisms of young children and older people are weaker.
- Old people get sick more easily.

Answering this question correctly corresponds to a difficulty of 507 score points on the PISA 2006 science scale. Across OECD countries, 62% of students answered correctly. This question assesses the students' competencies in explaining phenomena scientifically.

ACID RAIN SCORING 10.1

Full credit:

- Responses that mention any one of: car exhausts, factory emissions, *burning* fossil fuels such as oil and coal, gases from volcanoes or other similar things.
    - Burning coal and gas.
    - Oxides in the air come from pollution from factories and industries.
    - Volcanoes.
    - Fumes from power plants.
    - They come from the burning of materials that contain sulfur and nitrogen.
- Responses that include an incorrect as well as a correct source of the pollution.
    - Fossil fuel and nuclear power plants. *[Nuclear power plants are not a source of acid rain.]*
    - The oxides come from the ozone, atmosphere and meteors coming toward Earth. Also the burning of fossil fuels.
- Responses that refer to "pollution" but do not give a source of pollution that is a significant cause of acid rain.
    - Pollution.
    - The environment in general, the atmosphere we live in – e.g., pollution.
    - Gasification, pollution, fires, cigarettes.
    - Pollution such as from nuclear power plants.

Answering this question correctly corresponds to a difficulty of 506 score points on the PISA 2006 science scale. Across OECD countries, 58% of students answered correctly. The question assesses students' competencies in explaining phenomena scientifically.

ACID RAIN SCORING 10.2

Full credit: A. Less than 2.0 grams

Answering this question correctly corresponds to a difficulty of 460 score points on the PISA 2006 science scale. Across OECD countries, 67% of students answered correctly. This question assesses students' competencies in using scientific evidence.

ACID RAIN SCORING 10.3

Full credit: Responses such as:

- To show that the acid (vinegar) is necessary for the reaction.

- To make sure that rainwater must be acidic like acid rain to cause this reaction.
- To see whether there are other reasons for the holes in the marble chips.
- Because it shows that the marble chips don't just react with any fluid since water is neutral.

Partial credit: Responses which compare with the test of vinegar and marble, but do not make clear that this is being done to show that the acid (vinegar) is necessary for the reaction.

- To compare with the other test tube.
- To see whether the marble chip changes in pure water.
- The students included this step to show what happens when it rains normally on the marble.
- Because distilled water is not acid.
- To act as a control.
- To see the difference between normal water and acidic water (vinegar).

Answering this question correctly corresponds to a difficulty of 717 score points on the PISA 2006 science scale. Giving a partially correct answer corresponds to a difficulty of 513 score points on the PISA 2000 science scale. Across OECD countries, 36% of students answered correctly. The question assesses students' competencies in identifying scientific issues.

PHYSICAL EXERCISE SCORING 11.1

Full credit: Yes, No, Yes in that order.

Answering this question correctly corresponds to a difficulty of 545 score points on the PISA 2006 science scale. Across OECD countries, 57% of students answered correctly. The question assesses students' competencies in explaining phenomena scientifically.

PHYSICAL EXERCISE SCORING 11.2

Full credit: Yes, No in that order.

Answering this question correctly corresponds to a difficulty of 386 score points on the PISA 2006 science scale. Across OECD countries, 82% of students answered correctly. This question assesses students' competencies in explaining phenomena scientifically.

PHYSICAL EXERCISE SCORING 11.3

Full credit:

- To remove *increased* levels of carbon dioxide *and* to supply *more* oxygen to your body. *[Do not accept "air" instead of "carbon dioxide" or "oxygen".]*

- When you exercise your body needs more oxygen and produces more carbon dioxide. Breathing does this.
- Breathing faster allows more oxygen into the blood and more carbon dioxide to be removed.

- To remove *increased* levels of carbon dioxide from your body *or* to supply *more* oxygen to your body, but not both. *[Do not accept "air" instead of "carbon dioxide" or "oxygen".]*
  - Because we must get rid of the carbon dioxide that builds up.
  - Because the muscles need oxygen. *[The implication is that your body needs more oxygen when you are exercising (using your muscles).]*
  - Because physical exercise uses up oxygen.
  - You breathe more heavily because you are taking more oxygen into your lungs. *[Poorly expressed, but recognises that you are supplied with more oxygen.]*
  - Since you are using so much energy your body needs double or triple the amount of air intake. It also needs to remove the carbon dioxide in your body.

Answering this question correctly corresponds to a difficulty of 583 score points on the PISA 2006 science scale. Across OECD countries, 45% of students answered correctly. This question assesses students' competencies in explaining phenomena scientifically.

GM CROPS SCORING 12.1

Full Credit: Both correct: No, Yes in that order.

GM CROPS SCORING 12.2

Full credit: D. To include various growth conditions for corn.

Answering this question correctly corresponds to a difficulty of 421 score points on the PISA 2006 science scale. Across OECD countries, 74% of students answered correctly. The question assesses students' competencies in identifying scientific issues.

BIODIVERSITY SCORING 13.1

Full credit: A. Native Cat and Parasitic Wasp.

The process being assessed is demonstrating knowledge and understanding.

BIODIVERSITY SCORING 13.2

Full credit: C. The effect would be greater in food web B because the Parasitic Wasp has only one food source in web B.

The process being assessed is drawing or evaluating conclusions.

BUSES SCORING 14.1

Full credit: C. The water will spill over side 2.

The process being assessed is demonstrating knowledge and understanding.

BUSES SCORING 14.2

Full credit: Gives an answer in which it is stated that the power station also contributes to environmental pollution, such as:

- No, because the power station causes environmental pollution as well.
- Yes, but this is only true for the city itself; the power station however causes environmental pollution.

The process being assessed is demonstrating knowledge and understanding.

CLIMATE CHANGE SCORING 15.1

Full credit: Carbon dioxide is the main factor causing an increase in atmospheric temperature/ causing climatic change, so reducing the amount emitted will have the greatest effect in reducing the impact of human activities.

- The emission of CO_2 causes significant heating to the atmosphere and therefore should be lessened. *[Note: The term "significant" can be considered as equivalent to "most".]*
- According to figure 1 reduction in the emission of carbon dioxide is necessary because it considerably heats the earth. *[Note: The term "considerable" can be considered as equivalent to "most".]*

Partial credit: Carbon dioxide is causing an increase in atmospheric temperature/causing climatic change.

- The burning of fossil fuel such as oil, gas and coal are contributing to the build up of gases in the atmosphere, one of which is carbon dioxide (CO_2). This gas affects the temperature of the earth which increases causing a greenhouse effect.

The question assesses the ability to communicate conclusions based on evidence.

FLIES SCORING 16.1

Full credit: Responses in which three variables (type of flies, age of insecticide, and exposure) are controlled, such as:

- Compare the results from a new batch of the insecticide with results from the old batch on two groups of flies of the same species that have not been previously exposed to the insecticide.
- Some flies could be taken. If they would both be put in a separate box you could use a new spray and an older spray and see what the results are. *[Note: Although the same species is not mentioned, it is implied that the flies are the same type, and that the flies have not been previously exposed.]*
- Make one big batch of spray. Have 2 groups of flies and spray each group every six months. Spray groups one with the big batch, and group 2 a new batch each time. *[Note: Although the same species is not mentioned, it is implied that the flies are the same type, and that the flies have not been previously exposed.]*

Partial credit:

- Responses in which two of the three variables (type of flies, age of insecticide, and exposure) are controlled, such as:
    - Compare the results from a new batch of the insecticide with the results from the old batch on the flies in the barn.
    - Try a new bottle of it, then wait till it gets a bit older and the flies come back and then try again. *[Note: Reproduction of what the farmer experienced, controlling the age of the insecticide and type of flies ("the flies" is interpreted to mean the same flies).]*
- Responses in which one variable only of three variables (type of flies, age of insecticide, and exposure) is controlled, such as:
    - (Chemically) analyse samples of the insecticide at regular intervals to see if it changes over time.
    - Take batches of the insecticide to a laboratory every few months and have its strength tested.
    - Spray the flies with a new batch of insecticide, but without mentioning comparison with old batch.
    - Do the same thing but buy new insecticide each time, hence proving if his theory is right or wrong.
    - (Chemically) analyse samples of the insecticide but without mentioning comparison of analyses over time.
    - Maybe if he sent a fresh batch of the poison to the lab with a batch of the old stuff and get them retested the results may prove his theory.

The process being assessed is identifying evidence.

FLIES SCORING 16.2

Full credit: Responses that gives as one explanation a) that flies with resistance to the insecticide survive and pass on that resistance to later generations (also credit for "immunity" although it is recognised that it is not strictly analogous to "resistance"), as well as one of these b): a change in the environmental conditions (such as temperature), or a change in the way the insecticide was applied.

- Explanation 1: With the repeated use of the same insecticide the flies were becoming immune to the formula. Explanation 2: Over time chemicals in the insecticide rose to the top of spray can leaving water diluted (ineffective) at the bottom.
- Explanation 1: The flies were becoming immune to the spray. Explanation 2: Heat may make it decompose and temperature change.
- Explanation 1: Maybe the flies developed a defence gene so the insecticide would not work. Explanation 2: He (the farmer) used less each time. *[Note: Defence gene is allowed as an alternative to resistance.]*

Partial credit: Gives one explanation of type a) or type b).

- He might not have sprayed it properly.
- The flies could have built up an immunity.
- There were different types of flies each time. *[Note: A clear distinction is made between different types of flies in this example; it is not referring to new flies coming into the area.]*
- Explanation 1: The temperature got very hot and affected the insecticide. Explanation 2: the farmer did not spray the insecticide on the flies properly

The process being assessed is recognising questions.

CALF CLONES SCORING 17.1

Full credit: Responses that gives an acceptable main idea, such as:

- The idea of whether cloning of calves is possible.
- The determination of the number of calf clones that could be produced.
- That cloning was possible. *[Note: The fact that calves/cows have not been mentioned should be disregarded.]*

The process being assessed is recognising questions.

CALF CLONES SCORING 17.2

Full credit: Yes, Yes, Yes.

The process being assessed is evaluating conclusions.

CORN SCORING 18.1

Full credit: Yes, Yes, Yes.

CORN SCORING 18.2

Full credit: One of the following names: glucose, sugar(s), carbohydrate(s), saccharide(s) or starch.

CORN SCORING 18.3

Full credit: D. Data about the amounts of each of the four gases in the atmosphere.

FIT FOR DRINKING SCORING 19.1

Full credit:

- Responses referring to ground water being filtered through the ground
  - When it goes through sand and dust the water is cleaned.
  - It has been naturally filtered.
  - Because when water goes down through the ground it will be strained by rocks and sand.
- Responses referring to the ground water being encapsulated and therefore protected from possible pollution; OR that surface water is more easily polluted
  - Ground water is inside the earth and therefore air pollution cannot make it dirty.
  - Because ground water isn't open, it is located under something.
  - Lake and rivers can be polluted by the air and you can swim in it and so on, that's why it is not clean.
  - Because lakes and rivers are polluted by people and animals.
- Other correct responses, such as:
  - Ground water is water without much food for bacteria so they will not survive there.
  - Ground water is not in the Sun. There is blue-green algae.

The competency being assessed is explaining phenomena scientifically.

FIT FOR DRINKING SCORING 19.2

Full credit: C. Gravel and sand sink to the bottom.

The competency being assessed is explaining phenomena scientifically.

FIT FOR DRINKING SCORING 19.3

Full credit: Responses referring to removing, killing or breaking down bacteria (or microbes or viruses or germs)

- To make it free from bacteria.
- Chlorine kills bacteria.
- To kill all the algae.

The competency being assessed is explaining phenomena scientifically.

FIT FOR DRINKING SCORING 19.4

Full credit:

- Responses referring to boiling the water
  - Boil it.
- Responses referring to other methods of cleaning that are possible to do safely at home
  - Treat the water with chlorine tablets (e.g., Puratabs).
  - Use a micropore filter.

The competency being assessed is explaining phenomena scientifically.

FIT FOR DRINKING SCORING 19.5

Full credit: All three correct: No, Yes, No, in that order.

While classified as explaining phenomena scientifically, this question is a low-level form of this competency because it can be answered by simple recall of knowledge.

TOOTH DECAY SCORING 20.1

Full credit: D. Bacteria produce acid.

Students are required to select a conclusion based on the given information, so the question assesses the competency of using scientific evidence.

TOOTH DECAY SCORING 20.2

Full credit: B. The more sugar people eat, the more likely they are to get caries.

The competency being assessed is using scientific evidence.

TOOTH DECAY SCORING 20.3

Full credit: Yes, No in that order.

The competency being assessed is identifying scientific issues.

HOT WORK SCORING 21.1

Full credit: Yes, No, No, in that order.

The competency being assessed is explaining phenomena scientifically.

HOT WORK SCORING 21.2

Full credit: A. 70 ºC and 10 ºC

The competency being assessed is explaining phenomena scientifically.

MOUSEPOX SCORING 22.1

Full credit: B. A mutation in mousepox DNA might allow the virus to infect other animals.

The scientific process being assessed is explaining phenomena scientifically.

MOUSEPOX SCORING 22.2

Full credit: Yes, No, Yes in that order.

The competency being assessed is explaining phenomena scientifically.

MOUSEPOX SCORING 22.3

Full credit: Yes, Yes, Yes.

This question assesses both the competencies of explaining phenomena scientifically and of identifying scientific issues.

STICKLEBACK BEHAVIOUR SCORING 23.1

Full credit: Questions such as:

- What colour elicits the strongest aggressive behaviour by the male stickleback?
- Does the male stickleback react more aggressively to a red-coloured model than to a silver-coloured one?

- Is there a relationship between colour and aggressive behaviour?
- Does the colour of the fish cause the male to be aggressive?
- What fish colour does the stickleback find most threatening?

The competency being assessed is identifying scientific issues.

STICKLEBACK BEHAVIOUR SCORING 23.2

Full credit: No, No, Yes in that order.

The competency being assessed is using scientific evidence.

STICKLEBACK BEHAVIOUR SCORING 23.3

Full credit: C, A, C, B in that order.

Partial credit: Three of the four entries correct.

The competency being assessed is using scientific evidence.

TOBACCO SMOKING SCORING 24.1

Full credit: B. To transfer oxygen from the air that you breathe to your blood.

The competency being assessed is explaining phenomena scientifically.

TOBACCO SMOKING SCORING 24.2

Full credit: Yes, No, No in that order.

The competency being assessed is explaining phenomena scientifically.

TOBACCO SMOKING SCORING 24.3

Full credit: D. Half are randomly chosen to use patches and the other half do not use them.

The competency being assessed is identifying scientific issues.

TOBACCO SMOKING SCORING 24.4

Full credit: No, Yes, No in that order.

The competency being assessed is identifying scientific issues.

STARLIGHT SCORING 25.1

Full credit: C. The brightness of city lights makes many stars hard to see.

The competency being assessed is explaining phenomena scientifically.

STARLIGHT SCORING 25.2

Full credit: A. The larger the lens the more light is collected.

The competency being assessed is explaining phenomena scientifically.

ULTRASOUND SCORING 26.1

Full credit: Responses such as:

- It must measure the time the ultrasound wave takes to travel from the probe to the surface of the foetus and reflect back.
- The time of travel of the wave.
- The time.
- Time. Distance = speed / time. *[Although the formula is incorrect, the student has correctly identified "time" as the missing variable.]*
- It must find when the ultrasound finds the baby.

The competency being assessed is explaining phenomena scientifically.

ULTRASOUND SCORING 26.2

Full credit: Responses such as:

- X-rays are harmful to the foetus.
- X-rays hurt the foetus.
- X-rays might cause a mutation in the foetus.
- X-rays can cause birth defects in the foetus.
- Because the baby could get some radiation.

The competency being assessed is explaining phenomena scientifically.

ULTRASOUND SCORING 26.3

Full credit: Yes, No, Yes in that order.

The competency being assessed is explaining phenomena scientifically.

LIP GLOSS SCORING 27.1

Full credit: Responses indicating that you would add less wax AND/OR add more oil.

The competency being assessed is using scientific evidence.

LIP GLOSS SCORING 27.2

Full credit: D. Fatty lumps of the mixture float on the water.

The competency being assessed is using scientific evidence.

LIP GLOSS SCORING 27.3

Full credit: B. The soap acts as an emulsifier and allows the water and lipstick to mix.

The competency being assessed is using scientific evidence.

EVOLUTION SCORING 28.1

Full credit: Responses that refer to gradual change (progression) in leg skeleton structure over time, such as:

- The leg skeletons are much the same but have gradually changed.
- The digits/toes fused during the period 55 to 2 million years ago.
- The number of digits has decreased.

The competency being assessed is using scientific evidence.

EVOLUTION SCORING 28.2

Full credit: No, Yes in that order.

The competency being assessed is identifying scientific issues.

EVOLUTION SCORING 28.3

Full credit: C. Evolution is a scientific theory that is currently based on extensive evidence.

The competency being assessed is explaining phenomena scientifically.

BREAD DOUGH SCORING 29.1

Full credit: C. The dough rises because a gas, carbon dioxide, is produced.

The competency being assessed is explaining phenomena scientifically.

BREAD DOUGH SCORING 29.2

Full credit: D. The cook should compare experiments 3 and 4.

The competency being assessed is identifying scientific issues.

BREAD DOUGH SCORING 29.3

Full credit: Yes, No, No in that order.

The competency being assessed is explaining phenomena scientifically.

BREAD DOUGH SCORING 29.4

Full credit: B. Their molecules move faster.

The competency being assessed is explaining phenomena scientifically.

TRANSIT OF VENUS SCORING 30.1

Full credit: C. Viewing the Sun through a telescope may damage your eyes.

The competency being assessed is explaining phenomena scientifically.

TRANSIT OF VENUS SCORING 30.2

Full credit: A. Mercury.

The competency being assessed is explaining phenomena scientifically.

TRANSIT OF VENUS SCORING 30.3

Full credit: Responses referring to transit/Saturn/Neptune only.

Identifying keywords to search for scientific information on a given topic is a component of the competency identifying scientific issues.

HEALTH RISK SCORING 31.1

Full credit: An appropriate reason is given for doubting that the statement supports the owner's argument, such as:

- The substance causing the breathing problems may not have been recognised as toxic.
- Breathing problems may have been caused only when chemicals were in the air, not in the soil.
- Toxic substances may change/break down with time and show up as non-toxic substances in soil.
- We do not know if the samples are representative of the area.
- Because the scientists are being paid by the company.
- The scientists feared losing their jobs.

The competency being assessed is using scientific evidence.

HEALTH RISK SCORING 31.2

Full credit: Responses should focus on possible relevant differences between the areas investigated, such as:

- The number of people in the two areas might be different.
- One area could have better medical services than the other.
- There could be different proportions of elderly people in each area.
- There might be other air pollutants in the other area.

The competency being assessed is identifying scientific issues.

CATALYTIC CONVERTER SCORING 32.1

Full credit: Responses such as:

- The conversion of carbon monoxide, or nitrogen oxides, to other compounds is mentioned.
- Carbon monoxide is changed into carbon dioxide.
- Nitrogen oxides are changed into nitrogen.
- It changes harmful fumes into non-harmful fumes. E.g., CO into CO2 (90%).
- Carbon dioxide and nitrogen are not as harmful as carbon monoxide and nitrogen oxides.

The competency being assessed is using scientific evidence.

CATALYCTIC CONVERTER SCORING 32.2

Full credit: Answers which express the essential idea that atoms are rearranged to form different molecules (using both of these words), such as:

- Molecules break up and atoms are re-combined to form different molecules.
- Atoms rearrange to make different molecules.

Partial credit: Answers which express the essential idea of rearrangement, but does not refer to both atoms and molecules OR does not distinguish sufficiently between the roles of atoms and molecules, such as:

- Atoms rearrange to make different substances.
- Molecules are changing into other molecules.
- Atoms and molecules are combining and separating to make less harmful gases. *[The different roles of atoms and molecules are not sufficiently distinguished.]*
- $2(NO_2) = N_2 + 2O_2$.

The competency being assessed is explaining phenomena scientifically.

CATALYCTIC CONVERTER SCORING 32.3

Full credit: Acceptable responses should relate to achieving a reduction in harmful gases entering the atmosphere.

- Not all the carbon monoxide is converted into carbon dioxide.
- Not enough conversion of nitrogen oxides to nitrogen is taking place.
- Improve the percentage of carbon monoxide being converted to carbon dioxide and the percentage of nitrogen oxides being converted to nitrogen.
- The carbon dioxide produced should be captured and not allowed to escape into the atmosphere.

The competency being assessed is using scientific evidence.

MAJOR SURGERY SCORING 33.1

Full credit: No, Yes, Yes in that order.

The competency being assessed is explaining phenomena scientifically.

MAJOR SURGERY SCORING 33.2

Full credit: Student mentions both the need to ensure that there are no bacteria/germs on the instruments AND that this stops the spread of disease.

- To stop bacteria getting in the body and infecting the patient.
- So that no germs get into the body of another person going in for major surgery.

Partial credit:

- Student mentions the need to ensure that there are no bacteria, BUT not that this stops the spread of disease.
  - To kill the germs on them.
- Student mentions that this stops the spread of disease, BUT not that it is because any bacteria on the instruments are killed.
  - So the patient is not infected.
  - To prevent any transfer of disease.

The competency being assessed is explaining phenomena scientifically.

MAJOR SURGERY SCORING 33.3

Full credit: D. To provide necessary nutrition.

The competency being assessed is explaining phenomena scientifically.

MAJOR SURGERY SCORING 33.4

Full credit: No, No, Yes in that order.

The competency being assessed is using scientific evidence.

WIND FARMS SCORING 34.1

Full credit: C.

The competency being assessed is using scientific evidence.

WIND FARMS SCORING 34.2

Full credit: B.

The competency being assessed is using scientific evidence.

WIND FARMS SCORING 34.3

Full credit: A. The air is less dense as altitude increases.

The competency being assessed is explaining phenomena scientifically.

WIND FARMS SCORING 34.4

Full credit: One specific advantage and one specific disadvantage are described.

Advantage:

- Do not discharge carbon dioxide (CO_2).
- Do not consume fossil fuels.
- The wind resource will not be used up.
- After the wind generator is established, the cost for electric generation is cheap.
- No waste and/or no toxic substance will be emitted.
- Using natural forces or clean energy.
- Environmentally friendly and will last for a very long time.

Disadvantage:

- Generation on demand is not possible. *[Because the wind speed cannot be controlled.]*
- Good places for windmills are limited.
- The windmill could be damaged by too strong wind.
- The amount of power generated by each windmill is relatively small.
- Noise pollution occurs in some cases.
- Birds are sometimes killed when they crash into the rotors.
- Natural views are altered. *[Visual pollution.]*
- Expensive to set up.

Partial credit: Either a correct advantage or a correct disadvantage is described (as shown in the full credit examples) but not both.

The competency being assessed is explaining phenomena scientifically.

ANNEX A
PISA scales

The PISA test design makes it possible to use statistical techniques to simultaneously estimate the ability of all students taking the PISA assessment, and the difficulty of all PISA questions, locating these estimates of student ability and question difficulty on a single continuum. The relative ability of students taking a particular test can be estimated by considering the proportion of test questions they get correct. The relative difficulty of questions in a test can be estimated by considering the proportion of test takers getting each question correct. In this way, it becomes possible to estimate the position of students and of questions on a continuum referred to as the PISA literacy scale in either reading, mathematics or science.

The scales stretch from very low levels of performance through to very high levels. When thinking about what such a scale means about student proficiency, it can be observed that a student whose ability estimate places him/her at a certain point on the PISA scale would most likely be able to successfully complete tasks at or below that location, and increasingly more likely to complete tasks located at progressively lower points on the scale, but would be less likely to be able to complete tasks above that point, and increasingly less likely to complete tasks located at progressively higher points on the scale. Figure 1 depicts a scale, stretching from relatively low levels at the bottom of the figure, to relatively high levels towards the top. Six questions of varying difficulty are placed along the scale, as are three students of varying ability.

Figure 1
The relationship between items and students on a proficiency scale

For more information on PISA scales, please consult the technical reports listed below.

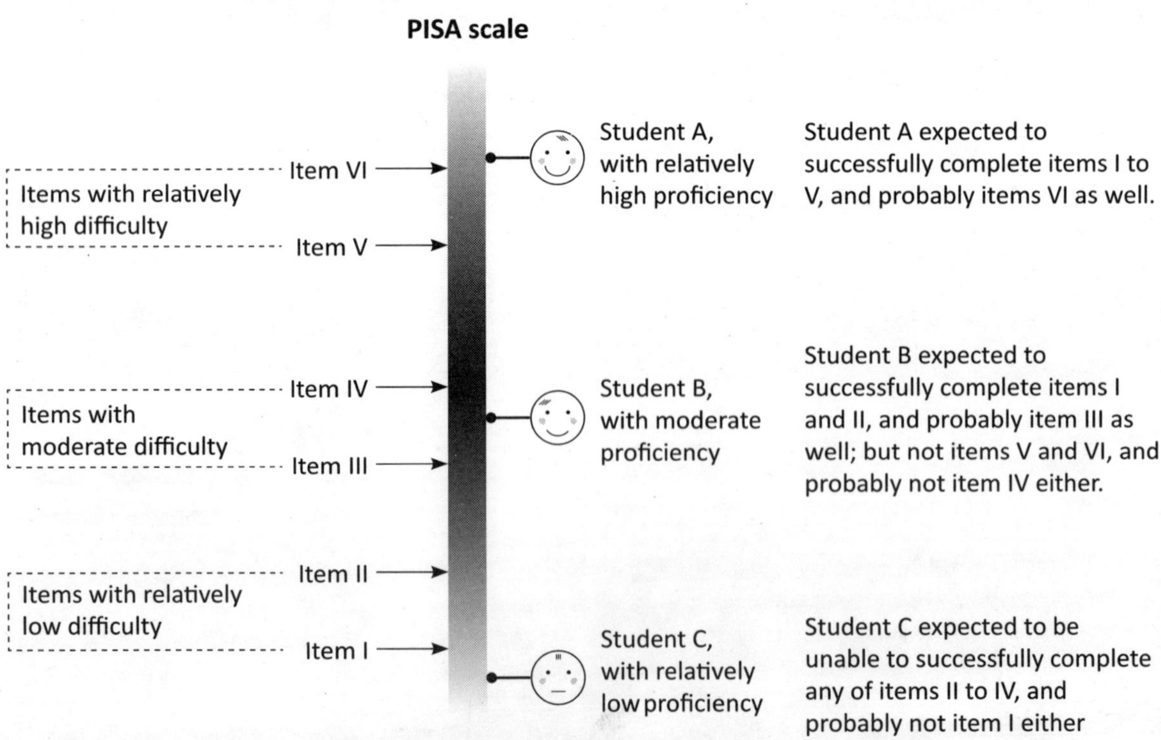